ACCLAIM   T0026355

THE SHORTEST HISTORY OF ENGLAND

"A vivid, supercharged tour through British history,
showing that many of the tensions of today have been
present throughout."
—John Kampfner, author of
Why the Germans Do It Better

"An engaging, informative sprint through the story
of our little island."*—The Independent*

"I've read hundreds of books on English history, but this is
the first one that clearly explains the North-South divide."
—Christopher Fowler, author of
the Bryant & May mysteries

"Brilliant insights on every page, and the multiple entry
points and clever use of graphics bestow an easy-to-read,
magazine-y feel."*—BookBrunch*

"At last, a chance to get to grips with the entire history of
England, and all in a few hours."*—The Mail on Sunday*

"A fantastic read. I would recommend it to anyone."
—Pat Kenny, Newstalk radio host

"Thorough and absorbing . . . steps back from the current
madness with admirable clarity."*—The New European*

"Such a thought-provoking read. . . .
The maps and charts are so useful."
—Dan Jackson, author of *The Northumbrians*

THE
SHORTEST
HISTORY
OF
ENGLAND

**Empire and Division from
the Anglo-Saxons to Brexit—
A Retelling for Our Times**

JAMES HAWES

THE EXPERIMENT

NEW YORK

Originally published in the UK by Old Street Publishing, LTD, in 2021. First published in North America in revised form by The Experiment, LLC, in 2022.

The Experiment, LLC
220 East 23rd Street, Suite 600
New York, NY 10010-4658
theexperimentpublishing.com

THE EXPERIMENT and its colophon are registered trademarks of The Experiment, LLC. Many of the designations used by manufacturers and sellers to distinguish their products are claimed as trademarks. Where those designations appear in this book and The Experiment was aware of a trademark claim, the designations have been capitalized.

The Experiment's books are available at special discounts when purchased in bulk for premiums and sales promotions as well as for fund-raising or educational use. For details, contact us at info@theexperimentpublishing.com.

Library of Congress Cataloging-in-Publication Data

Names: Hawes, J. M. (James M.), author.
Title: The shortest history of England : empire and division from the
    Anglo-Saxons to Brexit / James Hawes.
Description: New York : The Experiment, 2022. | Series: The shortest
    history | "Originally published in the UK by Old Street Publishing, LTD,
    in 2021." | Includes bibliographical references and index.
Identifiers: LCCN 2021058901 (print) | LCCN 2021058902 (ebook) | ISBN
    9781615198146 (paperback) | ISBN 9781615198153 (ebook)
Subjects: LCSH: Great Britain--History.
Classification: LCC DA30 .H39 2022 (print) | LCC DA30 (ebook) | DDC
    941--dc23/eng/20211208
LC record available at https://lccn.loc.gov/2021058901
LC ebook record available at https://lccn.loc.gov/2021058902

ISBN 978-1-61519-814-6
Ebook ISBN 978-1-61519-815-3

Cover design by Jack Dunnington
Text design by Old Street Publishing, LTD
Original maps and illustrations by James Nunn

Manufactured in the United States of America

First printing March 2022
10 9 8 7 6 5 4 3 2 1

To my mother, Janet Hawes, née Fry,
who dodged V-1s in Cricklewood

"The English have lost their sense of themselves as an ancient shared culture . . . In English schools, history is taught in a strangely episodic manner—Roman, Tudors, Second World War—so students have no continuous historical narrative . . . The English don't even know their country geographically. Most southerners have little interest in what goes on up north, and most northerners wouldn't be able to find Guildford on a map."

LOUIS DE BERNIÈRES
Financial Times, January 29, 2020

Contents

Preface

In 1944, on her way to school in Cricklewood, my mother heard a V-1 cut out above her. She threw herself flat on the pavement. Some twitch in the Nazi gyroscope decided that glass and rubble would rain down all around her, but that she would live to tell the tale.

My sons have heard it from her. So with luck, in 2094, one or other of them will be able to tell his grandchildren that he knows what it felt like to dodge a V-1 in London in 1944, because their great-great-grandmother told him.

A century and a half, hurdled by a family story. Try it with your own. Seven long generations like that—a short queue at the check-in to eternity, the old and the young holding hands—and we are back at the Battle of Hastings.

Our past whispers in our ears, whether we hear it or not, and makes us what we are. And given the state of England today, we English had better get to know ourselves a bit better. So where to begin? Well, we know almost to the hour when England emerged from archaeology, and entered history.

At dawn on August 27, 55 BCE—about fifteen long generations ago—a fleet appeared out of the night off Ebbsfleet in Kent, bearing none other than Julius Caesar.

PART ONE

From Caesar to the Conqueror
55 BCE–1087 CE

England Before the English

By 55 BCE, Rome had vaguely known for many years of a mysterious land beyond Europe inhabited by people the Greeks called the Pretaniki or Bretaniki. It was famous mainly as a source of tin, the vital metal that could transmute copper into brass or bronze. The Phoenician merchants who dominated this lucrative trade kept their business secrets to themselves, so when Caesar invaded from newly conquered Gaul, he knew that the Britons had dealings with the Gauls, that tin could be found there, and that the nearest part of the island was called Kantion, but that was about it.

> Having called to him the merchants from all parts, Caesar could learn neither the size of the island, nor what or how numerous were the nations which inhabited it, nor what system of war they followed, nor what customs they used.
>
> —Julius Caesar, *The Gallic War*

Caesar's fleet crossed the Channel in a single night, but could find no decent anchorage; his attempted landing at Ebbsfleet was met with a reception so ferocious that it never got off the beach. He tried again the following year. This time he made it as far as the Thames Valley, which was enough for him to learn that the Britannici were not a single people at all.

Inland, there was an old-established population, whereas "the maritime portion" (i.e., the southeastern coastal region) had recently been settled by raiders from the "country of the Belgae." Indeed, a Belgic leader had recently claimed some kind of overlordship in Britannia. Modern archaeologists agree that there was a distinctive Aylesford-Swarling/Atrebatic culture in the Southeast at this time, closely linked to the Belgic Gauls.

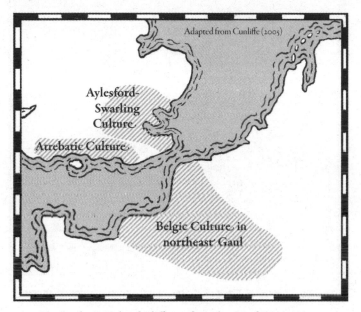

The Southeast is already different from the rest of Britannia in 54 BCE: Belgic cross-Channel culture in Caesar's day

Caesar and his army didn't stick around, but the elite of Britannia were suitably awed. Some thirty years later, the Greek geographer Strabo described Britannia as virtually a Roman property, whose chieftains came to dedicate offerings in the capitol. By 43 CE, Emperor Claudius decided that it had developed enough to be worth invading and taxing properly.

Claudius really only cared about the tribes already advanced enough to be making and using coins. The limit of their territory is no coincidence. It is also the line of the Jurassic Divide, where young sandstones, clays, and chalks give way to older shales and igneous rocks.

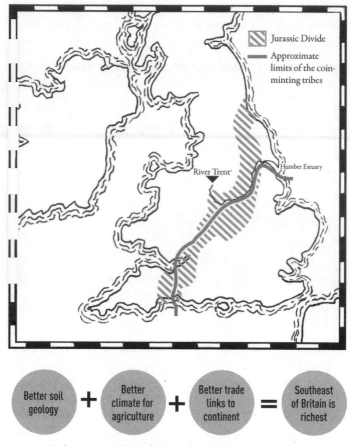

Geology, geography, and climate conspire timelessly in favor
of the Southeast

By 100 CE, the Southeast was a peaceful, prosperous colony. Its people, wrote the historian Tacitus, were obviously related to the Gauls. Beyond, to the north, were people "clearly Germanic in origin," while those in the west were like the Iberians. It now occurred to the Romans—as it occurred to almost every later ruler of the Southeast—that, since they controlled the richest part of the island, they should also rule those other peoples.

They failed. In what is today known as Scotland, resistance was so tough that the Romans fell back and built Hadrian's Wall, which still entrances walkers. What we now call Wales and the north of England were only ever ruled and taxed at spearpoint. Roman civilization in Britannia was effectively limited to what is today southern England. The only other truly Romanized areas were along the great roads that led to the northern bastion of York and connected the vital garrisons at Caerleon and Chester (the line of this road is still basically the western border of England). Thus the Romans, having found southeastern Britannia already different, made it far more so.

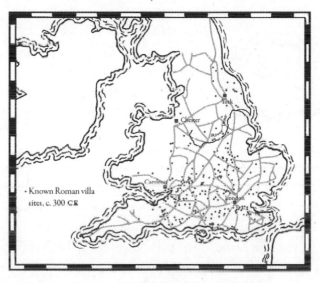

· Known Roman villa sites, c. 300 CE

It was in the fruitful plains of the Southeast that the Latinized Britons were concentrated, in a peaceful and civilian land, where the site of a cohort on the march was a rarity, where Roman cities and villas were plentiful and Roman civilization powerful in its attraction.

—Trevelyan

The Channel didn't cut Britannia off from the rest of the empire, but was the vital link. Britain was "within sight of Gaul" (Tacitus) across "a very narrow strait of the sea" (Ammianus) that could be crossed "in about eight hours" (Strabo). When the Rhineland was starving in 359, the future Emperor Julian didn't even attempt to convoy grain by land from neighboring Gaul. Instead he built 800 ships, sent them to Britannia, and "the voyage being short, he abundantly supplied the people" (Zosimus).

Toward the end of the third century CE, this sea road came under threat from people whose descendants would one day call themselves the English.

Enter the Saxons

Coin of Carausius

In 286, writes Eutropius, "Franci et Saxones" infested the Channel. This is the first written mention of the Saxons. A successful general called Marcus Aurelius Carausius was sent out to deal with them. However, Carausius soon declared himself emperor and built a short-lived cross-Channel realm with support from the very Franks and Saxons he'd been dispatched to defeat. It's distinctly possible that the Roman fortifications that still stand along the southeastern coast date from his reign.

In 367, the Saxons took part, along with the Picts (then the inhabitants of present-day Scotland), the Scots (what we nowadays call the Irish), and the Franks (who would one day found France but were at this stage just another German tribe) in the "barbarian conspiracy" (Ammiananus) that threatened the complete destruction of Roman Britain. Imperial rule was briefly restored, but in 383–4, the Roman armies left Britannia to fight other Romans. The last great Roman general, Stilicho, brought the legions back to Britannia and restored a kind of order in 399.

Documentary evidence from this time is very scanty, but we have one fascinating piece: the Notitia Dignitatum, a list of the Empire's military and customs commands. One such command is the fortified shore of southeastern Britannia, held by the *"comes litoris Saxonici"*—the Count of the Saxon Shore. This is the only mention of the Saxon Shore. Nobody is sure what it means, because the Notitia exists only as far later copies, and the Latin is degenerate. But all the other commands in the *Notitia* are named after the local populations, not the potential enemies, which strongly suggests that as early as 400, the Channel coast was actually settled by Saxon auxiliary troops and their families, serving Rome. Archaeology has evidence to back this idea up.

The first known English three-dimensional figure, from Spong in East Anglia. Archaeologists are in no doubt that it is Germanic; it comes from a cemetery whose "earliest burial dates from around 400–420"

This early presence may explain why the other people of Britain called—and still call—all Englishmen *Saxons (sassenach, saesneg)*, though the Saxons were soon followed by other tribes. But what should we call them? The name *Anglo-Saxon* was not invented for another 450 years or so (under Alfred the Great) and the land only started being called *Engla-londe* in the early tenth century. *The tribes who would one day call themselves the English* would be accurate, but cumbersome. So we'll just use *the English* as shorthand for all Germanic settlers, though it's unhistorical. In any case, what really matters is why they came.

Invasion or Invitation?

The Roman legions finally left Britain in 407, to fight in endless civil wars. The southern Britons now found themselves taxed yet undefended, so they felt "the necessity of revolting from the empire, and living no longer under the Roman laws" (Zosimus). Our only real source for what happened next is *The Ruin of Britain* (c. 540) by the Romano-British monk Gildas. He records, in Latin, his people regretting their rash break with the Empire and making a famous last plea for Roman help, known as the Groans of the Britons, in around 450:

> The barbarians drive us to the sea, the sea drives us to the barbarians, between these two means of death we are either killed or drowned.

But these barbarians weren't Saxons. Gildas doesn't mention Germanic tribes at all in these years. The deadly enemies of civilization in Britain were "two foreign nations, the Scots from the Northwest [i.e., the Irish], and the Picts from the north," who came *in coracles* (wooden-framed, leather-skinned boats, as found on the Celtic fringes of the British Isles). And since Rome could no longer help, the Romano-British turned to another European people.

> AD 443 This year sent the Britons to Rome & bade them assistance against the Picts, but they gave them none, for that they fought with Attila, King of the Huns, *& then sent they to the English & English-kin nobles* [author's emphasis].
> —*Anglo-Saxon Chronicle**

---

* The *Anglo-Saxon Chronicle*, hereafter just the *Chronicle*, is actually multiple chronicles that were (most scholars agree) begun in the reign of Alfred the Great, as an effort to draw together all existing history. There's no way of testing how accurate it is about events four hundred years earlier, but it's all we have.

The English didn't invade. They were invited from Europe to save Romano-British civilization from home-grown barbarians. In return they were offered land in the richest part of the island.

> AD 449 King Vortigern gave them land in the Southeast of this land withal that they should fight with the Picts. They then fought with the Picts & had victory wheresoever they came.
>
> —*Chronicle*

Soon, though, the English broke out of their agreed enclave. There was nothing special about this. All over fifth-century post-Roman Western Europe, the Germanic warriors who had largely staffed the Late Roman army were on the move in the Migration Period. Something unique, though, did take place in southeastern Britannia.

The Founding Uniqueness

Everywhere else in Europe, the Germanic invaders came, they saw, they conquered—and then they assimilated. In England,

and only in England, they entirely replaced the culture they found. This is England's founding uniqueness. It explains why the modern English find their immediate neighbor-language, Welsh, utterly strange, yet can still almost understand German swearing from around 850: *hundes ars in tino naso*, meaning (of course) *hound's arse in thine nose.*

So why did the Germanic migrants only stay Germanic in England? Partly, it was because Britannia had already declined and fallen into a land run by local warlords whom Gildas calls tyrants. All the incoming English found were ruins—and seeing nothing worth adopting, they stuck to their own culture. They could do so because of the other vital difference: the sea.

The Channel didn't protect Britannia: It made total conquest possible. Elsewhere in Europe, the Germanic conquerors were all-male war bands. An entire tribe—old people, nursing mothers, small children and all—couldn't survive long overland journeys through hostile territory. The English, though, could ship whole clans across to the Saxon Shore in a day or two, landing at well-built, long-familiar Roman ports.

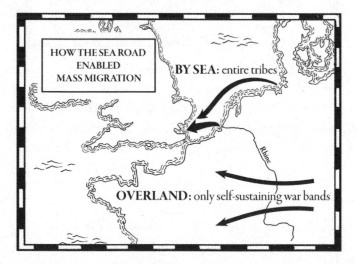

> When news of their success and the fertility of the country,
> and the cowardice of the Britons, reached their own home ...
> swarms of the aforesaid nations came over into the island.
>
> —Bede, *Historia Ecclesiastica Gentis Anglorum* (c. 731)

Everywhere else, the single male Germanic warriors intermarried with local women, so the Latinate languages—and Christianity—survived. The English brought their own womenfolk with them, so they stayed English pagans.

The Curious Case of the Disappearing Language

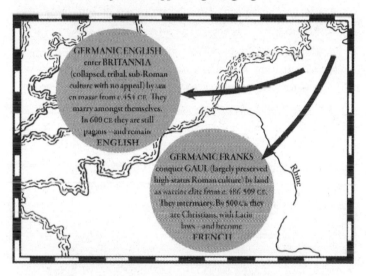

The English conquest was so complete that nothing remains of the Romano-British language in modern England except dreamlike fragments like the *yan-tan-tethera* way of counting sheep in the north of England (one-two-three in Celtic) or *hickory-dickory-dock* (eight-nine-ten).

The Victorians, familiar with the notion of ruthless, racial colonization, had no doubt what this meant:

> Those who fought against our forefathers were killed and those who submitted were made slaves . . . Now you will perhaps say that our forefathers were cruel and wicked men . . . But anyway it has turned out much better in the end.
> —*Old English History for Children*, Edward Freeman, 1869

Yet modern science shows that most of modern English people's DNA comes from the Romano-British.

> The majority of eastern, central and southern England is made up of a single, relatively homogeneous, genetic group [i.e., the Romano-Britons] with a significant DNA contribution from Anglo-Saxon migrations (10-40% of total ancestry). This settles a historical controversy in showing that the Anglo-Saxons intermarried with, rather than replaced, the existing populations.
> —"The Fine-Scale Genetic Structure of the British Population," *Nature,* March 18, 2015.

In England, then, the Romano-Britons survived, but switched languages, just as the vast majority of people later did in Wales, Scotland, and Ireland.

CULTURAL WIPEOUT:
Romano-British language virtually erased

BIOLOGICAL SURVIVAL:
Lowland Romano-British genes = 60–90% of modern English genes

The Wessex Deal

Gildas tells of successful native resistance led by a Romano-Briton called "Ambrosius Aurelianus," whom later writers have tried to identify as King Arthur. Be that as it may, archaeology and common sense suggest that as the English advanced from the Southeast, they met serious opposition. After all, the Britons, whom the early English called *waelisce* or *waehla* (from a Germanic word meaning "Romanized ones," also seen in *Walloon* and *Wallachia*) still hold out in the far west to this day, language and all, as the *Welsh*.

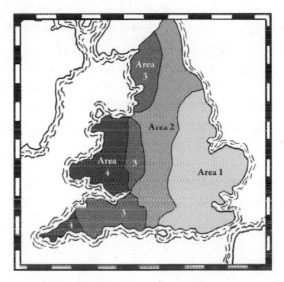

Kenneth Hurlstone Jackson's Map of River Names

Area 1 was conquered by c. 500, and thoroughly Anglicized. Area 2 was conquered by c. 600; here, many rivers still have Celtic names, suggesting an abiding presence. Conquest of Area 3 wasn't complete until c. 700; even small rivers still have pre-English names, suggesting that the population changed little. Area 4 resisted into modern times (Cornwall) or still does (Wales).

It seems that in Area 2, the Romano-British elite cut deals. Several names in the royal Wessex genealogy sound distinctly Celtic: *Cerdic, Caedwalla, Cenwahl*. The Venerable Bede makes a curious point about the victor after the men of Wessex defeated what sound like Gaelic warlords at Dryham, near Bath, in 577: "Caelin, King of the West Saxons, was known in the speech of his own people as Ceaulin." This suggests that early "English" Wessex was bilingual even at the very top. And indeed, the laws of King Ine of Wessex (c. 700) show beyond doubt that he ruled two cultures: the *waelisce* were generally second-class citizens, but they were protected by law. Some owned hundreds of acres (only 5–10 percent of the English themselves actually owned any land) and were deemed second in "blood-price" only to thanes of the royal household itself. Most strikingly of all, Ine commanded the *cyninges horswealh*, which translates neatly as the King's Welsh Horse. At Lady Mary Church in Wareham, five memorials to what must have been important people, inscribed with lettering clearly Celtic in origin, date from as late as 250 years after the birth of English Wessex.

The Romano-British of lowland Britannia were neither killed nor driven out. Instead, led by their elites, they adopted Englishness—and eventually the language—from the top down. Almost from the start, English identity wasn't a racial fate, but a political choice—a hard choice, no doubt, but a choice.*

After 600, that choice became far less drastic for the conquered natives, because Englishness itself was being dragged fast out of the pagan, Germanic world. Rome was back.

Bibles and Book Law

Every English cleric since Bede has loved the tale of how, around 590, Pope Gregory saw some boys at a Roman slave market. On

---

* You don't need much historical imagination to picture this. You can just talk to living people from the Highlands, Ireland, or Wales whose parents *deliberately* didn't pass on their own language because they thought that without fluent English (which their elites had long adopted), their children would be hopelessly disadvantaged.

being told they were Angles, he joked: "Well named, for they have angelic faces" (Bede). An Italian bishop, Augustine, was accordingly dispatched to convert them. The mission was enabled by the Franks, who had already been Christian for a century. Their king's daughter, Bertha, had recently married Ethelbert of Kent. At first he refused to convert, but he did allow Bertha to make over a Roman mausoleum in Canterbury for Augustine as the first English-speaking church.

By 601 Ethelbert had given in to Augustine, or the Franks, or his wife, and converted. He now set down the laws of his lands in writing. They stress the privileged position of the Church in society, and lay down in great detail the fines for various acts of rape and violence (12 shillings for cutting off an ear; 50 shillings for knocking out an eye; 12 shillings for having sex with a nobleman's maid—but only 6 shillings if she is a commoner's maid). Here is civilization coming in at ground zero.

These laws were written in English. This was unique: All the continental Germanic nations wrote down their laws in the prestige-language, Latin. In England, almost nobody spoke Latin anymore, so the everyday language was, from the dawn of literacy, given the awesome privilege of being written down. Until the Norman Conquest, the English, alone in Western Europe, were ruled in their own tongue.

Ethelbert was *Bretwalda* (paramount king) in England, so his example was instrumental. The next Bretwalda, Readwald of East Anglia, stayed pagan but allowed a Christian shrine in his pantheon. He's widely assumed to be the man buried in the magnificent ship tomb at Sutton Hoo, where the priceless treasures mix local pagan work with imported Christian and prestige goods.

Onward, Christian Soldiers

The Church went to work extirpating English paganism, and by 655 the last pagan English king, Penda of Mercia, was dead. Now, the question was which brand of Christianity would win. The Celts and some of the northern English wanted to stay independent of Rome, and stick to their own customs. Most English bishops wanted to line up with the Continent. At the Synod of Whitby in 663/4 Bishop Wilfred triumphed by posing the question: "Who holds the keys to heaven?" (Bede). No one could deny that it was Saint Peter, patron of Rome.

Their bridgehead secured, Rome's multinational Christian soldiers flooded in, led by a Greek, Theodore of Tarsus, and an African, Adrian of Canterbury. They showed how the most deeply held beliefs of common people can be changed by a determined new elite. Within a single generation, the English abandoned their ancient custom of burying the dead with grave goods for the afterlife.

> The practice of furnished burials came to an abrupt end in the AD 670s–680s. The disappearance of these rites coincided exactly with Theodore of Tarsus's period as primate . . . a far more radical shift in burial practice among the general population than previously considered possible.
> —*Current Archaeology*, November 6, 2013

Fresh from victory over their own pagans and Celtic heretics, English Christians saw themselves as the heroic shock troops of the Papacy. The oldest surviving Latin Bible of all is the stupendous Codex Amiatinus, a gift to the Pope from Bede's teacher, Coelfrid (642–716); the monks of Jarrow bought two thousand cattle just to make the vellum for it. Saint Boniface (c. 675–754) led a counterinvasion of the old English homelands in

Germany: Still able to talk to the Germans without a translator, he made good progress before winning martyrdom. Alcuin of York became the most trusted political advisor to Charlemagne. Astonishingly, their personal correspondence survives, showing how the English churchman advised the great Frankish king during his restoration of the Roman Empire in 800.

The Great Divide

By the end of the eighth century, the English had reached the limits of their expansion in Britain. In the North, the powerful kingdom of Northumberland was defeated by the Picts at Nechtansmere (c. 685). In the west, the Mercians under King Offa made a great effort to finally conquer the *waehlas* in 778–84. They failed, so they built a colossal dyke to deter cattle-raids and mark the border, patrolling it with mobile guards.

> Offa's Dyke is the largest, most impressive, and most complete purpose-built early medieval monument in Western Europe.
> —Dept. of Culture, Media and Sport, UNESCO application

Two centuries before the Conquest, the borders between the English and their neighbors were basically the same as they are today. And already people had noticed a North-South divide within the English themselves. Bede, writing in about 731, mentions the Humber nine times, every time as a variation on the idea that the Humber estuary "divides the Southern Saxons from the Northern."

Where exactly Bede placed the North-South line farther west is impossible to say—not least because modern Lancashire, Cheshire, Shropshire, and even Herefordshire were still disputed by the Welsh. Over time, though, the Trent became fixed in people's minds as a semi-border within the English.

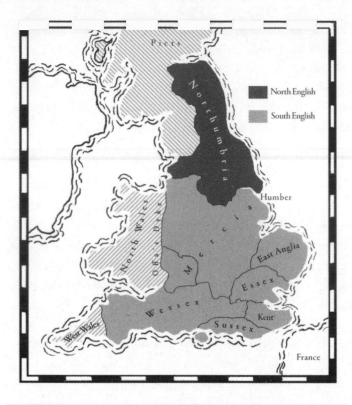

North English

South English

> The traditional symbolic dividing line between North
> and South was the river Trent ... a noticeable northern
> consciousness can be traced back as early as Bede.
> —Andrea Ruddick

The Church officially recognized this divide in Bede's lifetime:
In 733 its lasting, two-headed York-Canterbury structure was
settled. So did lawyers: In a charter of 736, Aethelbald of the
Mercians is "king of all the provinces which are generally called
by the name of the South English [sutangli]."

The Jurassic Divide, which had defined pre-Roman and
Roman Britannia, also shaped the English conquest. And

before long, this cultural divide within England was massively reinforced.

The South Alone Survives

The Vikings pillaged as far south as Pisa, so there was nothing special about their raids on Southampton (840) or London (842). In 865, however, English history again took a unique turn. A huge Viking force smashed into Northumbria and East Anglia—then carved up the land for settlement. England wasn't being raided; it was being colonized. After his defeat at Chippenham (January 6, 878), the one surviving English king, Alfred of Wessex, was reduced to a fugitive.

> Never before has such terror appeared in Britain as we have now suffered from a pagan race, nor was it thought that such an inroad from the sea could be made.
>
> — Alcuin, 793

Early Viking Attacks on England

Somehow, Alfred's Wessex had a unique resilience, perhaps because it had been born as an almost equal, law-based fusion of invading English and resident Romano-British elites. The memories of rural people easily span a mere couple of centuries.* It may be that Alfred of the Cerdicingas (as the Wessex royal family styled itself) was able to call, at the vital moment, on older, deeper loyalties than other English kings.

At any rate, Alfred was able to regroup, rally the shires, and defeat the Danes at the Battle of Eddington (878). Their leader, Guthrum, accepted baptism and agreed to the Treaty of Wedmore, then Alfred and Guthrum's Peace (878–880).

---

* In the 1980s, I was surveying a Norman motte in deepest County Carlow, Ireland. The farmer on whose land it stood pointed to a fine house down in the valley and said, with genuine bitterness, "That land was once ours and it will be again." The house was from the mid-eighteenth century.

Importing Unity

Alfred now wanted to unite the English—Saxons, Angles, and all. In his youth, he had twice visited the court of the Carolingian Franks at Aachen. There, the great medieval deal of Church-State rule established by Charlemagne (with advice from Alcuin) was firmly reinforced. Alfred imported it.

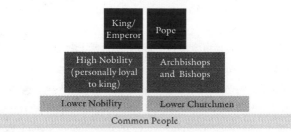

In Alfred's modernized England, as in Francia, kings could only become kings with the approval of the Church, ritually bestowed at the coronation. In politics, too, Frankish practices were aped. The result was a new kind of higher, imperial aristocracy.

> The collective oath of loyalty sworn to the king . . . looks straight back to Carolingian legislation.
>
> —Chris Wickham

One thing Alfred didn't import was rule through Latin. He couldn't. There weren't enough people left (he wrote) on either side of the Humber who could read it. But the unique tradition of ruling through English laws meant there were still people who could read English.

> I remembered how the knowledge of Latin had decayed throughout England, and yet many could read English.
>
> —Letter from Alfred to the Bishop of Worcester

It's assumed that the *Anglo-Saxon Chronicle* was born under Alfred's orders. His drive to unite all the English, in a time of dire necessity, meant that England kept its unique feature: The law and history stayed in the language of the common people.

Alfred also had his eye on the Danes in England. This helps explain a mystery at the birth of English literature. Why is *Beowulf*, the great national epic of Anglo-Saxon England, set in Scandinavia? The answer is that *Beowulf* was the perfect story for Alfred's new politics. A pagan, heroic tale set in Scandinavia, with Scandinavian heroes, but written down and recited in English, showcased the idea that there was a grand old Anglo-Scandinavian heritage common to all, in which society's vital glue was the personal loyalty of the elite to the king.

Alfred's Wessex-Frankish politics worked. In 886 he retook London from the Danes, and took a brand-new title for himself: Rex Anglorum Saxonum or Rex Angul-Saxonum. A few coins even proclaim him simply Rex Anglo (King of the English). He created the first royal navy, three times going to sea himself in ships built to his own design "full nigh twice as long as the others [i.e., the Viking ships] . . . neither shaped like Frisian ships nor Danish, but as he himself thought best that they need-worthily be made" (*Chronicle*).

By his death in 899, Alfred had built an English-speaking version of the most modern political culture in Europe and was "*cyning ofer eall Ongelcyn butan ðæm dæle þe under Dena onwalde wæs*" (king over all Anglekin but the deal [part] that was ruled by the Danes). Even so, that was a great deal. The North-South divide of Bede's day had been massively reinforced by Viking settlement and rule, with the cultural North now reaching almost as far south as the Thames Valley, and East Anglia definitely part of it. English place-names still trace the political boundary at the time of Alfred's death.

Scandinavian
place-names

.... Boundary of
the Danelaw

The Danelaw lives on: Scandinavian place-names in England today

United England, Subservient Britain?

Under Alfred's successors, the Wessex dynasty finally united England. His son and daughter, Edward the Elder and Athelflæd, the *Lady of the Mercians*, retook East Anglia and the Five Boroughs (in the Midlands). As part of their campaign to unite England, the Trent was finally bridged in 920. In 927, Edward's son Athelstan occupied Northumberland. For the first time, all the English—and the Danes—on the island of Britain were ruled by a single king.

> Athelstan, the great conqueror who had secured this happy result, was commemorated as the founder of something glorious and new: the united kingdom of what, in the native language of those who lived in it, was coming to be known as "Englalonde."
>
> —Tom Holland

Modern England was born. And immediately, the central conundrum of English and British history, down to our own day, arose.

A politically united England was clearly the dominant power on the island. So surely, the ruler of England should run the whole place?

In 937, Athelstan made good his claim in a battle so great that it was still remembered by the English two hundred years later: At Brunaburgh, he defeated Constantin, King of Scotland, Owain, King of Strathclyde, and the Viking warlord of Dublin, Olaf Guthfrithsson (whose family had recently ruled York).

Coin of Athelstan
REX TO BR = *Rex Totius Britanniae*

The Chronicle broke into heroic poetry, depicting the battle as the bloody culmination of all English history, while Athelstan's coins proclaimed him King of all Britain. Four of his half sisters married into continental royal families. At his death in 939, Englalonde was a major player in Europe, and claimed to rule all the island of Britain.

Benedictine Spin

Yet no sooner was Athelstan dead than the Vikings retook York, then Northumberland, then the Five Boroughs. After another fifteen years of war, England was redivided once again between the brother-kings Eadwig (South) and Edgar (North), until Eadwig died in 959. Edgar had to buy peace by handing over the northernmost English kingdom, Lothian, to the Scots. It was never retaken.

Edgar cemented his rule with another Frankish import: Benedictine monks, who were re-disciplining the Church and making it the irreplaceable helpmeet of kings. In 973, at Bath, Archbishop Dunstan masterminded the re-crowning ceremony, which still forms the basis of the coronation ritual. Soon afterward—according to his new Benedictine scribes—the kings of Wales and Scotland paid Edgar homage at Chester.

In truth Edgar didn't even rule all of England. His laws explicitly apply only to the English. "Among the Danes," things were to be done "according to as good laws as they can best decide on." A great chunk of England—the Danelaw—was still run by people with their own language, their own laws, and their own loyalties. This was to prove fatal: Within a generation of Edgar's death in 975, England would be a colony of Denmark.

The Decline and Fall of Anglo-Saxon England

Edgar left two underage sons by different women. He also left powerful men affronted by the wealth and power he'd transferred to the Benedictines. It was a formula for trouble.

The older boy, Edward, was crowned, but in 978 he unwisely visited his stepmother Aelfryth at Corfe, and was killed by her men before he'd even dismounted. In his place Aelfryth's own son by Edgar, Aethelred the Unready ("badly advised," a pun on his name, which meant "nobly advised") took the throne under her regency.

With English politics a bloodthirsty mess, the Vikings scented a new opening. After probing raids met with a feeble response, mass attacks followed. The Old English poem *The Battle of Maldon* (991) tells how an English commander and his officers actually behaved as if they were in *Beowulf*, challenging the Vikings head-on and fighting to the death rather than betray their lord.

Yet Maldon was celebrated by the English bards because it was the great exception. Much of the North and East felt more kinship with the Vikings than with the Wessex dynasty. This made an effective national resistance impossible. Instead, the Vikings were paid danegelds to go away. Unsurprisingly, they came back for more. Appeasement corrupted English society because Aethelred used his favorites as tax gatherers, and they took their own cut: no more danegelds, no more cut. Small wonder the *Chronicle* for these years repeatedly laments that plans to confront the Danes were undone by treachery.

Aethelred did make one bold strategic move, and it set wheels in motion that would decide the fate of English England. The Danish raiders often used ports belonging to Duke Richard of Normandy, whose own Viking ancestors had settled there only ninety years before. To bring the Normans onside, Aethelred married Richard's sister, Emma of Normandy, in 1002.

His Norman alliance secured, Aethelred tried to solve England's Danish problem. In November 1002, he ordered the massacre of "all the Danish men who were among the English race."* It backfired spectacularly because one of the dead was the sister of Sweyn, King of Denmark. Raiding England now became official Danish state policy, and the cost of the danegelds spiralled.

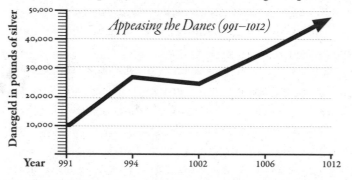

Appeasing the Danes (991–1012)

---

* To the Anglo-Saxons, the Vikings were all just *Danes* of one kind or another.

When Sweyn attacked in person in 1013, the Danelaw showed its true colors. Tellingly, the settled Danish population of England was still known to the *Chronicle*'s authors simply as the army:

> Earl Uchtred and all Northumbria quickly bowed to him, as did all the people of Lindsey and then the people of the Five Boroughs and soon all of the army.

Aethelred, Emma, and their sons fled to her brother's lands. England's royal family were now exiles in Normandy.

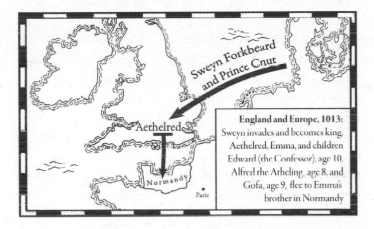

England and Europe, 1013: Sweyn invades and becomes king. Aethelred, Emma, and children Edward (the Confessor), age 10, Alfred the Atheling, age 8, and Gofa, age 9, flee to Emma's brother in Normandy

"This World Is in Haste and It Neareth the End"

So said Bishop Wulfstan in 1014 in his great *Sermon of the Wolf*. And indeed, English England was entering its end-time. When Sweyn died in 1014, the Danelaw naturally declared for his son, Cnut. In the South, the English *witenagemot* (moot of the wise men), sent word to Aethelred in Normandy that they'd have him back—but only if he agreed "to rule rightlier than he ere did."

This is a vital moment. The *witenagemot* didn't dispute Aethelred's dynastic right, but they insisted he had to rule *rightly*. This would be cited centuries later as proof that the king of England had always been chosen by parliament, under conditions. Aethelred agreed, returned across the Channel with Emma, and was restored (though only in the South, of course).

England was now the battleground for rival Vikings, as Aethelred invited King Olaf of Norway to help oust Cnut. According to the Norwegian *Heimskringla* saga, Olaf's men wound their anchor ropes around the piles of London Bridge and sent it falling down. Cnut fled to Denmark, and England had an English king again. Unfortunately, it was still Aethelred. He was soon back to his old ways, with his henchmen killing off rival nobles.

In 1016, Cnut mounted a new invasion and Aethelred died at last. Now, the loyally English South was ravaged by Cnut while the pro-Danish North was ravaged by Edmund Ironside, son of Aethelred. After several indecisive battles, Cnut and Edmund agreed to divide England between them.

The North-South line was the natural one: Edmund got Wessex (including London) and Cnut got the "Northern parts." When Edmund died later that year, Cnut inherited all of England, which now became the center of his Scandinavian empire.

Cnut Danifies England

Cnut wanted to legitimize his rule; Emma of Normandy (Athelred's widow) wanted her throne back; so they married. As part of the deal, Emma's sons were sent back across the Channel, to be guarded once more by her brother, Duke Richard.

> From the moment of Emma's marriage to Cnut, Normandy became a chief factor in English politics.
>
> —J. R. Green

Meanwhile, Cnut ruthlessly purged the high English aristocracy. Several were beheaded, their bodies publicly cast over the walls of London. The rest were replaced with Danish or Norwegian earls.

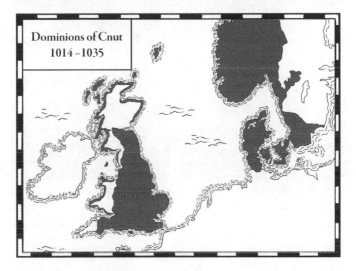

Dominions of Cnut
1014–1035

This Danish conqueror was the first king to officially call his realm *England*. He promised to abide by Edgar's laws, but unlike Edgar, who had admitted that only the English were bound by them, Cnut declared that they applied *"ofer eall Englaland"*—to the English and the Danes alike. This implied that you became rightful king of *Englaland* not by blood or force, but by sticking to established law: that the *law* made the *king*, not the other way around.

At first, Cnut ruled through Danish earls like Siward (immortalized by Shakespeare as the slayer of Macbeth). But within twenty years one Englishman had convinced the Danish king of his loyalty. Named Earl Godwin of Wessex, he was even married into Cnut's extended family. His half-Danish son and heir was named, in the Scandinavian manner, Harold Godwinson.

English Constitutionalism:
born in crisis and invasion
1014–1016

1014 A

Aethelred fettered by Witenagemot's conditional offer

1016 E C

Cnut promises to abide by Edgar's laws and
applies them to all of England

The years 1014–1016 would often be cited in later arguments about the
English constitution.

As in Athelstan's day, the unity of England lasted only as long
as the mighty king. At Cnut's death (1035), Harthacnut (his son
by Emma) was backed by Earl Godwin and "all the most senior
men in Wessex, while most of the thegns north of the Thames"
backed Harold Harefoot (his son by his first English wife,
Aelgilfu). Emma's two sons by Aethelred, Edward and Alfred,
lurked safely in their refuge in Normandy.

When Harthacnut died in a drinking bout at Lambeth in 1042, Edward "the Confessor" took the throne without a fight. After twenty-six years of rule by Danes, England had a (half-) English king again.

England's First French-Speaking King

Edward had spent almost his whole life across the Channel under the protection of his mother's relations. He was steeped in Norman culture, and his first language was French.

The king's childlessness was at once his weakness and his only strength, used to play off hopeful parties against each other. First he headed off Danish invasion by promising that if he died without an heir, the king of Denmark would inherit England. He then swiftly married Earl Godwin's daughter (even though Godwin had killed his younger brother, Alfred) to shore up his power in the South. Next, he moved to balance his new in-laws by inviting his own mother's people over. The *Chronicle* never calls them Normans. They are always Frenchmen (*Frensisce men*) because it was their language that set them apart.

By 1050, a French-speaking royal power-base was being created beyond London's ancient walls, around Edward's Westminster Abbey—the first English building in the imported Romanesque style. The vital archbishopric of Canterbury was given to a Norman. Other *Frensisce men* brought the latest European military technology, which baffled the scribe of the *Chronicle*.

A great mound of earth, topped with a large wooden tower, surrounded by an enclosure of wooden palisades. It was so new and so different that the monk didn't even have a word of his own to describe it. In the end he had to settle for the word the foreigners themselves used and called it a castle.

—Marc Morris

Game of Thrones

In 1051 the Godwins armed up for a coup against the Norman interlopers. Edward played on the North-South divide, summoning "Earl Siward, and Earl Leofric, and many people with them from the North" (*Chronicle*). An ad hoc alliance of the king, Normans, Welshmen, and northern earls drove the Godwins from England. According to one source, William of Normandy personally visited Edward at this time, and was promised the throne.

In 1052, Earl Godwin came back hard and forced Edward to exile most of the Normans. Over the next decade, the Godwins cemented their power. By 1064, now led by the half-Danish Harold, they controlled not only Wessex (almost all-southern England) but also the North, where Harold's brother, Tostig, was in charge. Now, though, two events fatally weakened Harold's position. First, he somehow found himself as the guest (or prisoner) of Duke William in France, where—according to the Normans—he swore to help William become king after Edward. Then, in 1064, Tostig's personal guard was wiped out at York as the Northerners rebelled against Godwin rule. The Welsh again joined them as they marched south. Edward grabbed the chance to tame his wife's family. Harold was forced to go in person to Northampton and inform the rebels that his own brother was being replaced by their choice, Earl Morcar. The furious Tostig, now Harold's mortal enemy, fled to Bruges, to plot revenge.

When Edward finally died, "what followed makes *Game of Thrones* look like a game of musical chairs" (Dan Snow). Harold had no blood-claim, but the *witenagemot* named him king anyway (another boost to future notions that parliament chose the ruler). He immediately had to go north to quell dissent. Then, with Halley's Comet burning in the skies and perplexing men's minds, he hurried back south, knowing that William would soon be coming.

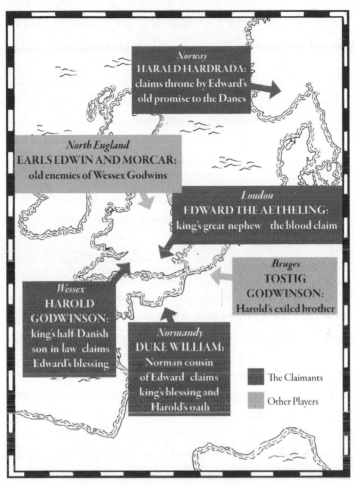

England and Europe on the eve of the Conquest

European power politics now intervened. Pope Alexander II, an Italian, was trying to break the German Emperor Henry IV's hold on the Papacy. In his backyard were the Norman warlords of southern Italy, William's close relatives. In return for their muscle, he blessed William's invasion.

Every adventurer in northern Europe knew that the Danes had conquered rich but disunited England within living memory.

They flocked to William's new papal banner, "scenting the booty that the conquest of England offered" (Ordericus Vitalis).

The North-South divide decided England's fate. Even as Harold awaited William's invasion, Harald Hardrada and his Norwegians linked up with Tostig at the Tyne (or perhaps, in Scotland), and struck south. The brother northern earls, Morcar and Edwin, old enemies of the Godwins, gathered at York and were beaten at Fulford Gate, but, unlike any of the other players that summer, both survived defeat, so it seems likely that their resistance was little more than a show. York then surrendered without a siege and the whole north of England acclaimed the king of Norway.

Harold was forced to race away from the Channel coast, William or no. He surprised the Norwegians basking in the sun at Stamford Bridge, their coats of mail (it was said) still in their ships, and wiped them out, with both Tostig and Hardrada dead. Just three days later, William landed at Pevensey in Sussex.

The Battle of England

Harold had been chosen as king by the *witenagemot* not because of any national, England-wide support, but because he was the great warlord of the South. The northern earls, Morcar and Edwin, lurked in their own power bases, refusing to link up with him, while William and his Norman troops were encamped in Wessex land, ravaging and spreading alarm. With no alternative, Harold confronted William immediately.

Anglo-Scandinavian warfare, with its classic shield-wall infantry formation, was fatally off the Continental pace. At Hastings, Harold's men became the first major army to face the brand-new tactic that would dominate European warfare for centuries: the heavy cavalry charge, with the lance held under the armpit.

A detailed and very early Norman account says that Harold was
deliberately targeted by a four-man hit squad:

The Bayeux Tapestry. Harold, surely, is the figure on the right, cut down by a
cavalryman who has broken through the shield-wall, rather than the knight
trying to remove an arrow from his eye.

William the Anglo-Norman

It took William over six weeks to reach London. If England had been a remotely united country, it would have gathered to resist him. Since it wasn't, the elite concentrated on saving themselves. When William approached the vital Thames crossing at Wallingford, the English commander there, Wigod—one of the most powerful men in the country—simply handed it over and married his daughter to a Norman knight on the spot. William let it be understood that if everyone acted like Wigod, there would need be no drastic change. Before entering London, he issued the so-called *William Charter*, in English.

> William the King greets . . . all the citizens in London, French and English, in friendly fashion; and I inform you that it is my will that your laws and customs be preserved as they were in King Edward's day, that every son shall be his father's heir after his father's death.

Earls Morcar, Edwin, and Waltheof were allowed to stay in place, on payment of large sums. At his coronation in Westminster, William used the English ceremony.

When Harold's Godwin relatives struck back from Ireland, they found little support. In 1067 the ordinary citizens of Bristol held the city against them, for William. The following year, Exeter did rise for them, but after eighteen days of siege by William himself (whose army included Englishmen), they fled and the citizens got remarkably civilized terms of surrender.

It looked as though all England might become a genuinely Anglo-Norman land, like the Anglo-Danish realm of such recent memory. As ever, though, the North was different. At first the Conqueror tried to govern there through established Anglo-Danish ruling families. When that didn't work, a

Norman earl was imposed. The men of the North, who had massacred Tostig's retinue in 1064, went one better in 1069 and slaughtered the new Norman earl along with all his men. Then they summoned the Danes, the nation that really scared William throughout his reign. The longships, says the *Chronicle*, were met by "the Northumbrians and all the people, riding and marching with an immense army rejoicing exceedingly."

William's patience was at an end: the Harrying of the North was a scorched-earth policy so murderously complete that twenty years later, the Domesday Book wrote off one third of all Yorkshire as "wasteland."

The English Elite Desert England

In 1075, Earl Waltheof of Northumberland, the last Englishman with real power, was invited to join an internal Norman rebellion against William. At the last minute, he confessed to the Conqueror, and the rebellion was crushed—with help from native English levies. Waltheof was eventually executed, despite his confession, in 1076. By this time the English warrior elite had nothing left to bargain with, so they fled the country en masse, actively enabled by William. In a fleet variously described as 235 or 350 strong, they went off to fight for the Byzantine Empire, and founded the first New England in the Crimea.

> ### The First New England
> The *Edwardsaga* from thirteenth-century Iceland states that "they called [their towns] both London and York, and by the names of other great towns in England" . . . the "native tongue" of the Varangian Guard continued to be English as late as the mid-fourteenth century.
>
> —Caitlin Green

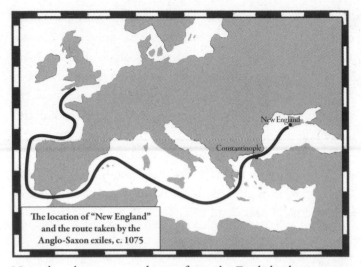

The location of "New England"
and the route taken by the
Anglo-Saxon exiles, c. 1075

Now that there was no danger from the English, there was no reason for William to delay rewarding his own impatient men. For the next decade and more, the English were robbed, under the guise of legal process, in courts run by Normans where the natives were only allowed to answer specific questions and had to use translators. The *Domesday Book* (1087)—named by the English themselves, because (it was said) you had no more chance of disputing it than you would have on Judgment Day itself—set it all down. By William's death, only about 5 percent of England remained in English hands.

> A small armed group speaking a language incomprehensible to the majority of the population controlled virtually all the landed wealth.
>
> —*Oxford History of England*

The Great Question
The lack of resistance by the English, who outnumbered the Normans by about a hundred to one, bewildered the invaders.

Two early Anglo-Norman historians, both with English mothers, shook their heads in disbelief. William of Malmesbury (c. 1095–1143) wrote of "miserable provincials ... so feeble that they failed after the first battle to seriously rise up and make an attempt for their freedom." Ordericus Vitalis (1075–c. 1142) depicts the English as interested only in feasting and drinking, caring nothing for freedom.

Luckily for English pride, however, there are good reasons.

1. **The North-South divide:** No English leader except, briefly, Athelstan, had ever been able truly to mobilize the whole country.

2. **Lack of natural redoubts:** Most of Southern England was near-perfect country for the invincible new Norman cavalry.

3. **No functioning native elite:** The English elite had been corrupted by Aethelred, Danified by Cnut, decimated at Hastings, and had finally fled the country in c. 1076.

4. **The Medieval Warm Period:** By 1100 the skeletons of ordinary Englishmen were distinctly taller than in 1000. No peasantry rebels if their bellies and barns are full.

5. **The Church:** It alone had given Anglo-Saxon England any real unity. Now, it was fully on the side of the Normans.

6. **Civilization:** The English had lived through decades of blood-drenched Anglo-Danish politics. Even after the Conquest, Earl Waltheof was still having rival Englishmen murdered as they sat down to dinner. The *Chronicle* itself, though listing William's acts of brutality and greed, reminded English readers that "betwixt other things is not to be forgotten that good peace which he maked in this land." Any king who maintained law and order was better than what had gone before.

The Normans hammered England into a genuine cultural unit for the first time. Ordinary people from Northumberland and Kent could barely understand one another—in 1066 and for centuries afterward—but their new rulers all spoke the same way, whether their mottes and castles were in Durham or Devon.* By the Conqueror's death, they were firmly in the saddle, on their high horses, talking their fancy foreign, looking down their noses at the English and over their shoulders at France. It was going to stay that way for a very long time.

---

* Norman French was more like modern Catalan than modern French. The way we say *Hainault* and *Theydon Bois* isn't bad English French, but proper Norman French.

PART TWO

The England of Two Tongues
1087–1509

*During the century and a half which
followed the Conquest, there is, to
speak strictly, no English history.*
—Lord Macaulay

A Chance for the English

According to the chronicler Ordericus Vitalis, as William lay dying in France he was hit with deathbed guilt.

> I have persecuted the natives of England beyond all reason ... Having gained the throne of that kingdom by so many crimes I dare not leave it to anyone but God.

So while he officially gave Normandy to his eldest son, Robert, he left the English succession open. Most Norman aristocrats wanted a single realm, with Robert in charge. But William's second son, Rufus, had other ideas. He raced across the Channel so fast that he was the first to bring news of his father's death. Then he appealed to the native English.

> He sent after Englishmen, and told them of his need, and yearned for their support, and promised them the best laws that ever yet were in this land.
>
> —*Chronicle*

Who exactly did Rufus *send after*? We don't know, but there must still have been identifiable leaders among the conquered English. And they decided that a Norman king based in England—one who was asking for their help—was less bad than reinvasion from France:

> The Englishmen went to the assistance [of Rufus] ... They came to the castle at Tonbridge, wherein were Bishop Odo's knights and many others who wanted to hold it against the king. And the Englishmen broke into the castle. —*Chronicle*

A vital group of Normans in England also broke for Rufus. This was the *ministerial nobility*—lower-order Normans who worked for the king as a sort of proto-civil service (real grandees thought such things beneath them). In England, there were lots of them because the Conqueror had restaffed the whole administration. They wanted a smooth transfer of power, and so backed Rufus, who was already on the throne. In 1087–8, Normans based in England made common cause with the ethnic English against Normans from Normandy. This was the birth of a distinct Anglo-Norman realm.

As king, Rufus used England mainly as a tax pump for his endless attempts to conquer Normandy. When, on August 2, 1100, he was killed by an allegedly misaimed arrow while hunting in the New Forest with his younger brother, Henry, nobody mourned. In fact, the royal corpse was left lying there for several days, while, as William of Malmesbury tactfully put it, "all were intent on other matters." Henry certainly was. He raced straight to Winchester, seized control of the Treasury, and had himself declared king the next day.

Rufus had shown how useful the native English could be. Henry, knowing that his older brother, Robert, would be coming for him, went one better: He swiftly married Matilda, great-granddaughter of Edmund Ironside and the last surviving link to the royal line of Wessex. The *Chronicle* (still maintained by devoted English monks) rejoiced: The new queen was "of the right Engla-lands king-kin."

Some of Henry's Norman elite were less impressed, calling him and his wife "Godric and Godiva" behind their backs to mock their Englishness. But his strategy worked. When Robert indeed invaded from Normandy in 1101, Henry was able, as Rufus had been, to mobilize the natives. It seems he could even speak some English himself, for William of

Malmesbury describes him personally teaching his levies how to avoid a second Hastings:

> He frequently went through the ranks, instructing them how to elude the ferocity of the cavalry by opposing their shields and how to return their strokes. By this he made them willingly long for battle, perfectly fearless of the Normans.

Robert backed down again. Henry must have known how vital his English play had been, for in 1103 his only son was named William *Adelin*, from the old English princely title *Aetheling*. A genuine Anglo-Norman synthesis, massively weighted to the Normans but with at least some role for the English, now seemed possible. Then disaster struck.

The *White Ship* sinks

The White Ship

On November 25, 1120, Henry set sail from Barfleur for England. The seventeen-year-old Prince Adelin followed on another vessel, the *White Ship*, with a band of hearty, young, aristocratic companions, determined to overtake his father. The ship hit a rock in the harbor-mouth and went down, taking the part-English heir down with it.

> No ship was ever productive of so much misery to England.
> —William of Malmesbury

A new hope for Henry came in 1133. His daughter, Matilda (named after her English mother), at last had a son—another Henry—by her husband, Geoffrey, Count of Anjou. But skipping a generation like this—and in the female line—was sure to be challenged by the Conqueror's own grandson, Stephen of Blois. Faced with the prospect of rival invasions from France as soon as Henry died, the Anglo-Norman aristocracy looked for ways to nail down their own special position in England.

Owning English History

They began to call themselves *les Engleis*. Of course, that didn't mean that they were the same as the actual *English*. The Engleis might cry *drinc heil!* as they raised their glasses, but that was just a way of claiming a right to their land, like a modern landowner in Scotland whose one word of Gaelic is *slainte!* They spoke only French, and the gap between them and the conquered natives was absolute. As a typical Engleis author wrote (in Latin): "God chose the Normans to exterminate the English nation."

The Normans now reworked the bloody English past into French or Latin tales of chivalry. Here is the sort of thing the elite of England were listening to at dinner, eighty years after the Conquest:

> *Dunc parlat Kenut mult sagement / E dist: Edmund, un poi atent o sui Daneis e vus Engleis / E noz peres furent dous reis.*
>
> Then Cnut spoke very sagely, and said: Edmund, wait awhile, I am Danish and you English, and our fathers were both kings.
>
> —Geffrei Gaimar, *L'Estoire des Engleis*,
> written in England, c. 1140

Today we'd call it cultural appropriation. The Engleis rewrote English history to suit themselves. *Deeds of Hereward* (c. 1125) recruits the resistance fighter Hereward the Wake as a "faithful servant" of King William. In c. 1135 Geoffrey of Monmouth, by far the most influential Engleis writer, transformed Arthur forever from an obscure warlord of the Dark Ages to a great chivalric hero. Geoffrey was the first non-Welsh author to mention Myrddin, whom he changed to Merlin (perhaps because Myrddin sounded too much like the French *merde*). As for the English, their main characteristic is treachery. The message was that Britain should be ruled by a single, non-English king and his united chivalry, whose first duty was to avoid civil strife.

The advice was timely. On November 25, 1135, fifteen years to the day after the disaster of the *White Ship*, Henry I gorged fatally on lampreys in Normandy. The *Chronicle* mourned him: "A good man he was, and there was much awe of him. A man dared not evil do to another in his time. Peace he made for man and beast." The English had given up all hope of getting rid of the French. The best they could hope for now was a strong, Anglo-Norman, *Engleis* king, who had at least some connection to England and who could maintain law and order.

They didn't get one.

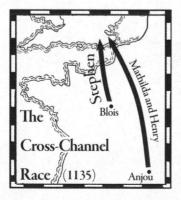

The Cross-Channel Race (1135)

When God and His Angels Slept

Stephen of Blois (Henry I's nephew) won the cross-channel race, fending off the rival French claim of Henry's daughter, Matilda, and her son Prince Henry of Anjou (aka Henry Plantagenet).

Like Rufus and Henry I, Stephen moved to win the backing of the natives, promising London its own assembly. This was a radical concession, and his own Norman elite saw it as weakness. For the hapless English themselves, a weak French-speaking king, unable to keep a strong French-speaking aristocracy in check, was the worst possible case:

> The traitors [i.e., rebel aristrocrats] understood that he [Stephen] a mild man was, soft & good, who did no justice . . . They burdened sadly the wretched men of the land with castle-works; when the castles were maked they filled them with devils & evil men. Then took they those people that they thought any goods had, both by night & by day, men or women & did them imprison, [being] after gold & silver, & pained them with untellable pains . . . They hanged them up by the feet and smoked them with full smoke.
>
> —*Chronicle*

Meanwhile, new troubles were brewing, and they would profoundly alter English history. Normans and Frenchmen had no inherited quarrels with the Scots and Welsh. Yet, being in possession of the richest part of Britain, they soon imagined they should rule the rest of it too. Unlike the English in 1066, however, the Scots and the Welsh had natural redoubts and deep-rooted elites. At Crug Mawr in 1136, the allied Welsh princes destroyed a full Anglo-Norman army, perhaps as large as the force at Hastings, when they used massed longbows for the first time. Two years later, a Scottish counterinvasion reached Yorkshire before it was defeated at the Battle of the Standard.

This was the start of centuries of warfare on the Welsh and Scottish borders that reinforced the ancient differences between the wealthy, pacified Southeast and the rest. It led to the creation of a super-aristocracy known as the Marcher Lords, who were entrusted by English kings with holding, and if possible extending, the disputed frontiers. Soon they controlled all of Cheshire, Lancashire, Durham, Shropshire, Worcestershire, Herefordshire, and Gloucestershire, as well as most of South Wales. Being in a permanent state of semi-mobilization, they could (unlike kings) call on battle-ready men at any moment.

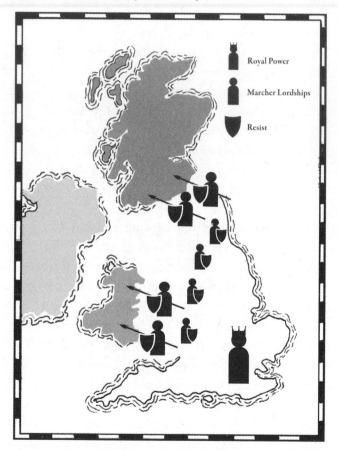

Centuries of warfare on the northern and western borders created an aristocracy strong enough to defy kings. England's unique freedoms were thus largely enabled by the continued resistance of the Welsh and Scots.

THE SHORTEST HISTORY OF ENGLAND

In 1139, England itself was invaded again—from France, naturally—by the Empress Matilda (in the name of her six-year-old son, Henry). The country collapsed into years of civil war and anarchy. Order was only restored by events in France. In 1152, the fabulously wealthy Eleanor of Aquitaine divorced the king of France and, at thirty, married Matilda's son Henry Plantagenet, now a ferociously ambitious nineteen-year-old.

Henry and Eleanor

With Eleanor's treasure backing him, Henry crossed the Channel. In July 1153 his army faced Stephen's across the Thames at Wallingford, but there was no fight. Chivalric deterrence operated in twelfth-century Europe: the heavy cavalry charge was matchless when it came to mowing down hapless foot soldiers, but if steel-clad horsemen met head-on at a combined speed of over forty miles per hour, the result was mutual aristocratic destruction. The Church brokered a deal: Stephen would keep the throne but Henry would inherit.

Stephen died within the year. Though Henry was abroad, he was so feared that he was able to take unchallenged possession. The *Chronicle* expresses the relief among the English at having a strong king able to keep his barons under control "for the great awe of him"—but the return of order sealed the fate of Old English culture. For almost three hundred years, the scribes of the *Anglo-Saxon Chronicle* had set down the story of their people. No other western nation has a record like this.

Its day was done. Henry II was French, not Norman, and ruled more of France than the king of France himself. The political, social, and cultural gravity from across the Channel was now irresistible. The book was finally closed on English England.

> In 1154, the English monks who wrote the *Anglo-Saxon Chronicle* abandoned their work forever. A great silence seems to descend on English writing.
>
> —Robert McCrum

The Most French Place on Earth

> French literature begins, to all intents and purposes, in Anglo-Norman England.
>
> —Ian Short, *Patrons and Polyglots*

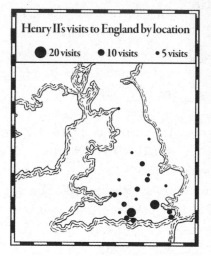

Henry II's visits to England by location

● 20 visits   ● 10 visits   • 5 visits

This vibrant cross-Channel culture made Southern England more different than ever. Henry spent the vast majority of his reign in France, and his visits to England were overwhelmingly to the South.

The new wave of Frenchification had a massive impact on ordinary English people. Survivors of the old English elite now abandoned them altogether, and became French-speakers. In *The Dialogue of the Exchequer* (c. 1180), the Lord Treasurer, Richard FitzNigel, explains:

The English and Normans having now dwelt together, and mutually married and given in marriage, the nations have become so intermingled that one can hardly tell today *(I speak of freemen)* who is of English and who of Norman race. [Author's emphasis]

That rider is vital. Freemen meant roughly the top 5–10 percent of the native English population. It was only these higher-status English—presumably survivors of once-great families who had kept their wealth by collaborating with their new colonial masters—who *intermingled*.

Why were the Norman incomers willing to admit the natives? There was a good reason. Despite the tradition of written English law, the Conqueror and his successors treated their new colony as a legal blank slate and tried to impose the feudal system. This claimed that all noble land was a personal loan from the king, and not necessarily hereditable.

To strengthen their ownership claims and defend themselves against grasping kings, the Anglo-Norman nobles adopted strict primogeniture, meaning that estates and titles descended only to the firstborn male heir. This was extremely rare: Elsewhere in Europe, all the children of an aristocrat (and all their children, and so on) inherited the title—and the legal privileges that went with it. In England, primogeniture created a tight, rich aristocracy whose younger sons and daughters had neither lands nor titles, and were legally no different than commoners.

Naturally these scions of the Norman aristocracy were keen to stay rich by any means possible—such as marrying the offspring of native Englishmen who had remained on the right side of the occupiers. This meant there was always a way into the Anglo-Norman elite. Around FitzNigel's time, the male descendant of Gospatric, the last English Earl of

Northumberland, married a Norman and took her name of *de Neville*. By this deal, the Norman woman stayed wealthy and the Englishman entered the Norman elite.

Colonial England

By 1180, the English elite had refashioned themselves in the image of their masters by making the great leap of adopting French language and culture. This is typical of what happens in a colony. In a normal country, things look like this (right).

Elite set apart by geneaology. Entry is very difficult.

General Population

Elite set apart by learnable language & culture.

General Population

That was how things were set up in most European countries until the French Revolution, and in many of them until the Great War. But in a colony, be it Roman, Anglo-Norman, or part of the British Empire, things look like the illustration on the left.

> Many historians have remarked on the openness, in comparison with France or Germany, of the English elite from the Middle Ages on . . . From very much earlier, they were ready . . . to admit incomers to their circle.
>
> —Derek Sayer, *American Journal of Sociology*

To get into the French elite, the survivors of the pre-Conquest elite had to speak fluent French on all important social or business occasions. By doing so, they set themselves publicly apart from the common English.

> The difference between French and English became one of rank, rather than of race. French was for the landlords and officers, English for the peasants and privates . . . "*rusticanus*" was the term used for a peasant ignorant of any language but English.
> —Sir James Holt, *Colonial England 1066–1215*

It took over a century for a profound consequence of 1066 to become clear: The ordinary English—90 percent of the population—were left with no leaders of their own. By adopting the language of the conquerors, and intermingling with them if allowed, the surviving English freemen hoped that their own families would retain some level of privilege after the deluge. That is what happens in colonies. The price was setting themselves publicly apart from the people they had once led. The result was a relatively open colonial elite lording it over a leaderless peasantry whose ancient national culture had been abandoned.

No other major Western European people experienced anything like this in the second millennium—until England visited it upon its neighbors. Becoming a pure colony was the third great uniqueness in English history (after being conquered by Germans, then settled en masse by the Vikings), and it was to mark these islands forever.

The Frenchification of English Law

Until Henry II's reign, local courts used both French and English, depending who was before them. Henry rammed through the creation of the royal assizes, traveling courts designed to provide swift justice. At the Assize of Clarendon in 1166, the signature feature of English law, the jury of "twelve of the more lawful men of the Hundred," was first set down (in Latin). The royal assizes were speedy and efficient, so use of them soon spread—and their proceedings were always conducted in French. Henceforth, from generation to generation, any ordinary English who came before the law were reminded that they were second-class citizens in their own nation.

King vs. Church

Henry II (left), face-to-face with his powerful archbishop

The only real brake on royal power in high-medieval Europe was the Church. Henry II thought he had found the perfect man to bend it to his will in Thomas à Becket, a humble-born but clever Anglo-Norman who had risen fast in colonial England. In 1162, Becket was created archbishop of Canterbury. The obedient functionary was now a made man in a great, Europe-wide organization, and instead of placing the English Church under the royal thumb, Becket became the champion of its rights.

At last, in 1170, Henry (in Normandy, as usual) fell into one of his notorious furies, crying out: "What miserable drones and traitors have I nourished and brought up in my household, who let their lord be treated with such shameful contempt by a low-born cleric?" Four knights set out to Canterbury, where they slew Becket in his own church. All Europe was horrified, and Henry was forced to do public penance. The Church had won the great showdown.

The episode left England with a powerful and confident Church, wary of monarchical power, which made it, most unusually for Europe, ready to ally with the aristocracy against the Crown. Forty years later, this would become vital.

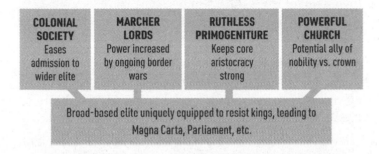

COLONIAL SOCIETY	MARCHER LORDS	RUTHLESS PRIMOGENITURE	POWERFUL CHURCH
Eases admission to wider elite	Power increased by ongoing border wars	Keeps core aristocracy strong	Potential ally of nobility vs. crown

Broad-based elite uniquely equipped to resist kings, leading to Magna Carta, Parliament, etc.

An Island Too Far

Henry was now bounced into an imperial adventure which was to distort English politics for centuries. In 1169, the Welsh marcher lord the Earl of Pembroke ("Strongbow") was hired to fight in an Irish civil war, and did so well that he looked set to create his very own Anglo-Norman-Irish-Welsh super-lordship.

No Roman, British, Anglo-Saxon, or Norman regime had ever claimed to rule Ireland, but Henry could not tolerate this. He sailed to Ireland himself in 1171 and demanded fealty from all, before declaring his beloved fourth son, John, Lord of Ireland. Theoretically, Ireland was conquered before Scotland or Wales, and Henry intended to actually crown John king of it once he got the Pope onside. But the native Irish kings fought back, John infuriated everybody in Ireland, Irish or Norman, and the plan had to be abandoned.

Richard, Henry's eldest living son, rebelled in arms and harried his father across France until Henry named him, rather than John, as his heir. In 1189, the exhausted king who had finally Frenchified England died in his real homeland, at Chinon.

The Devil Is Loose

Richard I wrote poems in both French and Norman French, and could read Latin, but there is no evidence that he could understand English, let alone speak it. He spent only seven months of his ten-year reign in England, which he treated as a cash cow for his crusading, selling off royal demesnes to fill his coffers and joking that he'd put London itself on the market if there were a buyer.

As the Crown's own resources were used up, Richard's officials were forced to raise special taxes and fees (this is the historical background to most modern versions of Robin Hood). Soon, the aristocracy rebelled against his low-born enforcer-in-chief, William Longchamp. In 1191, Longchamp tried to flee the country, disguised as a poor woman peddling a bundle of cloth. His cover was blown when somebody asked him how much he wanted for it: the bishop of Ely and chancellor of England didn't speak a word of English. Meanwhile, Richard was shipwrecked upon returning home from the Crusades and ended up a prisoner of the Holy Roman emperor. The emperor demanded 100,000 marks to let him go. Richard's brother, John, and King Philip of France offered 80,000 to keep him in jail, but royal officials in England raised the full sum and he was released. On February 4, 1194, Philip sent a warning message to John: "Look to yourself; the devil is loose."

Richard, however, forgave John, and spent the last five years of his life taxing the English even more heavily. At his death in 1199, John, who as the fourth son could never realistically have expected to become king, crossed the Channel with a small army to claim the throne of a half-bankrupt England, even though his teenage nephew, Arthur, duke of Brittany, was actually next in line.

The Road to Runnymede

John's borderline usurpation, and the empty coffers Richard had left him, put him in a weak position. The king of France used Arthur to blackmail him into conceding territory. Eventually open war broke out, and though John managed to seize Arthur (the youth mysteriously vanished shortly afterward), by 1204 he lost all his French possessions. This marks the birth of a purely Engleis aristocracy in England—albeit one that still spoke French.

For the next ten years, John plotted—and taxed the English—to regain his lost French realms. In 1214 he mounted a final bid in alliance with Otto IV, the Holy Roman Emperor. Although he was the bankroller, John wasn't present when the forces met at the epochal Battle of Bouvines. The French cavalry won the day, ushering in modern France as well as one of the great events in English history.

French and combined Imperial/English cavalry clash at Bouvines (1214)

The road from Bouvines to Runnymede was direct, short, and unavoidable.

—Sir James Holt

With John's European plan in ruins, the barons, backed by the muscularly independent English Church, brought him to bay at Runnymede in June 1215 and forced him to sign what became known as Magna Carta.

> Throughout the document it is implied that here is a law which is above the King and which even he must not break.
>
> —Winston Churchill

Magna Carta

Many of Magna Carta's clauses address now-obscure financial disputes between the king and the nobility. The most enduring are:

1: The English Church is guaranteed "independence of appointments from the Crown." This opening clause shows the central role the Church played in taming the monarchy.

14: Taxes can only be raised after a "general summons" of major landowners. Here is the germ of Parliament.

20: Fines to be proportionate and only given with "the oath of trustworthy men of the locality." Radical, since it implies that non-noble men can be involved in justice-giving.

39–40: The ones people today think of when they talk about Magna Carta: "No freeman is to be arrested, or imprisoned, or disseised, or outlawed, or exiled, or in any other way ruined, nor will we go against him or send against him, except by the lawful judgment of his peers or by the law of the land."

56–59: These clauses deal with the rights of Welshmen and the Scottish King, who had both helped the rebellion against John. Apart from everything else, Magna Carta confirms that Wales and Scotland are separate jurisdictions.

60: "All in the kingdom, and not only the barons confronting John, should observe the provisions of the charter in their dealings *with those beneath them*." [Author's emphasis] This implies something like an idea of universal justice for Englishmen.

Suffix A was radical indeed: the barons and the 'commune of the whole land' had the right to 'distrain and afflict' the king himself if he broke the Charter. Later this would be taken to mean that Parliament had this power.

The Charter was set down in Latin and immediately translated into the daily language of the English barons: *Icy comence la chartre le Rey Johan done a Renemede.* There was no written English version until 1534. Up till then, if you (or your lawyers) couldn't read French or Latin, Magna Carta was none of your business.

John didn't mean a word of it. He persuaded the Pope to annul the Charter, then filled the land with mercenaries from northern France. The barons countered by inviting the king of France to save England from pillage by outsiders. Prince Louis accordingly sent an advance party of knights to London in late 1215, before mounting a full invasion the following year, landing at Thanet. John fled to Winchester, and Louis was proclaimed (though not crowned) king of England.

The two sides were still locked in warfare—consisting mainly of great sieges, as at Rochester and Dover—when John died of dysentery. Matthew Paris, monk and historian, delivered the ultimate condemnation: "Foul as it is, Hell itself is made fouler by the presence of John."

Strange Aliens vs. Naturals

John's son Henry was only nine years old in 1216 when he became king, and large areas of England were under French control. His throne was saved by victory over Louis at Lincoln. The boy-king's council quickly reissued the Charter. In 1225, old enough to rule, Henry reconfirmed it personally, of his own free will, in exchange for taxes. Magna Carta now became constitutional holy writ—literally, for the bishops declared that anyone who broke it, including the king, could be excommunicated. The unique tradition which had begun in a misty way with Ethelred and Cnut was now set down on vellum: *Even the king of England himself had to obey the law.*

Under Henry III, England became still more French. The new Westminster Abbey (begun 1245) was built to honor Edward the Confessor, who had invited French-speakers over to help him rule, and was modeled on the latest French cathedrals. Henry's half-siblings, relatives, and hangers-on crossed the Channel by the shipload.

Civil war now broke out in England between rival groups of Frenchmen, who pronounced French differently, which is why we have pairs like *guardian/warden* and *gallop/wallop*. The English-born Frenchmen, known as *natureus*, were led by Simon de Montfort. They had one great advantage over their rivals, the *estranges aliens*: They could talk to the natives. And they did. When de Montfort forced Henry to accept the Provisions of Oxford (1258), letters explaining the agreement were sent out across the land. For the first time since 1067 (and the last for many years) the common people of England heard the words of their rulers read out in English as well as French.

Et se nul v nus viegnent encunt ceste chose nus voulons et comandons ke tuz nos seaus et leaus le teignent a enemi mortel.
(13th-century French)

And gif oni other onie cumen her ongenes we willen and hoaten that alle ure trewe heom healden deadliche ifoan.
(13th-century English)

And if any person or persons go against this, we will and command that all true to us hold them as deadly foes.
(Modern English)

The Provisions of Oxford placed the king under the authority of a council of fifteen, and stipulated that parliaments be held three times a year. According to Parliament's official website, it was the "most radical scheme of reform undertaken before the arrest and execution of King Charles I."

Henry went back on the deal, and war broke out. In 1264, de Montfort's army, which was partly composed of ordinary Londoners, won a stunning victory at the Battle of Lewes, capturing both Henry III and his heir, Prince Edward. For the first time since the Conquest, we hear English political rejoicing in English. The bard of the "Song Against the King of Alemaigne" (1264) gleefully imagines Edward riding spurless *all the ryhte way to Dovere-ward*, never more to break his word.

De Montfort allowed the captive Henry to remain king, with all decisions subject to approval by Parliament. But when Prince Edward escaped and gathered an army of disaffected nobles, he was doomed. At the Battle of Evesham on August 4, 1265, the chivalric values of the age were suspended. De Montfort had dared to enlist the common people: Now he was treated as a common rebel, and targeted by a twelve-man hit squad who hacked him to pieces. Virtually all his followers were slaughtered on the spot. Henry III himself, a prisoner in de Montfort's ranks, was almost killed by accident because he wasn't wearing the badge Prince Edward had chosen to mark out his own men—the St. George's Cross. The national banner of England was born at the defeat of the first man who'd appealed in English to the English since 1066.

Simon de Montfort is dismembered on August 4, 1265, at the Battle of Evesham

The Limits of Power: Edward I

The royal power seemed so completely restored that Edward I tried one last time to impose pure feudalism. The barons stayed loyal, but refused to allow him to roll back Magna Carta: He was forced to agree that anyone who'd held land at the accession of Richard I in 1189 was legally secure, even from the king (this is the origin of the phrase "since time immemorial"). From now on, an Englishman's castle really was his castle, not just on loan from the king.

Thwarted at home, Edward turned his attention to foreign conquest. In 1278, he traveled to Glastonbury to witness the opening of Arthur's alleged tomb, then he put the myth of the Arthurian *Empire of Britain* into practice. In Wales he pursued a vast, methodical and ruthless campaign in 1282–83. Victory was set in stone, as a Savoyan military architect, James

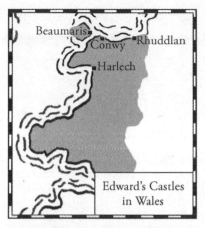

Edward I's attempt to quash the last
redoubt of the Romano-British

of St. George, created the greatest set of castles on earth, at colossal expense. Edward partly defrayed the cost by expelling all the Jews of England in 1290 and declaring that debts owed to them were now owed to him.

Scotland was next in Edward's sights. His wars offered the English a sort of comeback as most-favored native group under foreign-speaking commanders (the same offer the English would make later to Sikhs and Gurkhas). Before 1066, the English had fought the Welsh and Scots, but at times had also regional alliances with them, and had never claimed to be culturally superior. That idea was invented, as a handy sop to defeated English pride, by their new elite. *Langtoft's Chronicle*, the official record of Edward's 1294 campaign against Scotland, opens with the first example of modern English nationalism—in French:

> *Gales soit maldit de Deus e de Saint Symoun! Car tuz jours*
> *ad este pleins de tresoun. Escoce soit maldit de la Mere De!*
>
> Cursed be the Welsh in the name of God and St. Simon!
> For they have always been full of treason. May the Scots be
> accursed by the mother of God!

In a few places, though, Langtoft slots into his French the words he must have heard being used by Edward's English troops:

> *The fote folke puth the Scotes in the polke, and nakned their nages.*
>
> The foot-folk put the Scots in the poke, and made bare their backsides.

French was for the cavalry, English for the *fote folke* (as they apparently called themselves). And they knew it. The constant, daily presence of a culturally foreign elite reminded them, from generation to generation, of their own great national trauma. Robert of Gloucester, writing around 1290, neatly expresses the subjugation of the English:

> *Thus com lo engelond in to normandies hond.*
> *& the normans ne couthe speke tho bote hor owe speche . . .*
> *Vor bote a man conne frenss me telth of him lute.*
> *Ac lowe men holdeth to engliss & to hor owe speche.*
>
> Thus came, lo! England into Normandy's hand.
> And the Normans could only speak their own speech . . .
> Unless a man knows French, men think little of him.
> But low men hold to English and to their own speech.

Even so, the English were willing to fight their neighbors under French-speaking officers—the ancestors of the "Ruperts" whom modern English soldiers secretly despise yet still obey.

The vast expense of fighting the Welsh and the Scots was the chance for the English elite's very own device—Parliament—to come of age. If England had been a normal country with its own ruling class, Edward might have tried to tame the aristocracy by giving the peasants (who could be taxed more easily) rights over their own property. That is exactly what happened in France during this era. But Edward, as a French-speaking king, could hardly side with English-speaking peasants against his own French-speaking nobility. So he admitted that he needed to negotiate—*parley*—with them. The 1295 Model Parliament gave things the basic shape we still know today.

> In France, the manor lost; the peasant won. In England, the manor won; the peasant lost.
>
> —Sir Robert Morier

For all the huge expenditure, Edward never truly quelled Wales. And in 1307, as he lay on his deathbed at his field HQ in Cumbria, he received news that his forces in Scotland had been defeated by Robert Bruce. His wars hardened all three nationalisms in Britain, leaving "a legacy of division that has lasted from his day to our own" (Marc Morris). They also enshrined Parliament as co-ruler of England.

Which the Community Shall Have Chosen: Edward II

In 1308, Edward II was crowned in French, rather than Latin. This was because his barons wanted him personally, beyond all doubt, to mouth a radical new clause in their own everyday language. It still exists in the Coronation Oath: The king agreed to obey laws that did not yet exist, but which might come about in the future if the "community of the realm"—Parliament—chose.

> *Sire, grauntez vous a tenir et garder les leys et les custumes droitureles les quiels la communaute de vostre roiaume aura eslu?*
>
> Sire, do you promise to maintain and defend the rightful laws and customs which *the community of your realm shall have chosen?*

Edward didn't see which way the wind was blowing. He heaped titles and money on his Gascon favorite, Piers Gaveston, until in 1312 the barons rose in open rebellion and murdered Gaveston outside Kenilworth Castle. The royal fortunes were soon in a tailspin. The Scots destroyed Edward's much larger army at Bannockburn in 1314. In 1320, his forces suffered ignominious defeat in France, and in order to keep any land at all there, he had to visit the king of France to do personal homage.

On the journey, Queen Isabella began an affair with Roger Mortimer. She refused to return home with Edward, staying behind to mount yet another invasion of England from across the Channel. Edward was captured, then murdered in 1327—the gory details have been disputed ever since—leaving Isabella and Mortimer as de facto rulers of England. Tensions with the young king soon escalated, and in 1330 the seventeen-year-old Edward and a band of followers ambushed and executed Mortimer at Nottingham Castle. So began the reign proper of Edward III, which lasted an extraordinary forty-seven further years.

The Hundred Years' War

By 1346, having agreed to a truce with the Scots and won control of the Channel in the great naval battle of Sluys (1340), Edward III was ready to pursue his claim to the French throne and mount a full-scale invasion. At Crécy (1346) the English and Welsh longbowmen mowed down the French cavalry. Nine years later, at Poitiers (1356), the Black Prince, Edward III's son, routed them again.

> The English archers took one step forwards, drew their bowstrings to their ears, and loosed their arrows, in such unity and so thickly that it seemed like snow.
>
> —Froissart, *Chronicles*

With French armies now frankly shy of pitched battle, France became a happy hunting ground for a generation of English looters and pillagers. Decades of war against the French made it strange for the English nobility to speak French in front of their own men, and it is in these years that they—though not the king and his court—finally began to use English as their daily language. The greatest boost to Englishness, however, came from natural causes.

Plague: Lucky for Some

The Great Death (as it was called at the time) killed 30–45 percent of all the people in England in 1349–50. It came back in 1361–64, 1368–69, and 1371–75. By the end of the fourth epidemic, the population had halved, and it did not fully recover for two hundred years.

"In 1300 a knight might choose to be represented on his tombstone as a young knight in all his vigor; by 1400 graphic depictions of skeletons and decay as a warning of mortality were in vogue." —Barbara Tuchman, *A Distant Mirror*

Fan-vaulting, Gloucester, 1351

But plague doesn't hurt property. The survivors among the wealthy got even wealthier through unexpected inheritances. They expressed their gratitude in gifts to the church, leading to spectacular new architectural masterpieces such as the first fan vaulting in England, in Gloucester Cathedral.

The real winners were the lucky among the English-speaking peasantry. We have to imagine medieval English rural society as working on two separate levels. The French-speaking lords of the manors wanted income out of their estates; they didn't care which English-speaking peasants were their tenants, so long as they paid the rent. But among the English-speaking peasantry themselves, luck, work, and cunning had led to a second-tier class system of its own.

> When a peasant leaves the manor or dies without heirs, the other tenants offer a sort of small land-market and bid for his land . . . [hence] this emergence of peasants richer and more prosperous than their fellows.
>
> —R. H. Tawney

Like their aristocratic counterparts, these better-off peasants formed extended families by marriage. If half the extended family died in the Black Death, the survivors would be doubly wealthy, bumped up suddenly into a new rural middle class.

Yet even the poorest peasants benefited from the Black Death, because land was no good without people to work it. With fewer peasants about, wages soared.

> [They] do withdraw themselves from serving great men and others, unless they have livery [i.e., free food and drink] and wages double or treble of what they were wont to take.
>
> —Statute of Labourers 1351

By the harvest season of 1349, a reaper could demand 8 denarii (English pennies) a day, with free food on top, when a cow could be bought for a shilling (equal to 12d). The regime tried to impose wage controls with draconian threats, but this new market couldn't be bucked. Lucky peasant farmers with unexpected inheritances and plenty of surviving relatives of working age (who could be paid in board and lodging) prospered so much that they were able to lease noble lands that weren't viable for aristocrats who had to pay wages in cash.

Inheritances, new tenancies, and land leases all meant legal documents. For the first time in almost three hundred years, there were ordinary English people with cases to bring to law, and the money to do it. In 1362 the Statute of Pleading decreed that all pleas should be "counted in the English language." The original statute was still in French, and in practice the lawyers of England ignored it: In the half-century after the plague, demand actually rocketed for writers versed in legal French. Still, the new status of English had been officially recognized, and was famously summed up thus:

> lered [learned] and lewed [ignorant], olde and yonge, Alle vnderstonden english tongue
>
> —*The Mirror of Life*, c. 1350–75

Yet this means exactly what it says. Even if *alle vnderstonden* English, anyone who wanted to be someone still had to speak French too.

> Chyldren in school, against the usage and manner of all other nacions, beeth compelled to leave there own language and for to construe there lessons and there things in Freynsch, and haveth since the Normans come furst into Engelond. Also gentilmen children beeth y-taught for to speke Freynsch from tyme that they beeth y-rokked in there cradel . . . and uplandish men will liken themselves to gentilmen, and try with gret bysynes for to speke Freynsch, for to be better thought of.
>
> —John of Trevisa [slightly updated]

What of the ordinary English who couldn't afford to abandon their own culture or didn't want to uplandishly ape their betters? William Langland's *Piers Plowman*, written in English around 1380, has what may be the earliest reference to the "rymes of Robin Hood." It seems the English had long been retelling stories of the great resistance fighter in his forest redoubt, and dreaming of a long-lost "Merrie England." Now, a generation after the Black Death and three centuries after the Conquest, they tried to make it real.

At Last, an English Rebellion

Edward III died in 1377 and his grandson was crowned Richard II at ten years of age. Under his uncle, John of Gaunt, the nobility tried to turn the clock back to pre–Black Death days, enforcing lapsed feudal rights to unpaid labor on their estates to avoid paying the new, higher wages. But the Black Death had left a new class of English who were prosperous and even literate, despite being still legally peasants. They now faced being made to do unpaid work for the local aristocrat, in keeping with French or Latin laws. What had once seemed inescapable now seemed outrageous.

At last, the common people of England had rebel leaders sprung from their own ranks, who literally spoke their own language. When the final straw came with the Poll Tax of 1381, it wasn't the poorest English who revolted, but those in the richest corner of England—which was, as ever, the Southeast.

> In a short time there were fiue thousand gotten togither of those commons and husbandmen . . . beheading all such men of law, iustices, and iurors as they might catch, and laie hands vpon . . . they purposed to burne and destroie all records, evidences, court-rolles . . . And so likewise did they at Westminster, where they brake open the eschequer, and destroied the ancient bookes and other records there.
>
> —Holinshed, *Chronicles*

The rebels targeted lawyers, books of law, and records—the very pillars of rule through foreign tongues. John Wycliffe, Oxford scholar and leader of the Lollard heretics, demanded the Bible in English and a nationalized church for the people *her in Ynglonde*. The preacher John Ball, released from prison by the rebels, asked at Blackheath: "When Adam delved and Eve span, who was then the gentleman?"

With order in London collapsing, a king of England was forced, for the first time since 1066, to speak to his people, in person, in English. Wat Tyler, leader of the rebels, came to Richard II not on foot, but mounted: the *fote folke* were now in the saddle. Tyler even took the king by the arm and called him "brother." The Mayor of London could not tolerate this, and struck Tyler down. At the moment of high peril, Richard rose to the occasion, breaking away from his men and addressing the crowd.

> [Richard] went up by himself to the insurgents, who were putting themselves in battle array. "Sirs," said he, "what do you want? You have no other captain but me; I am your king: keep at peace."

Richard had instinctively seen that the rebels' anger wasn't aimed at the king. It was the semi-foreign nobility they really hated. They wanted to hear the Bible, read the laws, and speak to power in their own language. They wanted, in short, to undo the Conquest. So when their handsome young king rode forward alone, and spoke to them in English—calling them "gentlemen"!—they trusted him, and were (of course) hunted down afterward.

Richard recovered his power, but things would never be the same again, because it wasn't just that the English peasantry were growing restive. The Engleis aristocracy was starting to break apart, and in a very English way.

The Times They Are A-Changing Back

Since 1066, the French-speaking elite had given a gloss of cultural unity to a country where ordinary men from the South and the North could barely understand one another:

> It seemeth a great wonder how English, that is the birth-tongue of English men, and their own language and tongue, is so diverse of sound in this island . . . Al the longage of the Northumbres, and specially at York ys so scharp, slyttyng, and frotyng, and vnschape, that we Southern men may that longage scarcely understonde.
>
> —John of Trevisa, 1385

Richard's 1395 portrait. After the close shave of 1381, he adopted the supposed arms of Edward the Confessor to court popularity—and then became the first king since Edward to deliberately play on the North-South divide within England.

By the fourteenth century, the ancient divide had infected even the French-speaking elite. Chivalric heralds separated the nobility of England into *Norroy* (North realm) and *Surroy* (South realm, later *Clarenceux*), with the border being the Trent. Oxford and Cambridge used the same river to split their students into *Australes* (South) and *Boreales* (North), each "nation" (as they were called) with its own administrators.

Since the Conquest, the Normans had been able to plaster over this divide, and ambitious Englishmen had always tried to imitate them. But as the fifteenth century dawned, this began to change.

> Now, in the year of oure Lord a thousond thre hondred foure score and fyve . . . gentil men habbeth now moche yleft for to teche their childern Frensch.
>
> —John of Trevisa (slightly updated)

As the French-speaking culture of the elite weakened, older forces in England raised their heads. The Peasants' Revolt had been in the south, so Richard looked northward. From Cheshire he recruited the first-ever personal royal army; in 1398, at Nottingham, he announced that he didn't trust the men of *"Londoun, and of xvii shires lyying aboute."* Unless the southerners paid him a vast sum, he would gather a great army and "*destroie thaym*." The same year, he exiled his cousin, Henry Bolingbroke (who fled to France) and seized the vast Duchy of Lancaster, buttressing his strength in the North.

Naturally, the South turned hostile. Bolingbroke took advantage of Richard's absence in Ireland to return, and men flocked to his banner. By the time Richard got back, his support was melting away. He surrendered to Bolingbroke, who was crowned Henry IV on October 13, 1399.

The Old Order Falls

Henry IV, with a weak claim to the throne, made a populist appeal to ordinary English folk, becoming the first king since Edward the Confessor to accept the crown in English. He then had the *Record and Process* (originally in Latin) of why he had deposed Richard II read out in English too.

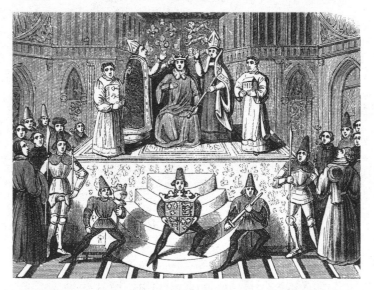

The first blatant usurper since the Conquest was also the first to make his accession speech in English.

It was spin, because Henry's private messages to his nobles were still all in French, but it worked. The following year, after the failed Epiphany Rising, supporters of the deposed Richard II (still alive in captivity) fled to Cirencester. The gang included some of the highest nobles in the land. In previous generations, awe of the Normans might have cowed the townspeople. But now the Englishmen of Cirencester grabbed their bows and pinned the aristocrats indoors all night with a hail of arrows. The next day, defying orders to bring the rebels before the king for judgment, the Gloucestershire men led the captured aristocrats ignominiously away on foot, while they themselves rode their horses. Then they "*smoot of the lordis heddis.*" For the first time since Durham in 1069, a company of fully armed aristocrats had been defied, defeated, and slaughtered by English commoners.

A great disruption was coming, as the post-Conquest order collapsed.

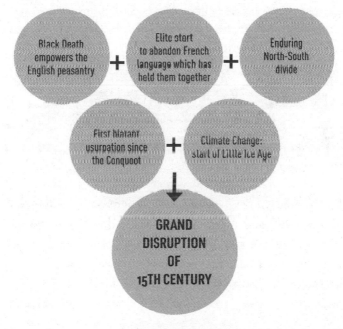

Carving Up England

With great alterations in the air, the warlords of England began to think the unthinkable. In 1403, the Mortimers (Richard II's legitimate heirs) united with the mighty Percys, virtual rulers of Northumberland, and Owain Glyndwr of Wales to rebel against Henry IV. The king marched his army up from the South at breakneck speed, intercepting the northerners before they could link up with the Welsh, at Shrewsbury on July 21, 1403.

As if the Conquest had never happened, northern and southern Englishmen, led by English-speaking aristocrats, faced off in pitched battle. Their fearsome longbows were now unleashed on each other, and the history of the nation turned the flights of two arrows. One killed Henry Hotspur, son of the Earl of Northumberland, and his army lost heart. The other smashed six inches deep into the face of Prince Hal—the future Henry V—just below his eye, but he stayed on the field until victory was won, and was saved in a near-miraculous operation by the surgeon John Bradmore.

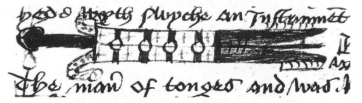

John Bradmore's sketch of the instrument he created to remove the arrow in Prince Hal's skull.

Yet the rebels regrouped and in 1405 agreed to the Tripartite Indenture. This extraordinary deal, set down in Latin and witnessed by the king of France, aimed at nothing less than carving up England forever. Glyndwr, Mortimer, and Percy were each to get a brand-new realm "for himself and his successors" (*sibi et successoribus*). A 2,500-strong French army landed at Milford Haven to support the plot, but it was too late. Henry had time to defeat the Northerners first; Glyndwr, the Mortimers, and the French then simply gave up.

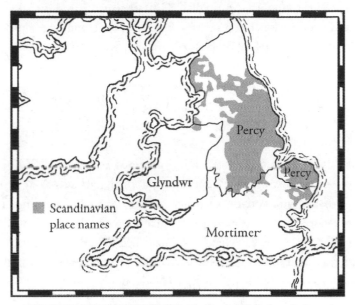

THE TRIPARTITE INDENTURE. The border of the Percys' planned Northern English realm is extremely close to that of Viking settlements in the century before the Conquest. The plotters of 1405 didn't know this, of course. They didn't have to: Everyone knew the North and the South were different.

English unity had been saved, but the price was a serious transfer of power to Parliament. Henry had needed its support to get through the crisis, and members of Parliament (MPs) took their chance: In 1406, the Lords and Commons sat for a record 139 days, including the first ever all-night sitting, and forced the king to subject even his household expenditure to inspection. Henry desperately tried to revive the royal authority in the traditional way—war with France—but his campaigns were abject failures. Sick and worn out, he died in 1413, having caught his son trying on the crown while he was (just) still alive.

Once More unto the Breach: Henry V

Henry V knew he needed Parliament onside if he wanted to keep the old dream of France alive, so he issued proclamations asking for support—in English. His father had paved the way at his coronation, but now the language of the common people reached new levels of official acceptance.

> Henry V's use of English marks the turning point in establishing English as the national language of England.
> —John H. Fisher, *The Emergence of Standard English*

Henry got his invasion, but it all seemed to be going badly wrong when the French cornered his small, sickness-ravaged force at Agincourt on October 25, 1415. Luckily for Henry, the caste-bound aristocracy of France were hopelessly wedded to the heavy cavalry charge of their ancestors, despite recent defeats by the Flemish and the Turks. It was Crécy all over again as the English archers had a field day.

A contemporary picture of Agincourt. The painter knew who had really mattered: All the action is between the non-noble archers, while the aristocratic knights are almost offstage.

After this spectacular triumph, Henry was married to Catherine, daughter of the king of France. Briefly, it seemed as though the Conquest had been turned on its head and that France would now be ruled by English-speakers. In reality, the English hold was too weak to tax the French citizenry, so the costs of the occupation had to be met from English taxes, and quickly became unsustainable. Henry was still campaigning in France when he died in August 1422, leaving England with its heir a mere nine-month-old baby.

Fit for Any Mischief

By mid-century, with the memory of Joan of Arc (d. 1431) inspiring the French resistance, the English position was crumbling. The young Henry VI was married off to the French princess Margaret of Anjou in an effort to buy peace. It didn't work. In 1450 the last English army in Normandy was annihilated. Defeated and unpaid English soldiers flooded back to a bankrupt country.

> The return of the garrisons and armies from overseas filled England with knights and archers, accustomed to war, license, and plunder and fit for any mischief.
>
> —Trevelyan

As in 1381, the men of Kent rose in 1450 and occupied London in Jack Cade's Rebellion. Henry VI fled to Kenilworth, while for three days Cade turned the entire social order on its head.

> The said captain rode about the city bearing a naked sword in his hand . . . wearing a pair of gilt spurs, and a gilt helmet and a gown of blue velvet, as if he had been a lord or a knight, and yet was he but a knave.
>
> —*Davies Chronicle*

Cade complained that King Henry's "fals cowncell" had led England to disaster: "his comon people is dystroyed, the sea is lost, Fraunce is lost, the kynge hym selffe is so set that he may not pay for his mete nor drynke." Cade's solution was that Henry should place his trust in *the hyghe and myghty prynce* Richard, Duke of York. The trouble was that, as a direct descendant of Edward III on both his mother and his father's side, Richard had a serious claim to the throne himself. His moment seemed to have come when Bordeaux, English for three hundred years, was lost in the summer of 1453, swiftly followed by the whole of Aquitaine. Only Calais now remained. Henry VI suffered a complete mental breakdown when he heard the news. York maneuvered to take over, but then, to everyone's surprise, Margaret bore Henry a son in October 1453, and the king seemed to recover his sanity.

The Hundred Years' War for France was lost; immediately thirty years of war for England began.

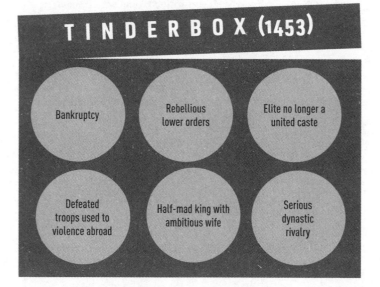

TINDERBOX (1453)

Bankruptcy	Rebellious lower orders	Elite no longer a united caste
Defeated troops used to violence abroad	Half-mad king with ambitious wife	Serious dynastic rivalry

North vs. South: The Wars of the Roses

Fifty years earlier, the southern Mortimers and the northern Percys had planned to split England between them. Now their descendants became deadly rivals in a war to rule the whole country, both sides of the Trent. In 1455, at the First Battle of St. Albans, Richard of York (heir to the Mortimers) and Richard Neville (aka Warwick the Kingmaker; mighty in the South but also the only rival to Percy hegemony in the North) lined up against the king and the Northumberland Percys.

At first it looked like an almost random series of alliances, vendettas, and betrayals, but as the war dragged on, the underlying pattern became clear. Since the York family powerbase was (confusingly) in the Welsh Marches, the native Welsh broke for the Lancastrians (named because their own family powerbase was the great Duchy of Lancaster). An English earl of 1051 would have easily understood what was happening: It was the warlords of the North and Wales against the warlords of the South, fighting for control of London and the throne.

By 1461, the Lancastrians were seen by all as the Northern party. When Queen Margaret appeared outside London after her great victory at St. Albans on February 17, 1461, the Londoners so feared her *Northern-men* that they locked the city against her.

> Thenne kyng Harry, with Margarete his quene and the Northern-men, went and returned homewarde toward the North again: whyche Northurnemenne as they went homwarde did harmes innumerable, taking men's cartes, waynes, horses and beastis, and robbed the peple.
>
> —Friedrich W. D. Brie, *The Brut*
> Written before 1471 (slightly updated)

The Southerners pursued Margaret and her Northern army across the Trent. At Towton on March 29, 1461, both sides massed all the men they could: perhaps thirty-five thousand Yorkists and forty thousand Lancastrians. The gulf that existed between those men is illustrated by a famous anecdote of William Caxton, father of English printing.

> Some Northern merchants, becalmed off the Kent coast, went ashore in search of supplies: And one of them named Sheffelde, a mercer, came into a house and asked for meat; and specially he asked after eggs; And the good wife answered that she could speak no French.
>
> —William Caxton, 1490

The Northern and Southern foot-folk who lined up at Towton could barely understand one another. And they were no longer led by rival members of a French-speaking caste who might jockey violently, but who in the end wanted to keep their colonized English subjects under control. Now, the aristocrats of England all spoke English and they had begun to act like old-fashioned English warlords, each with his own local powerbase, intent not just on winning, but on wiping out his opponents. It was as if 1066 and chivalry had never happened.

> The war saw the complete breakdown of the medieval code of chivalry . . . In 1460–61 alone, twelve noblemen were killed in the field and six were beheaded off it, removing a third of the English peerage.
>
> —Ed West

The scene was set—smack on the old North-South border— for England's bloodiest day.

Around twenty thousand Englishmen died, when the entire population was not much more than 2 million. Today, that would equal five hundred thousand fighting-age Englishmen being killed, at close quarters, in a single afternoon.

One of many skulls found at Towton, bearing witness to the savage close-quarter fighting

The Yorkists won the day, and the extraordinary slaughter should have ended the war. Yet the Lancastrian heir, Prince Edward, was safe in France, where King Louis XI had a clear interest in keeping the English fighting amongst themselves. There, Sir John Fortescue wrote a little Latin history of England for him. Here it is, in a 1577 translation:

The realm of England was first inhabited of the Britons. Next after them the Romans had the rule of the land And then again the Britons possessed it. After whom the Saxons invaded it, who changing the name thereof did for Britain call it England. After them for a certain time the Danes had the dominion of the realm, then Saxons again. But last of all the Normans subdued it, whose descent continues in the government of the kingdom at this present.

Four centuries after the Conquest, even as their—now English-speaking—elite slaughtered one another, the kings of England still saw themselves as direct descendants of the Normans.

With Edward the Lancastrian heir alive, and Warwick the Kingmaker changing sides for personal reasons, the war went on until, at Tewkesbury on May 4, 1471, the last real Lancastrian army was smashed. The by now usual post-battle executions included that of Prince Edward himself. With him safely dead, there was no reason for the Yorkists to keep his mad father, Henry, alive as a puppet. Edward of York was crowned as Edward IV, and the Wars of the Roses were (it seemed) over.

This Sun of York: An English England Again, At Last?

The wars caused surprisingly little damage to the English economy. For a century beforehand, the English had done all their fighting in France. Warriors on both sides knew that the castles and towns of England had hopelessly outdated defenses, so instead of retreating behind walls, they chose to settle things in the open field. As a result, aristocrats had fallen like nine-pins but there had been no great sieges, little laying waste of the countryside, and not much interruption of trade. A French chronicler wrote enviously:

> Neither the countryside nor the people are destroyed, nor are buildings burned or demolished. Disaster and misfortune fall only on those who make war, the soldiers and the nobles.
> —Philippe de Commynes, cited by John Gillingham

This had shifted social power to non-aristocrats, making English fully acceptable at last. There were now English-speakers rich and educated enough to want those great prestige items, books—but after four hundred years of French-speaking rule, there were very few English books to be had. In 1473, William Caxton, a multilingual English trader based in Flanders, having seen the latest German information technology at work, scented a gap in the market. He set himself up with copied machinery, either in Bruges or in Ghent, and produced the first printed book in English: *The Recuyell of the Historyes of Troye*, translated by himself from the French. Three years later, he set up his machines in London, and began churning out English books at unheard-of speed.

England was more English than it had been since 1015. It had even grown its very own building style: a unique form of late Gothic—*Perpendicular*—which would entrance later architectural patriots:

Backwards travels our gaze . . . Back through the brash adventurous days of the first Elizabeth and the hard materialism of the Tudors, and there at last we find them, or seem to find them, in many a village church, beneath the tall tracery of a perpendicular east window and the coffered ceiling of the chantry chapel . . . They would speak to us in our own English tongue.

—Enoch Powell, April 1961

But there was nothing more truly English than the North-South divide, and it now sparked the final, unexpected act of the Wars of the Roses.

The Most English King?
Even with the wars apparently over, the North needed special handling, so Edward IV appointed his brother, Richard of Gloucester, to run the new Council of the North (1472). This allowed Richard to build up his own power base at York. By

1483, he had virtually royal authority there. When Edward IV died that year, Richard mounted a York family coup, taking the throne as Richard III. Edward's sons were never heard of again.

The most reviled king in English history was the first and only ever to claim (in the document known as the Titulus Regius) that his right was based on the "common opinion of the people" and the "publique voice." In fact, though, the "publique voice" was split. Southern England rebelled almost immediately, and Richard was forced more and more to rely on northern henchmen.

> The catte [Catesby], the ratte [Ratcliff], and Lovell our dogge rulyth all England under the hogge
> —Anti-Richard propaganda of the day (Lovell's emblem was a hunting dog and Richard III's a white boar)

Richard III, represented (left) by an early Tudor artist and (right) by the actor Laurence Olivier. In both pictures, his body is as lopsided as his realm.

The North-South divide in English minds outweighed any superficial politics, as southern dislike of Richard's northern enforcers turned the constellation of 1455–71 on its head and revived the Lancastrian cause.

New Dynasty, New Country, New Elite

At Rennes Cathedral, on Christmas Day 1483, Henry Tudor, last hope of the Lancastrians, was publicly engaged to Elizabeth, daughter of Edward IV, sister of the murdered princes. Two years later, in 1485, the second-last successful invasion of England set out from Harfleur on August 1, landing at Milford Haven in Wales.

Henry was part Welsh, which meant he had two out of the three power blocs of the Tripartite Indenture of 1405 in his pocket: It was now the South and the Welsh against the North. When the forces met at Bosworth, Richard saw his allies wavering. He risked all on a direct personal charge at Henry, who took cover amidst his French mercenaries until Richard's key commander, Sir William Stanley, made the vital decision to turn his coat. The real last battle of the Wars of the Roses—probably bigger than Bosworth itself—took place on the Trent, at Stoke Field, on June 16, 1487. Henry's southern English and Welsh forces routed the Yorkist northerners, Irishmen, and German mercenaries.

The war for England was over. But it was no longer just England. For a thousand years, the Welsh had resisted. Now, they stopped—not because they had been beaten, but because they saw the new king as one of their own. England had only just emerged again as a true nation, yet now it was ruled by a king whose great-grandfather had fought for his own nation against the English.

Henry VII wasn't just Welsh: He was as self-consciously European as any medieval king. He had spent the past fourteen years in France, and modeled himself on modern French royal taste. That meant Renaissance Humanism, whose signature was a new, rational statecraft (as described by Niccolò Machiavelli) in which kings were to be served and guided by an elite who had studied the classics.

For the next four hundred years, the entire English upper class was expected to have good French, decent Latin, and a smattering of ancient Greek. Anyone who could speak only English was *proletarian*, *hoi polloi*, not *comme il faut*—and if you didn't understand those insults, well, it just went to show. Oxford and Cambridge demanded both ancient Greek and Latin from all applicants until 1919, with Latin still required until 1960.

There was worse coming for the foot-folk. English, much changed but still their own language, had just become fully respectable again after centuries—yet now Henry's new men (*homines novi*) of learning began to import words wholesale from French, Latin, and Greek.

By 1490, William Caxton could already see what was happening. Caxton had been accused of using "curious terms which could not be understood of common people." Keen to "satisfy every man" (and find as many readers as possible) he took an old English book from his shelves.

> the English was so rude and broad that I could not well understand it . . . [It was] more like to Dutch than English . . .
>
> —Prologue to *The boke yf Eneydos*, 1490

In the end, Caxton had to admit defeat. Since it was impossible to please both commoners and gentlefolk, he plumped for the more lucrative market:

> This book is not for every rude and uncunning [ignorant] man to see but to clerks and very gentlemen that understand gentleness and science.

The English language itself was splitting into two levels.

The Tudor State

The Wars of the Roses had culled the old military aristocracy (there were only twenty-nine lords left in 1485) so Henry had an epochal chance to rebalance power in favor of the Crown and its "new men." The Council Learned in the Law rode roughshod over the nobility in a radical, modernizing partnership between King and Parliament, against the old aristocracy. Henry had observed this new model of state-building during his long exile in France.

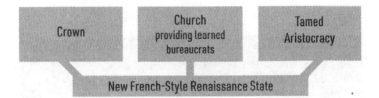

| Crown | Church providing learned bureaucrats | Tamed Aristocracy |

New French-Style Renaissance State

Henry also followed European rulers into the New World. In 1496, the Italian explorer John Cabot was given a royal warrant. He returned in triumph the following year, having discovered North America. Within two years, the king was backing a home-grown English explorer, William Weston of Bristol:

> We intend that he shall shortly with God's grace pass and sail for to search and find if he can the new-found land.
>
> —Henry VII to Cardinal Morton, c. 1499

Tudor legitimacy was secured when, in 1501, Henry married his son and heir, Prince Arthur, to Catherine of Aragon, a member of the mighty Habsburg family, rulers of half of Europe. Arthur died almost immediately, but that wasn't allowed to spoil the diplomatic party. Even though Arthur had apparently boasted that he "had spent the night in Spain," everyone handily agreed that the marriage had never been consummated. This meant Catherine could be kept on ice in England until Henry's younger son, another Henry, was old enough to marry her instead.

At Henry VII's death in 1509, the elite was more multilingual than ever, and the Church of Rome, ruling hand-in-hand with the Crown, was the bedrock of daily life. Bequests from rich and poor for prayers to be said for their souls were more popular than ever, and mighty works of devotion arose or were made over. Nothing suggested that England was about to take off on an entirely new path.

Effigies of Henry VII and his wife Elizabeth in the Lady Chapel of Westminster Abbey, constructed shortly after the king's death.

PART THREE

The English and Empire
1509–1763

The Thwarted European

To Henry VIII, being King of England was just the start. Charles V, the Holy Roman Emperor, and Francis I of France were both about his age, and Henry saw himself as their equal in Europe. He began by reasserting the old claim that he was rightful heir to France.

Henri Grace à Dieu (1514) was the most powerful and expensive warship afloat. The name signaled Henry's obsession.

Having immediately married, as planned, the Habsburg princess Catherine of Aragon, he allied with her family to invade France in 1512, and again in 1513. His forces won the Battle of the Spurs, but for all the expense there was no tangible gain.

Piqued, Henry made peace with France and announced that he would stand as a rival candidate to be the next Holy Roman Emperor. He even had it put about by his agents that he could speak German.

Playing power games with the big boys of Europe cost big money, yet England only had a quarter of the population of France, a fifth of the Holy Roman Empire. And with the English economy in such a fragile state, raising taxes was a dangerous business.

The entire Old World was disrupted in this era by the Little Ice Age, which hit food supplies, and by the sudden, inflationary injection of precious metals from the New World. England, though, had one special trouble. This was *enclosures*, the great flashpoint of popular discontent for the next three centuries.

The Enclosing of England

Until the late fifteenth century, almost all farmland in England was on the open-field system, where people's land was held in strips rather like large allotments. The idea was that everybody would have a share of good land, poor land, and fallow land.

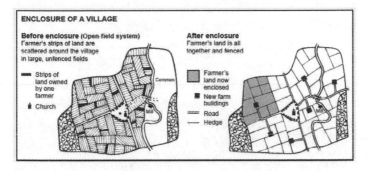

Putting strips of land together meant that wealthier farmers could try out new farming techniques or crops without having to negotiate with everybody else in the village. So when a lord wanted to enclose his lands, he could count on the support of his better-off tenants. The great issue was the common land. Here, everybody could keep a few geese, goats, or pigs—even a cow or two.

> The king, or the Lord of the Manor, might have owned an estate in one sense of the word, but the peasant enjoyed . . . rights which enabled him, or her, to graze stock, cut wood or peat, draw water or grow crops.
>
> —Simon Fairlie

To subsistence farmers, this was often the difference between mere survival and being able to make a tiny amount of money—enough, perhaps, over thrifty generations, to drag a laboring family into the lowest rungs of the tenantry. Common land provided a small but important chance of social mobility.

Rules about who could keep what on the common land varied
greatly, depending on local traditions and verbal agreements.

When a manor was enclosed, however, the lawyers had no
time for unwritten traditions. The common land was divided
up too, and awarded to farmers in proportion to their existing
holdings. That meant the lord got most of it, and people who
already had official tenancies were next. Laborers without their
own land found it difficult to prove that they had ever had any
right to the common land: Without written evidence, it was
easy for lords to argue that they'd only used it on sufferance.

The very idea of a landless, illiterate peasant appealing against
the court was absurd. The poor often ended up with nothing—
or with such tiny and inconvenient plots that it wasn't worth the
work of fencing and ditching them in, so they were sold to bigger
owners for a pittance. The impact was worst when landlords
turned over their newly enclosed land to the great cash crop of
the day—sheep for wool—which required far fewer laborers.

Enclosures made landowners richer, helped the better-off peasantry, and created the most destabilizing thing for any society:
a class of poor folk with no hope of ever bettering themselves.

The Unquiet Land

As ancient rural communities collapsed, people flooded into towns and cities, especially London. In its dog-eat-dog streets, they were easy prey to demagogues. In 1517, the Evil May Day Riots erupted after a renegade priest told his congregation that foreigners "ate the bread from poor fatherless children." Things got so out of control that the constable of the Tower of London fired artillery from his battlements at the rampaging citizens.

Cardinal Thomas Wolsey (1473–1530), Henry's chief advisor, tried to restore the royal finances, and hence order, by making surveys of England so detailed they've been called a *Second Domesday*. Despite the fall of the Roman Empire, the English invasions, the Vikings, the Conquest, the High Medieval boom, the Black Death, and the Wars of the Roses, the North South divide was almost exactly the same as in 300 CE.

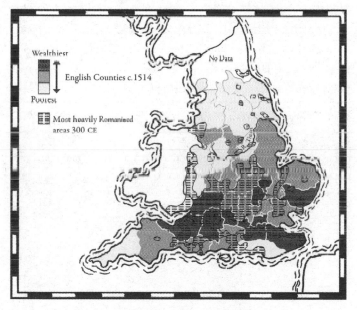

The most heavily Romanized areas in 300 CE were still the richest in England
in the early 16th century

Armed with this information, and following the latest French theories on state-building, Wolsey imposed an unheard-of level of central control and taxation, much resented by landowners. He also tried to introduce French-style Roman law, earning himself the hatred of London's influential common lawyers. But so long as he had Henry's trust, he was all-powerful. With the Treaty of London (1518) and the great royal moot in France at the Field of the Cloth of Gold (1520), he presented Henry as the peacemaker of Europe.

Henry was a pillar of the European establishment: In 1521, he personally denounced a troublesome priest from Germany called Martin Luther, and the grateful Pope awarded him the title Defender of the Faith (which his descendants still use).

Then the New World disrupted the balance of the Old.

Enter the New World

In 1519, the Habsburg family's worldwide possessions were united when Charles V inherited them all and was (despite Henry's candidacy) elected Holy Roman Emperor. His vast new realm threatened to dominate all Europe.

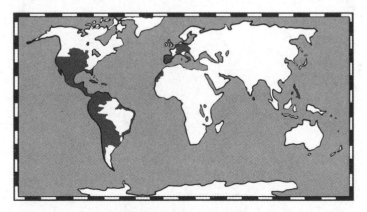

Empire of Charles V from 1519. The phrase "an empire on which the sun never sets" was coined for it.

When this mighty new empire crushed the French at Pavia (1525), Henry saw not disaster, but his great chance. He swapped sides again, demanding a full-scale invasion of France. Wolsey had no choice but to obey. A special tax was announced, optimistically named the Amicable Grant. But Henry's French obsession was pushing England too far: Parliament resisted and thousands of peasants rose in open revolt. Henry had to back down, blaming Wolsey for it all.

He was thirty-four. His dreams of ruling France and of becoming Holy Roman Emperor were thwarted; his subjects were restive; and he still didn't have an heir. He convinced himself that his marriage was cursed because Catherine of Aragon had been his brother's wife, and that his new paramour, Anne Boleyn, would give him a son.

Wolsey pressured Catherine to declare that her brief 1501 marriage to Henry's brother had indeed been consummated. When that failed, he lobbied the Pope to declare her a liar. But Catherine had close relatives in high places, and one—the mighty Charles V—happened to have just stormed and occupied Rome itself. For the Pope, it was no choice. Fifteen years of aggression and duplicity had left Henry with no serious ally in Europe, outgunned at the vital moment. The crisis was the opportunity for a new alliance of religious radicalism and political ambition.

Such Men Are Dangerous: Reformers and Radicals

In Cambridge, the scholars of the White Horse Circle (named after the pub where they met) looked across to Europe in awe at the career of Martin Luther.

Luther had turned himself from a mere priest and lawyer, like them, into an international influencer, feared by the Pope and courted by princes. His trick had been to master the new mass media of the cheap, printed pamphlet, talk to the common people in their own language, and offer Germany's rulers (nervous lest the Catholic Church become a mere tool of the Habsburgs) control of their very own *Protestant* state churches.

The Cambridge men took note. Their radical associates, safe in exile in Antwerp, cranked up the printing presses. On February 2, 1529, Henry was leading the traditional Candlemas procession at Westminster when an incendiary pamphlet entitled *A Supplication for the Beggars* was thrown and scattered at the procession.

Packed with made-up statistics and wild accusations, it offered a conspiracy theory calculated to appeal to commoners and king alike. What was the cause of the ancient oppression of the English people? Why was the country in such dire economic straits? Who was stopping Henry from solving his dynastic problems? It was Rome! If only the foreign rule of Rome were broken, there would not only be a financial dividend for all the English and a grand renewal of national vigor—it would also mean total power for Henry.

Then shall these great yearly exactions cease. Then shall not your sword, power, crown, dignity, and obedience of your people be translated from you. Then shall you have full obedience of your people. Then shall the idle people be set to work. Then shall matrimony be much better kept. Then shall the generation of your people be increased. Then shall your commons increase in riches. Then shall the gospel be preached. Then shall none beg our alms from us. Then shall we have enough and more than shall suffice us; which shall be the best hospital that ever was founded for us.

—*A Supplication for the Beggars*, 1528–29

The author, Simon Fish, was no lone wolf. He shared exile in Antwerp with the great Bible translator, William Tyndale, who claimed that Rome was guilty of the Conquest itself. After all, hadn't the Pope supported the Conqueror, sending "a banner to go and conquer England?" Tyndale offered Henry VIII a heady vision of total power:

> The king is, in this world, without law; and may at his lust do right or wrong, and shall give accounts but to God only.
> —*The Obedience of Christian Man*, 1528

Henry was tempted. And vitally, he was backed by powerful members of the elite. England's aristocrats and London's common lawyers (many of whom were also MPs) both wanted Wolsey off their backs. Having virtually ruled England by sole dint of the royal favor, Wolsey had no allies when it was withdrawn. He died in November 1530 en route to London to face charges of treason. Yet still the king held back from an open breach with the Church "from fear of his subjects" (according to Anne Boleyn herself). Catherine of Aragon was popular. To get rid of her, Henry needed public backing from England's most trusted institution.

Parliament Seizes the Day

Both houses of Parliament jumped at the chance to replace the Church as the great tool of royal power. Wolsey's erstwhile sidekick, Thomas Cromwell, dusted off fourteenth-century laws called *praemunire* and made the breathtaking claim that the entire English clergy were traitors because the Papacy was a foreign power. A circle of radicalization developed, with power-hungry men in London doing things unthinkable a mere few years before.

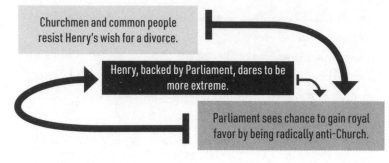

Churchmen and common people resist Henry's wish for a divorce.

Henry, backed by Parliament, dares to be more extreme.

Parliament sees chance to gain royal favor by being radically anti-Church.

The new Archbishop of Canterbury, Thomas Cranmer, pronounced Henry's marriage to Catherine of Aragon null and void. In the Act in Restraint of Appeals (1533) it was declared:

> England is an Empire, and so hath been accepted in the world, governed by one Supreme Head and King.

The Act of Supremacy (1534) made this law. England was now completely sovereign, like no other major nation in Europe. But it soon became clear that the common English and their elite meant entirely different things by *England.*

What Do They Know of England Who Only England Know?

To the ordinary English, England (or *Englonde,* or *Ynglonde*) meant the land where they were born, lived and died—where ordinary people spoke English. To the multilingual elite, it meant what the act said: "England is an Empire." In other words, it was wherever in the world Henry and his loyal Parliament ruled.

This empire straightaway set out from its epicenter in the South of England. It never cared remotely about nationalism. Indeed, the Northern English resisted the new empire of the Protestant South more strongly than some of the Celts: Wales was finally assimilated to England in 1536 without a shot being fired, whereas in 1536–37, thirty-five thousand armed Northerners gathered at York and seriously shook Henry's throne in the Pilgrimage of Grace, until they were hoodwinked by royal promises to abandon the Reformation: Hundreds were executed, including several members of the Northern aristocracy. Wales, the North—then Ireland: in 1541, Henry was proclaimed its first English King. Finally, Scotland: from 1543, Henry pursued the *rough wooing*, trying to impose the marriage of six-year-old Prince Edward to two-year-old Mary, future Queen of Scots, by military force, as a prelude to full incorporation. And even France: In 1544–46 the area around Boulogne was ethnically cleansed in a brutal campaign, and resettled with the first planned overseas English colonists.

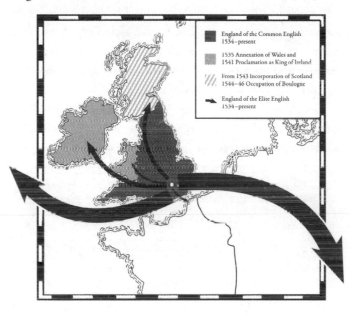

All Power to the South

The new Empire of England was funded by a vast royal asset grab. In the Dissolution of the Monasteries (begun 1536), about a quarter of all the land in England and Wales changed hands within a few years. Henry carted ancient treasures away by the wagonload and monastic property was sold off for him by Cromwell's Court of Augmentations.

The prices were knockdown because this wasn't ordinary business. It was a political sell-off: The new owners would never want monasticism back, and would thus be tied to the new order. If you were in the right place (London) with the right idea (ruthless opportunism), the right connections (to Cromwell's henchmen), and the wherewithal (ready money), it was a time of dizzying opportunity.

Even in England, there had never been social mobility like this. The later dictator, Oliver Cromwell, was a member of the gentry (vital to his career) only because his great-great-great-grandfather, Morgan ap William, a cash-rich Welsh brewer in London, was married to Thomas Cromwell's own sister and hence able to profit by the Dissolution: The family changed their name to Cromwell by way of thanks.

A new, broader ruling order was born, more centered on London, backed by scholars at Oxbridge, with Parliament its natural home, and Protestantism its very own religion.

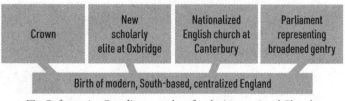

The Reformation Paradigm: no place for the international Church, the common English, or the North

Selling the Reformation

But of course, the Dissolution and the Reformation had to be sold to at least some of the common people as more than just a change of guard among the elite. And sold it was, using all the resources of the new, centralized Tudor state and new media, as an English national uprising against a foreign elite and their venal collaborators.

Cranmer's traveling preachers and Cromwell's printing presses (which employed top international artists like Hans

Holbein's portrait of Thomas Cromwell

Holbein) told the ordinary English that attacking the foreign-language elite culture of England was not only allowed; it was the King's will itself. The whole story of England was retold. The great shrine of St. Thomas à Becket, who had dared to resist a king, was destroyed and his bones personally burned by Cromwell "so that no more mention shall be made of him never." A state-sponsored traveling theater company, The Lord Cromwell's Players, paved the way for Shakespeare's historical plays by making the rambunctious public theater into a place where the English learned of their (supposed) history: In *Kynge Johan* (1538), the king who had been forced to grant Magna Carta was recast as an anti-Papal national hero. Like the Russian Bolsheviks to come in the 1920s, England's Reformers nailed down their coup by using new media and the power of the state to rewrite or erase history. Unlike the Russian Bolsheviks, they had the benefit of a ready-made—and genuine—story of foreign cultural oppression. They didn't fail to use it.

> Tyndale [reformer and translator of the Bible into English] associates himself fully with the popular legend of the Norman Yoke, which attributed all evils to the Norman Conquest of the free Anglo-Saxons . . . his addition of an anti-papal element added to the popularity of the old myth.
>
> —Christopher Hill

The Reformers found their keenest foot soldiers in the Southeast: the same area where the peasant rebels of 1381 had especially targeted books in foreign tongues. This was no coincidence. In the 1530s, as in 1381, it wasn't the poorest ordinary English who were most radical, but the best-off and most literate (in the advanced Southeast, about 10 percent of the English could read). They were already big men among their fellows: Having the Bible in English would make them fully equipped community leaders, because they would now have direct access to the great handbook for society, at present owned and ring-fenced in Latin by the real elite. The Reformation offered a chance for the English yeomanry to at last retake the social position they'd lost after 1066.

Slamming on the Brakes

Henry VIII saw what was going on. The common English were getting out of control: "The Word of God [he cried to Parliament] is disputed, rhymed, sung and jangled in every ale-house and tavern." Now that he had the monks' wealth and his longed-for son (Edward, born 1537), the king wanted an end to the disruption.

The *Six Articles* of 1539 restored almost all Catholic practice except obedience to the Pope. In 1543, ordinary Englishmen of the rank of yeomen or under were banned from owning, reading, or even hearing the Bible in English. Now, Catholics were burned for treason (denying the royal supremacy) while Protestants were burned for heresy (breaking the *Six Articles*). On at least one occasion, both were burned on the same pyre.

Adding to the confusion, Henry kept changing his mind about the status of his daughters. Edward was indisputably the rightful heir, but the positions of Mary (Catherine of Aragon's daughter) and Elizabeth (Anne Boleyn's daughter) were less clear. Henry knew that each time he shuffled their ranking order, he risked popular opposition, so he demanded public backing from Parliament. Fearful and ambitious MPs rubber-stamped his wishes every time, but the effect was to make it look as if Parliament co-decided the next sovereign.

Old Coppernose: a debased shilling

The one-off windfall from the Dissolution was spent out. Henry was paying 13 percent to borrow, and the currency was so debased that foreigners refused to accept it (his nickname became Old Coppernose because the silver plate on his coins wore quickly through). The Empire of England was rolled back, in Europe and at home. Henry's flagship, the *Mary Rose*, was lost in 1545 when the French attempted to counterinvade; in 1546, he had to promise to sell Boulogne back to France; and the rough wooing of Scotland was called off.

By now, nobody's head was safe and the English hardly knew what was official religion and what was heresy. In his will, the king who broke with Rome begged the "Blessed Virgin and holy company of Heaven" to ease him into the afterlife. Henry VIII died on January 28, 1547, halfway through yet another round of executions, leaving England in the hands of new-made men ready for anything.

Nailing Down the Reformation

Edward VI was only nine on his accession. His uncle, Edward Seymour, promoted himself to Duke of Somerset—Protector Somerset—backed by John Dudley, the new Earl of Warwick. They set about ensuring that the Reformation that had made them could never be undone. By government diktat, the parish churches, chantries, and cathedrals of England were purged.

> This largely state-sponsored destruction . . . was a comprehensive dismantling and eradication of centuries-worth of medieval art and religious and cultural tradition.
>
> —Tate Museum

The common people had been promised a Reformation dividend, but Somerset quickly enacted the most ferocious poor law in English history. Anyone unemployed for three days had to do any work offered them, just for food. Otherwise, the would-be employer could enslave them for two years, and "cause the said Slave to work by beating, chaining or otherwise in such work and Labour how vile so ever it be." The old, rambunctious Catholicism, with its scores of feast days and festivals, was replaced with state-disciplined Protestantism.

> Our holy and festival days are very well reduced also unto a less number; for whereas (not long since) we had under the pope four score and fifteen, called festivals, and thirty *profesti*, beside the Sundays, they are all brought unto seven and twenty.
>
> —William Harrison, 1577

Too late, the ordinary English rose up to defend their old freedoms. In 1549, the Prayer Book Rebellion in Cornwall was crushed with extraordinary brutality: According to one chronicle, nine hundred prisoners had their throats cut in ten minutes. The peasants of Kett's Rebellion took Norwich before launching a wild charge at Dudley's well-ordered force:

> One of these cursed boys, putting down his hose, and . . . turning his bare buttocks to our men, with an horrible noise . . . did that, which a chaste tongue shameth

His star high, Dudley did away with Seymour, and in May 1553 married his son to Lady Jane Grey, a great-granddaughter of Henry VII, getting the bedridden Edward to declare Jane's male heirs his successors. At the last moment, the document was altered to make Jane herself next in line. With Dudley's only possible rivals, Mary and Elizabeth, both unmarried women, England looked set for a brand new dynasty when Edward died, aged fifteen, on July 6, 1553.

England's First Queen

Princess Mary had other ideas. She boldly raised her own banner in East Anglia, scene of the recent rebellions. Dudley's support melted away, and Mary was welcomed as their true queen by the citizens of London. Her countercoup restored the Catholic Church and gave England its first ever queen to reign in her own right.

It also made her believe that she could rule without Parliament. She ignored its pleas to marry an English Catholic and insisted on Philip of Spain, the son of Emperor Charles V. The people might be vague about theology, but they were not about to be ruled over by a Spaniard. In 1554, Mary only survived popular rebellion by swinging London's elite in a great speech carefully spun at England's famous love for the Virgin Mary:

> I can not tell how naturally the Mother loveth the Child, for
> I was never the mother of any, but . . . I being your Lady and
> Mistress, do as earnestly and as tenderly love and favor you.
>
> —Queen Mary, Guildhall, February 1, 1554

This second triumph left her fatally convinced of her own mission. Lady Jane Grey was executed, and Princess Elizabeth only narrowly escaped. Despite all opposition, her marriage to Philip went ahead.

When Mary's longed-for child turned out to be a false pregnancy, she decided that God was punishing her for tolerating heretics. Hundreds of Protestants were burned. In 1556, her husband prevailed upon her to join in an anti-French war. It was a debacle, and England lost Calais, its last foothold in France. By her death in late 1558, Mary had doomed Catholicism in England by making it seem linked to executions and foreign dominance.

Southern Privilege

Elizabeth had only just survived the political and religious chaos, and she was determined to stabilize a riven country. When it came to religion, so long as people conformed publicly, she "would not open windows into men's souls." *The Act of Settlement* (1559) and the *39 Articles* (1563) left things so deliberately vague that, to this day, there are Anglicans who are barely distinguishable from Baptists and Anglicans who scarcely differ from Catholics.

The political situation was less tractable. Under her father, Parliament had tasted power; her sister, Mary, had ignored its advice to her cost. Now it was ready to flex its muscles. In 1567, Robert Mulcaster, MP, translated Sir John Fortescue's fifteenth-century Latin treatise on English law. There it was, for all to read—and the English did indeed read it repeatedly for the next century: The sovereign had to rule together with Parliament.

> The Kynge of Englande can neither change laws without
> the consent of his subjects, nor yette charge them with
> strange impositions against their will . . . forasmuch as they
> are made not only by the Prince's pleasure, but also by the
> assent of the whole realm . . . the Parliament of Englande.

Then there was the age-old question of whether the North would accept the rule of the South. Theology was the window-dressing for revolt, but the real issue, as Elizabeth's Privy Council warned her, was that "north of the Trent men know no other Prince but only a Percy or a Neville." In 1569, the Northern Rebellion was crushed with a ferocity that would have impressed Henry VIII himself: At least six hundred were hanged.

England was being dragooned into a unity that in practice meant rule by the South. The Crown, the Church (now working directly for the Crown), Parliament (now co-rulers), the Law, and the new humanist learning were all based in the South. Three centuries before Received Pronunciation (RP) was invented, the first guidebook for English authors explained that using "good southern as we of Middlesex or Surrey do" was the only proper way to write:

> |Writers must not use| the terms of northern men . . . Nor
> in effect any speech used beyond the river of Trent . . . Ye
> shall therefore take the usual speech of the court, and that
> of London and the shires lying about London.
> —George Puttenham, *The Art of English Poesie* (1589)

The way into this new elite was clear: money, and a very specific kind of education, based on the classics and law French, in Oxford, Cambridge, and London.

> [Successful and thrifty commoners] ... setting their sons to the schools, to the universities, and to the Inns of the Court ... do make them by those means to become gentlemen.
>
> —William Harrison (1577)

The vast majority of ordinary English, who had been promised that the Reformation would be a great moment of national liberation, found themselves worse off than ever.

Just Another Nation: England Submerged

The climate grew harsher and harsher. Enclosures continued apace. Inflation crushed the real value of wages. The landless poor of England were now so desperate that Elizabeth was advised she could use them to settle her brand-new American lands for free.

> There are at this day great numbers ... in such penurie & want, as they could be content to hazard their lives, and to serve one yeere for meat, drinke and apparell only, without wages.
>
> —Richard Hakluyt, 1583

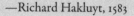

The "open" crown in this portrait signifies that Elizabeth was an empress, not a mere queen.

And now England was just one nation within the new empire of the *British Iles* (the term is first recorded in 1577). Elizabeth Tudor was no mere English queen. She was a multi-national Empress who wore the imperial crown. All her nations were equally her subjects. In 1563, she ordered a translation of the Bible into Welsh. The following year, she did the same for the Gaelic Irish.

A long new tale had begun: the re-submersion of the ordinary English, not under a French-speaking ruling class, but within a multinational empire, beginning at home in the British Isles, run by their very own imperialist elite. For the time being, however, this was disguised by a great moment of enforced unity.

The Island Fortress

In 1570, Elizabeth was declared a heretic and a "servant of crime" by the Pope, making her fair game to every potential Catholic assassin. Twice in that decade, the Protestants of Holland, fighting desperately against Spanish rule, offered her their entire country. Elizabeth was part of the new European confessional war, whether she liked it or not, but she was too canny to be bounced into open conflict with Spain. Instead she went for hybrid warfare, covertly backing Sir Francis Drake as he became the first Englishman to circumnavigate the globe, in 1577–1580.

Only one of Drake's five ships made it to the Pacific, but the *Golden Hinde* found the Spanish treasure fleet unprepared for any attack. He returned with such booty that Elizabeth's half-share in the profits was more than all her other Crown income for the year.

When the Dutch yet again offered themselves to Elizabeth (1584), she refused again, but sent a force of seven thousand men into the Low Countries to confront Spain directly at the Battle of Zutphen (1586). For almost five hundred years, English foreign policy had all been about invading—or being invaded from—France. For the next four hundred years, the army would go to the Low Countries and Northwest Germany, always in alliances to maintain the balance of power, while the navy sailed the globe.

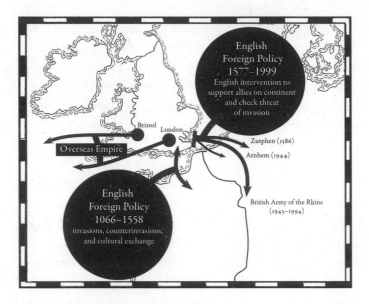

Jehovah Blew, and They Were Scattered

In 1588, the Spanish Armada set sail, bent on regime change in England. The new elite had their heads on the line and the ordinary people had ancient memories of traumatic foreign conquest: The Armada became a great moment of national unification, skillfully channeled by Elizabeth.

> And therefore I am come amongst you at this time, not as for my recreation or sport, but being resolved, in the midst and heat of the battle, to live or die amongst you all; to lay down, for my God, and for my kingdom, and for my people, my honour and my blood, even the dust.
>
> —Elizabeth at Tilbury, 1588

The Armada's defeat, and the destruction of two later armadas (1596–97) by wind and weather alone, allowed the regime to claim that the Protestant English were God's chosen people.

After the Armada

The Catholic threat defeated, Elizabeth returned to fighting off radical Protestants. In 1593, it became a capital offense not to attend the Church of England. At important moments, centrally printed special sermons were sent by courier to every parish in the land. The Church was the first English national mass medium, and controlling it became central to politics for the following century.

For now, though, all conflict was prorogued by the glory of Elizabeth. In sermons, pictures, poems, and pamphlets, the "Virgin Queen," the "Faerie Queen" was adored as a nationalized replacement for the Holy Virgin herself.

> She cheerfully received not only rich gifts from persons of worth, but Nosegays, Flowers, Rose-mary branches, and such like presents, offered unto her by very mean persons . . . hereby the people, to whom no musicke is so sweete as the affability of their Prince, were so strongly stirred to love and joye.
>
> —John Hayward

Beyond this political theater, the common people got still poorer. In the 1590s, the poorest actually starved to death while speculators bought grain up and stashed it away until the price rose even further.

The government tried vainly to control this deadly free market. One man fined for grain hoarding in 1598 could write in French if he needed to, though he had (according to a university-educated rival) "small Latin and less Greek." And he had come to London at the perfect time to be a writer in English.

How Shakespeare Speaks to All English People

The English were ready to become theater lovers. With their age-old religious art, rites, and popular celebrations now forbidden, they had become used to listening very carefully to the spoken Word, even if they only half-understood things (getting it right might be life or death). Thomas Cromwell had established the stage as the one place where color, noise, and spectacle were still allowed—though only in the service of teaching supposed national history. And in the post-Armada rush of unity, the high and low of England were ready, for the first time since the Conquest, to mix in the same public spaces.

This allowed Shakespeare to tread the linguistic tightrope of the English language, and talk for once to everybody. The first great historical play (*Henry VI*) opens with courtly, Latinate language and classical references, but later suggests that this is un-English ("Submission, Dauphin? 'Tis a mere French word; We English warriors wot not what it means"). At other times, he does what English lawyers did (and do) with doublets such as "lands and tenements." Lady Macbeth's bloodied hand would "the multitudinous seas incarnadine" (Latinate)—straight away explained as "making the green one red" (Germanic).

> English has the odd facility of offering the chance to say most things in two ways.
>
> —George Watson

We can imagine Shakespeare's actors looking up to the elite in the balcony seats at one moment, then talking down to the standing groundlings the next. It held together because for once, the English genuinely felt united.

> The moment was of supreme importance—such a moment can never come again. Its rise, maturity and decline coincided with Shakespeare's dramatic career . . . After the strain was over and the heroic days departed . . . things began to fall apart.
>
> —A. L. Rowse

Handing Over England

Elizabeth clung to power by refusing to name an heir. Even to discuss the succession was punishable by death. Radical Protestants were waiting to drive the Reformation forward. Hard-line Catholics hoped that the clock could still be turned back. The country was only held together—yet simultaneously paralyzed—by its aging Virgin Queen. When she finally died on March 24, 1603, everybody knew it was the end of an era. Few thought the future would be decided without a fight.

> A nation that was almost begotten and born under her . . . how was it possible, but that her sickness should throw abroad an universal fear?
>
> —Thomas Dekker

Behind the scenes, though, Elizabeth and her chief minister, Lord Salisbury, had concocted a plan to avoid political-religious civil war: England would be handed over to a foreign king.

England Abolished?

England had been at war with Scotland almost incessantly since the twelfth century. James VI of Scotland (whose great-grandmother had been Henry VIII's sister) was only accepted as James I of England because Salisbury presented him as the sole way to avoid civil war. Every Anglican vicar was ordered to remind his parishioners that James had been crowned "without any Bloodshed, tumults or uproars to the disturbing of the public peace of this his Majesty's realm . . . contrary to all men's expectations."

The new king found his realm deeply unstable. Extreme reformers wanted him to be the warlike leader of Protestant Europe. Instead, he abandoned Elizabeth's eternal war with

Spain, tolerated some Catholic practices, and tried to hold the center ground by commissioning the mighty King James Bible in 1604. It wasn't enough for extreme Catholics. On November 5, 1605, Guy Fawkes and his gang tried to blow him, and Parliament, up.

By then James had already proposed a radical solution to the divisions within England: Abolish it entirely as a separate nation.

> Wherefore We have thought good to discontinue the divided names of England and Scotland . . . and do intend and resolve to take and assume unto Us . . . the Name and Style of King of Great Brittaine.
>
> —James I, proclamation of October 20, 1604

England's elite didn't care what their country was called. But they cared very much who ran it. If they gave James his wish, and thereby a separate power base in Scotland, their power— exercised through London's Parliament—would be massively reduced.

And so the question that would dominate English politics for centuries first raised its head with James I. Was the Southeast of England to remain supreme, or would its power be challenged by an alliance of countries called *Great Brittaine*? In James's reign, this struggle was framed as one between the king, with his would-be "Empire of Great Britaine" (as the mapmaker John Speed called it in 1612), and the Parliament of England.

MPs and lawyers—they were frequently both—burrowed into old books of English law to find cases. Under Henry VIII, it had been found unlawful that "whore-houses, called the stews, were suppressed by [royal] proclamation." The great judge of the age, Sir Edward Coke, declared that this legal precedent applied equally to a brothel or to a parliament, so that "the King hath no prerogative but that which the law of the land allows him."

James warned MPs that if they didn't give him the funds he demanded and back his scheme for the union of England and Scotland, "they must not look for more Parliaments in haste." Some men wanted to bring things to a head then and there, but others feared the consequences of openly opposing a king. This split allowed James to keep ruling.

The Birth of Overseas Empire: Starvation and Emigration

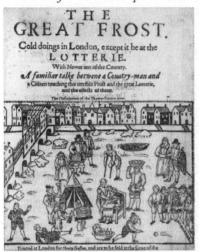

In 1608 winning the great Lotterie was one escape route; emigration would soon provide another.

The rulers of England were wise to be wary of social upheaval. The Little Ice Age was approaching its deepest phase. From 1608, fairs were regularly held on the frozen Thames. As agriculture became marginal in the North and even the Midlands, enclosures became a matter of life and death. In 1607, dozens of rebellious Northamptonshire peasants, trying to stop their commons from being enclosed, were slain on the spot. Dozens more were later hanged, drawn, and quartered. The English social order was barely holding.

One new escape valve was emigration. In the first half of the seventeenth century, perhaps fifty thousand people (from a population of around four million) made the dangerous voyage to the royal colonies in America. Many signed themselves over to indentured servitude for years just to pay for the crossing. Their lot was often no better than slavery.

> The arrival of the first twenty or more Africans [in Virginia, 1619] did not require the colony to fashion special laws of slavery based on race because the law which treated servants as chattel was sufficient.
>
> —William Terence Martin Riches

Aware of this, a group of Nottinghamshire peasants decided to head for parts of the New World beyond royal control: "those vast and unpeopled countries of America, which are fruitful and fit for habitation, being devoid of all civil inhabitants, where there are only savage and brutish men, which range up and down, little otherwise than the wild beasts." In 1620, they boarded the *Mayflower*.

Later imperialists would proclaim that the English-speaking empire was proof of some unique, racial capacity. The reality was that France, for example, was no less keen on empire and had adventurers aplenty—but it never had large numbers of landless peasants so desperate that they would risk their lives in barely discovered countries on the far side of the world. The English-speaking empire arose because life was so bad for the common English.

A Capital Enemy: Charles I and Parliament

By James I's death in 1625, the tension between him and Parliament had almost paralyzed government. His twenty-four-year-old son Charles zigzagged wildly as he tried to find ways and funds to sidestep, win over, or browbeat Parliament. Disaster finally struck in 1628: Three costly English naval expeditions failed to stop the French king from taking the great Protestant stronghold of La Rochelle (this is the background to *The Three Musketeers*). With his defeated troops and sailors mutinying for lack of pay, Charles was forced to call Parliament and ask it to raise taxes.

MPs pounced—literally. On March 2, 1629, they physically held the Speaker of the House down in his chair, keeping the session going so that they could pass emergency votes. Henceforth, anyone who advised the king to raise taxes without Parliament, and even anyone who paid such taxes, was "a capital enemy to this Kingdom and Commonwealth."

Yet still, to actually rise in arms against a king was a step too far. Charles called Parliament's bluff, and ruled without it for ten years, funding his regime by reviving medieval taxes, like Ship Money, that did not require parliamentary approval.

Civil War: The Empire of Great Britaine vs. Parliament

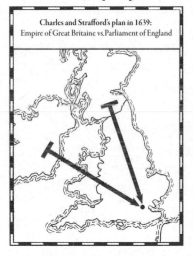

Charles and Strafford's plan in 1639:
Empire of Great Britaine vs. Parliament of England

The crisis finally came when Charles moved to use the Empire of Great Britaine against the Parliament of England. His military commander, the Earl of Strafford, had seemingly managed to pacify Ireland at last in the 1630s, giving Charles a power base beyond the control of London's MPs. In 1639, Strafford tried to secure Scotland as well. It backfired fatally. The Scots rose in arms, Strafford's underfunded army collapsed, the Short Parliament refused to finance another force unless it was under their control, and the whole of Northumberland ended up under Scottish occupation.

A third of all English merchant ships were employed bringing coal from Newcastle to London, to see it through the harsh seventeenth-century winters. With this vital trade cut off, Charles had no option but to recall MPs. On November 3, 1640, Parliament gathered at Westminster. The king just wanted money to cow the Scots, but Parliament was determined to use the opportunity to nail down its dominance over all possible rivals.

Archbishop Laud had tried to use the power of the Church in the shires to circumvent the London Parliament's control of the law. Strafford had suggested that an army of King Charles's Irish subjects might crush the Parliament of England. Parliament declared both guilty of high treason, and the Council of the North at York was abolished.

On January 4, 1642, Charles entered the House of Commons with armed soldiers to arrest five leading members. He was too late. The birds, as he famously put it, had flown. Fearing the London populace, which backed Parliament, Charles fled to the capital's ancient rival, York. For the first time in English history, two powers in the country now tried, in print, to swing popular opinion. Both tried to sound moderate.

> **Parliament** (*from London, June 1642*): And these our humble desires being granted by your Majesty, we shall forthwith apply ourselves to regulate your present Revenue, in such sort, as may be for your best advantage . . .
>
> **King Charles** (*from York, in reply*): In this Kingdom the Laws are jointly made by a King, by a House of Peers, and by a House of Commons chosen by the People, all having free Votes and particular Privileges . . .

But a hidden motor was driving things, and it wasn't ideology. It was about ancient tribes. The North of England, the Cornish, and the Celts were determined to resist rule from the South, and they were ready to ally. This was what led to open, and ultimately brutal, war.

> The North and West were regarded by parliamentarians as the "dark corners of the land."
>
> —Christopher Hill

The Royalists dithered after narrowly winning the first battle, Edgehill (October 23, 1642). London held out for Parliament. Charles sat with his court—and his own Parliament— at Oxford, with solid support from Wales and the North. His forces won significant victories in 1643, and took England's second city, Bristol. Having made peace in Ireland, he could now recall troops from there too. By late 1643, he seemed poised to win.

Scotland Decides England's Fate

The Scots were now the joker in the pack, prepared to back either English side for a price. Charles, foolishly overconfident, made no concessions. Parliament, desperate, offered an extraordinary deal that reversed the power-relationship of centuries. If it won, it would cede long-contested Berwick-upon-Tweed and remake the Church of England in the fundamentalist image of the Kirk of Scotland. This promise was known as the Covenant.

As negotiations started, the Committee for the Demolition of Monuments of Superstition and Idolatry (July 1643) hiked up the assault on images and statues in England's southeastern churches and cathedrals, as a sign of good faith—and the radicals found their great leader, Oliver Cromwell.

Out instantly all you can! Raise all your Bands; Send them to Huntingdon; get up what Volunteers you can; hasten your Horses . . . I beseech you spare not, but be expeditious and industrious! . . . You must act lively; do it without Distraction! Neglect no means.

—Cromwell to the Commissioners at Cambridge,
August 6, 1643

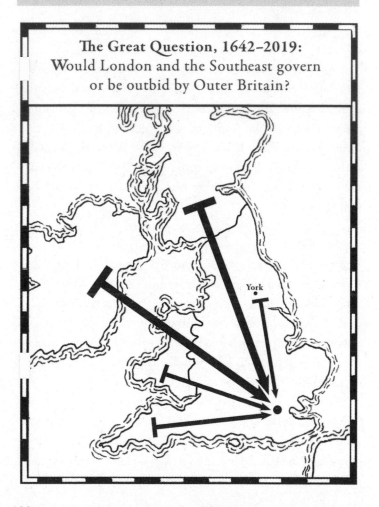

The Great Question, 1642–2019:
Would London and the Southeast govern
or be outbid by Outer Britain?

York

All Cromwell's zeal would have been no good without the Scots. At Marston Moor near York (July 2, 1644)—after Towton the greatest battle ever fought in England—over half the Parliamentary army were Scottish Covenanters. But for them, the Cavaliers would surely have won the day, and perhaps the war.

The Southeast at Bay

By late 1644, despite Marston Moor, the idea that the rulers of London and the Southeast should naturally rule the whole of Britain—perhaps even the whole British Isles—seemed thoroughly defeated. Ireland had regained de facto sovereignty. The Scots, whose alliance with Parliament was creaking, held Newcastle and Durham, controlling the vital coal trade. Wales was still solid for the king.

England itself was something like a failed state. Men across the rural Southwest formed local militias of Clubmen to defend against both sides. Cornwall and Devon signed a nonaggression pact as though they were independent countries. Two months after Marston Moor, Royalist Cornishmen shattered the Earl of Essex's army at Lostwithiel. In London, moderates were at loggerheads with "Cromwell and his junto" (as the parliamentarian Earl of Manchester called them). Then Cromwell proclaimed total war.

Total War and True English Hearts

It is now a time to speak, or forever hold the tongue. The important occasion now is no less than to save a Nation.
—Cromwell in Parliament, December 9, 1644

To "save a Nation"—that is, to preserve the dominance of Southeastern England—Cromwell needed to mobilize his own people at all costs. His New Model Army, founded at the start of 1645, was manned exclusively by those with "true English hearts." Battle-hardened soldiers were made officers in preference to gentlemen. Preachers were attached to every unit, inspiring men with a sense of righteous mission. The long-despised common English were now invited to see themselves as the Lord's Anointed. After the New Model Army smashed Charles's last serious force at Naseby (June 14, 1645), its fighters cornered a group of female Royalist camp followers and, as their extremist supporters openly exulted in print, slaughtered a hundred "harlots with golden tresses." The

horrors spilled off the battlefields: Between 1644 and 1647, dozens of women in the New Model Army's heartland of Cromwell's Eastern Association were tortured and executed by Mathew Hopkins, the "Witchfinder" General. The price of Parliament's victory was an uncontrollable religious-political radicalism.

Grandees and Agitators

Cromwell had told his men that they were fighting ungodly enemies for the ancient liberties of England. Some of them, known as Levellers (so called because they wanted to *level*— tear down—enclosure boundaries), took him at his word.

In June 1647, Leveller radicals in the army captured the King, abolished Christmas as a popish festival, and demanded the completion of the Reformation (as they still called it), by which they meant votes and land for all. They insisted that the promise given to the common people by Thomas Cromwell in the 1530s should be made good at last by Oliver Cromwell. In the Putney Debates (October–November 1647), Cromwell and Ireton—the Grandees—had to debate personally with Agitators, one of whom declared simply that their dream was "the time before the Conquest."

The Civil War gave the ordinary Southeastern English weapons. Literacy and printing gave their voices the power of mass media. Their mix of religious visions and political demands sounds very like Martin Luther King in 1960s America:

> O what mighty Delusion, do you, who are the powers of *England* live in! That while you pretend to throw down that *Norman* yoke, and *Babylonish* power, and have promised to make the groaning people of *England* a Free People; yet you still lift up that *Norman* yoke, and slavish Tyranny, and holds the People as much in Bondage, as the Bastard Conqueror himself, and his Council of War . . . Therefore, if thou wilt find Mercy, *Let Israel go Free!*
> —*The True Levellers' Standard Advanced*, 1649

It wasn't just this one pamphlet that blamed the Normans for the centuries in the wilderness. They almost all did. Six hundred years had passed, but the common people of England, their tales handed down from the old to the young, still recalled the Conquest as the great national trauma that had robbed them of their language, their laws, and their land.

Army vs. Parliament

Cromwell tried to tame his radicalized army by conniving at King Charles's escape from their clutches in November 1647, which gave him a pretext to demand total loyalty. He even had one Agitator shot in front of his own regiment.

From now on, he was forced to ride the populist tiger he'd unleashed. Though in private he raged against the Levellers, he had no choice but to publicly back the army against the more moderate Parliament. Non-radical MPs were kicked out in Pride's Purge (1648), before finally the Rump Parliament decided on the unthinkable. On January 30, 1649, King Charles was executed.

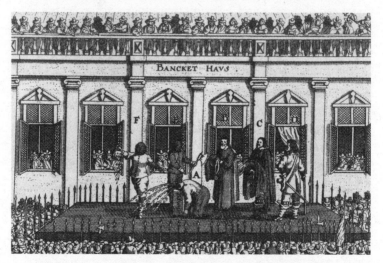

The execution of Charles I (detail from German engraving, 1649)

The People of England . . . shall from henceforth be Governed as a Commonwealth and Free-State, by the Supreme Authority of this Nation, the Representatives of the People in Parliament.

As they had a century earlier, the common people expected their new rulers to deal with enclosures—or at least, to let them do it themselves. In April 1649, the Diggers occupied common land at St. George's Hill in Surrey. They were followed by groups in Kent, Northamptonshire, and Buckinghamshire. Like the Levellers, they believed they were putting right a wrong that went directly back to the Norman Conquest.

> We shall with ease cast down, all those former enslaving Norman reiterated laws, in every King's reign since the Conquest, which are as thorns in our eyes, and pricks in our sides.
>
> —From *A Declaration from the Poor Oppressed People of England directed to all that call themselves, or are called Lords of Manors*

As at the first Reformation, the common people were swiftly put in their place. The Digger communes were destroyed, and England placed under military rule.

> At all places of Garrison there is a very strict examinations of persons . . . no traveller could pass without catechizing words: *As what is your name, whence came you, where dwell you, whither go you, and wherefore came you hither?*
>
> —John Taylor, "The Water-Poet," 1649

The Truly English Empire

With the Southeast back in control of England, Cromwell set about extending its rule over the British Isles. This was a different mission from earlier and later empire building. It made no concessions at all to local elites: Being beaten by the New Model Army put you at the mercy of radicalized common Englishmen convinced they were doing God's work.

In Ireland, religious slaughter was visited upon Wexford and Drogheda (1649). At Dunbar (1650), the Scots were routed and hundreds of civilians afterward massacred at Dundee. The dead king's son, Prince Charles, led an invasion from Scotland and was crushed at Worcester (1651), barely escaping to France.

> Upon all of us there still lies "the curse of Cromwell."
>
> —Churchill

Having imposed its brand of Englishness on Outer Britain with fire and sword, the army was in no mood to be ruled over by a more moderate elite at home. In 1653, it forcibly dissolved two Parliaments—the Rump and the Nominated Assembly—before declaring Oliver Cromwell king in all but name.

The only way to keep the radicalized army under control was to keep it at war. So Cromwell made new wars, against Holland and Spain. At first it worked, and for a time the English Republic was the terror of Europe. The turning point was the disastrous attack on the Caribbean island of Hispaniola (1655). With public confidence shattered and the finances tottering, the New Model Army was finally turned loose on the English people themselves, in the Rule of the Major-Generals (1655–57).

The Rule of the Major-Generals

For the first time since 1066, England was run by ordinary Englishmen: Almost all the major generals were non-gentry-born. They and their underlings were radicalized zealots who believed that taverns, Catholics, cockfights, political opponents, Maypoles, theaters, bishops, church music, and the undeserving poor were literally agents of the devil. The experience left the English with a lasting horror of anything remotely like military rule: For the next 150 years (unlike every other European nation) they strongly disliked seeing their own soldiers around the place except in time of war.

By 1658, the cost of maintaining the army had bankrupted the country: The English would accept no more taxes, and foreign bankers would lend no more. Parliament knew that confidence could only be restored by ending the radical experiment, so it offered Cromwell the crown in May 1658. But Oliver still couldn't escape his army: His generals wouldn't serve a king—even King Oliver I—so he had to refuse.

When he died on September 3, 1658, few mourned. His son, Richard, inherited the post of Lord Protector, but not his father's prestige among the soldiery. Without it, he was unable to control them and, in May 1659, threw in the towel. So did the army. In 1647, it had tried to impose Heaven by force; now it just wanted its backpay.

The End of the Populist Experiment

Almost all the English wanted a king again, but they wanted a freely elected Parliament to approve him first. In 1660, *Restoration* meant not only restoring the monarchy, but also the true power of Parliament. The one man with a viable force still at his command, General Monck, military ruler of Scotland, marched on London to make this happen. On May 2, the Convention Parliament agreed that Prince Charles, the royal heir-in-exile, should return and be crowned.

> Great joy all yesterday at London, and at night more bonfires than ever, and ringing of bells, and drinking of the King's health upon their knees in the streets.
> —Samuel Pepys, *Diary*, May 2, 1660

It was the end of England's populist experiment, and the end of the attempt to impose English rule on the British Isles by sheer force. Scotland and Ireland got their own parliaments back. The English were only too happy to forget such imperial ambitions: They just wanted a return of traditional order, and they celebrated wildly when Charles entered London on May 29, 1660.

Aping the French in Every Thing

Charles II, like many kings of England before him, was thoroughly French in his tastes. In the courts, Latin and law French (banished in 1651) came back. Styles in French fashion, art, architecture, and literature were often slavishly imitated.

> Really, the Law is scarcely expressible properly in English.
>
> —Sir Roger North, Attorney General, 1686–88

> It is Modish to Ape the French in every thing . . . [we] chop and change our language, as we do our Cloths, at the pleasure of every French Taylor.
>
> —Aphra Behn, 1688

Charles could not, however, copy his cousin, Louis XIV, in ruling absolutely. Even the Cavalier Parliament (1661–79) was a parliament, and though at first it got on swimmingly with Charles, restoring the Anglican Church to full power and rejigging the tax system to favor landlords, MPs grew restive after the national disasters of the last Great Plague (1665), the Fire of London (1666), and humiliating defeat in the Second Dutch War (1665–67).

What Parliament didn't know was that Louis XIV was secretly bankrolling Charles, and had even offered military assistance if MPs got out of hand. In return, Charles had promised to convert to Catholicism as soon as he could safely do so.

> The King of Great Britain ... is determined to declare himself a Catholic ... as soon as the welfare of his realm shall permit. His most Christian Majesty [i.e., Louis] promises to further this action by giving to the King of Great Britain 2 million livres tournois ... And to assist his Britannic Majesty with 6,000 foot soldiers.
>
> —The secret Treaty of Dover, 1670

Unaware of this, most English people couldn't understand why they were on France's side in the Third Dutch War (1672–74).

Parliament grew suspicious and in the Exclusion Crisis (1678–81) moved to ban Charles's Catholic brother, James, from the succession.

Whigs and Tories

The political elite of England split. One party (mockingly named after anti-Cromwell Irish brigands known as *Tories*, from the Gaelic for *fugitives*) maintained that a king was paramount and ruled by right of bloodline. The other (mockingly named after Scots Puritans known as *Whigs*, from the Gaelic for *horse rustlers*) believed that Parliament determined the succession, and had the right to limit any king's powers. As if by some instinct, the English at the birth of modern politics chose insults that mirrored the essential disunity of the British Isles.

The Whigs invented modern fake news to whip up the London *mob* (a brand new word, abbreviated from the Latin *mobile vulgus*—fickle mass). The entirely fabricated Popish Plot of 1678 claimed that Catholics were plotting to overthrow England. In fact, it was Whig extremists who tried to assassinate Charles and James on their way back from Newmarket Races in the Rye House Plot (1683). Public outrage gave Charles freedom to do more or less as he wanted. By his death in 1685, the Tories were ascendant and Charles was edging toward an absolute monarchy on the French model.

English Liberty and Continental Realpolitik

James II, the first Catholic ruler since Queen Mary, never faced widespread popular revolt. Many English loathed Rome and Louis XIV, but they feared another civil war more. So even when James's illegitimate nephew, the Duke of Monmouth, landed in arms at Lyme Regis in June 1685 and offered a Protestant alternative, most of the country stuck passively with their king. James's forces easily won the Battle of Sedgemoor, and vengeance was taken on the West Country by Judge Jeffreys in the Bloody Assizes.

James took this to mean that Parliament could now be sidelined. When MPs refused to back Catholic emancipation, he prorogued them for eighteen months before finally dissolving Parliament and trying to govern without it. The London mob cheered his opponents and burned effigies of the Pope—but still there was no actual revolt.

Then, in late 1687, James's second wife, Mary of Modena, announced she was pregnant. Many in England were aghast at the prospect of a Catholic dynasty, but for one Dutchman, William, Prince of Orange—king of Holland in all but name—it was an existential threat. William was married to Mary Hyde, James's daughter by his first marriage, and had been expecting her to become queen of England on his death. This would bring English support to his life-and-death struggle against Louis XIV's aggression. But with a Catholic son as his heir, James might easily be tempted, or (like his brother, Charles) bribed, into a full alliance with Louis.

With William fearing for Holland's future and Englishmen dreading a new Civil War, an extraordinary deal was made. Rebel members of England's elite would invite Dutch invasion.

In return, William would promise a free Parliament. Swiftly, he secured backing from France's rivals, the Habsburgs, and from the Pope himself. By the time the feared royal son—James Francis Edward Stuart—was indeed born on June 10, 1688, the master plan was ready.

Inglorious Revolution

On June 30, William received his invitation. The invasion was a masterpiece of spin. The Habsburgs and the Pope were assured it was an anti-French move, not an anti-Catholic crusade. The English, meanwhile, were assured the exact opposite.

> This our expedition is intended for no other design, but to have a free and lawful Parliament assembled, as soon as possible ... We have nothing before our eyes, in this our undertaking, but the preservation of the Protestant religion ... under a just and legal government.
>
> —William of Orange's Declaration, October 1688

William's fleet—placed under an English admiral for show—was so huge that it simultaneously saluted the forts of Dover and Calais. A lucky change of wind allowed it to evade the real English navy, which was still loyal to James, and it landed at Brixham on November 5, 1688. The Dutch swiftly took Exeter without a fight.

> The Dutch army, composed of men who had been born in various climates, and had served under various standards, presented an aspect at once grotesque, gorgeous, and terrible to the islanders. The citizens of Exeter, who had never seen so many specimens of the African race, gazed with wonder on the black faces, set off by embroidered turbans and white

feathers. Then with drawn broadswords came a squadron of
Swedish horsemen in black armour and fur cloaks.

—Macaulay

After three weeks of cat-and-mouse, William entered London
unopposed at the head of his own army, having ordered all
English troops to withdraw twenty miles from London.

Dutch Blue Guards took up all the posts around Whitehall
and Hyde Park; and London remained under Dutch
military occupation for 18 months.

—Jonathan Israel

It was obvious that the Prince of Orange and his army were
foreign, but ordinary Londoners were desperate to avoid a repeat
of 1642–45, so they bought the story that he had come only to
defy "Popery," preserve their "Laws and Liberties"—and restore a
"free Parliament," so that both "King and People" might flourish.

The Prince of Orange "Welcome to London" ballad, 1688

The promised free Parliament was indeed delivered, but behind the scenes William let MPs know that if they made the wrong decision, he would take his Blue Guards home, leaving the English to fight it out. On April 11, 1689, he and Mary were accordingly crowned as co-rulers.

The Triumph of Parliament

William was only in England because he desperately needed its muscle against France. Armed with this knowledge, MPs were able to force an epochal agreement: Parliament would fund a war—but only if it controlled the military. This was exactly how they had tried to hog-tie Charles I in 1639, sparking the civil war. Fifty years later, William III, more concerned with saving Holland than ruling England, agreed.

CIVIL LIST (embryonic civil service, still controlled by King)	VS.	"MILITARY-FISCAL" BUDGET (now controlled by Parliament)

Now, the more the country spent on war, the greater proportion of the tax-take came under parliamentary control. So MPs were delighted to back the "warr against France," as it was put in the founding document of the Bank of England (1694).

William—with his own Blue Guards naturally at the forefront—defeated James and his French-backed army in Ireland at the Battle of the Boyne (July 1, 1690). The Anglo-Dutch fleet eventually beat the French, and in the aftermath Louis XIV had to back down in the Netherlands and acknowledge William as king of England.

His own position was now secure, but William was childless. In 1702, he was succeeded by his sister-in-law, Anne—clearly only a stopgap because she had lost her last child in 1700 and was too old to have any more. With the succession in doubt, Parliament made its move. Ever since Magna Carta and de Montfort's parliaments, England's elite had tussled with its kings over who truly ruled. Now that struggle was finally decided. The Act of Settlement removed any Catholic from the succession, and George, the German son of Sophie, Electress of Hanover, granddaughter of James I, thereby leaped over fifty-six more direct Stuart claimants to become king of England.

The Perfect Offer

The new power balance between King and Parliament created a unique offer to international financial markets. In England, and only in England, your loans were guaranteed both by a real king who offered traditional solidity, and by a parliament run by a broad-based elite. This elite, concentrated in what was now the largest city in Western Europe, had been admitting successful tradesmen for centuries, and treated government as a business.

loaning money to an Absolute King: seems solid, but he might simply default.

loaning money to a Republic: businesslike folk, but who knows how long it will last?

loaning money to England: traditional monarchy + businesslike elite.

All power was now gathered in London. The English had no more need to disguise tribal fights as ideologies. They still called each other Whigs and Tories, but those were just handy insults. Now, it was all about making money.

> The Ministry distinguished with the name of Tory, was no other than another set of Whigs ... The question being not, who shall be king, but who shall hold places of profit under the king?
>
> —*The Gentleman's Magazine*, 1763

Everywhere else in Europe, royal governments taxed the people who made money, and channeled the funds to politically reliable, hereditary elites:

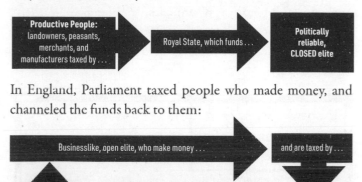

In England, Parliament taxed people who made money, and channeled the funds back to them:

Europeans began to borrow the word *gentleman* to describe this strange new fusion of aristocracy and business class, which existed nowhere else.

Parliament serviced its debts, rather than defaulting on them (as France did in 1759 and 1770), so people were ready to lend it money, the sinews of war. The great eighteenth-century struggle for empire was not won because of any intrinsic English superiority over France, but because England was able to borrow far more cheaply. Except, it wasn't England anymore.

Scotland Changes Everything

In 1707, this new "polity programmed for commerce and war" (Brendan Simms) officially got a new name: Great Britain. The lowland Scottish elite wanted a free trade deal with rich England, seats in its mighty London Parliament, and kickbacks. They got all three.

The Union changed England. When Daniel Defoe traveled the new realm to write the first guidebook to it, *A Tour Thro' the Whole Island of Great Britain* (1724–27), he treated the Anglo-Scottish border as meaningless, and lumped Northern England and Scotland together. The dividing line was, of course, the Trent. Defoe compared crossing it to Caesar crossing the Rubicon.

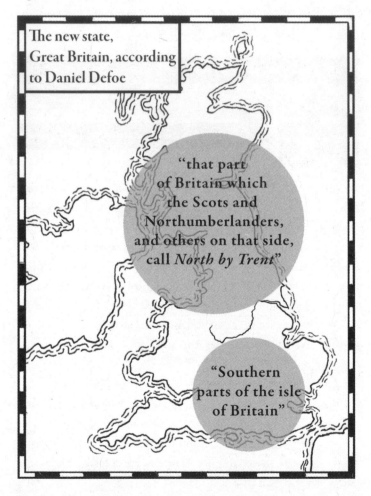

The new state, Great Britain, according to Daniel Defoe

"that part of Britain which the Scots and Northumberlanders, and others on that side, call *North by Trent*"

"Southern parts of the isle of Britain"

The division within Great Britain wasn't a national one between England and Scotland, but an economic and cultural one between Southern England and the rest. This remains so to the present day.

Joining the Un-English Elite

The new kingdom of Great Britain—in dynastic union with the kingdom of Ireland and the Electorate of Hanover—was almost permanently at war with France, but that didn't mean its elite stopped using the language. The multilingual gentry of Georgian England spoke—and above all, wrote—an English that was more Frenchified, and more obsessed with Classical culture, than ever. Edward Gibbon's vastly successful *Decline and Fall of the Roman Empire* (1776) was the model of educated style for a century:

> It is not my intention to detain the reader by expatiating on the variety, or the importance of the subject, which I have undertaken to treat; since the merit of the choice would serve to render the weakness of the execution still more apparent, and still less excusable.

This is English, but any uneducated Englishman, eighteenth-century or modern, would need a translation. And that was the whole point. This wasn't anybody's natural language; it was the property of no ethnic group. It was something that you had to learn—that anybody could learn if they could afford the right sort of education. Precisely because of that, it was perfectly fitted to become the social glue of the new Great British elite. The gentry, lairds, and clan chiefs of Outer Britain were being offered something very different to the Bible-thumping English nationalism of Cromwell's day.

They were being invited to join a strange new realm whose own German kings barely spoke English themselves, whose language was a deliberately artificial, half-French English, and whose true culture was revealed in stone.

From Dover to Donegal, from Truro to Inverness, brand-new houses, built to strict new, imported rules, proclaimed that their owners belonged not to any one nation, but to a pan-European elite. Yeoman farmers and country vicars built scaled-down versions in every village. Long ago, England had been united under Norman kings, by an elite who spoke French and built castles all over the land. Now, the British Isles were united under German kings, by an elite who spoke French, Latin, and Greek and built classical mansions all over the islands. Anyone who was anyone also had to have a classically proportioned townhouse in the imperial headquarters, London, and to take their holidays and network at the spa town of Bath, which had just been rebuilt—in the Classical style, naturally—for this sole purpose.

The Pump Room at Bath. Its Greek inscription means *Water Is Best.*

The Defeat of the English Peasantry

It was all Greek to the common people of England. They were just as left behind in this new, classically branded empire as the Highlanders of Scotland, the Welsh-speakers of Wales, and the

Gaelic peasantry of Ireland. The long, creeping wave of enclosures now blew up into the final assault. It all went through the
courts, of course, but peasants had no chance there. Parliament
may have ordered in 1731 that "all [court] proceedings shall be
in the English tongue and language only, and not in Latin or
French," but lawyers' English was still peppered with law French
and Latin phrases. Besides, what peasant could afford a lawyer?
And if the English peasantry still tried to treat what had once
been common land or forest as public property, the Black Act
of 1723 was there to put them right: It turned a whole range
of traditional, rambunctious country pursuits—poaching,
robbing orchards, and suchlike—from simple misdemeanors
to capital crimes.

What the modern English fetishize as the traditional
English countryside—fine Georgian buildings in a landscape
of hedgerows—was created by the wholesale importation of a
foreign architecture and the destruction of traditional English
country life, by force if need be. For English rural people who
came afterward, all that was left was to mourn:

> To cheat plain honesty by force of might
> Thus came enclosure—ruin was her guide . . .
> And workhouse prisons raised upon the site.
>
> —John Clare (c. 1820)

> Warkworth meadow was common to the inhabitants of
> three neighbouring villages . . . When they made good
> their threat to march on the new fences they were met by
> a company of mounted gentlemen led by the local justice
> who rode over them and "broke their Disposition."
>
> —J. M. Neeson

> I have no particular tenderness of peasants, but the fact remains that in many different countries they have been able to live in a special world of their own, at ease with their own customs, manners, clothes, food, drinks, songs and dances. The same folk in England lost all this and were never quite able to replace it with anything else
>
> —J. B. Priestley, *The English*

Since enclosures dramatically increased the nation's agricultural output, argued the philosopher David Hume and the economist Adam Smith, surely they must be good for everyone? Not so, answered radicals Tom Paine and Richard Price (and conservatives worried about killing off the stout peasantry): How could something obviously bad for the majority of individual Britons be good for Great Britain? Modern debates about trickle-down economics have their roots in enclosures.

The Mighty Hybrid

Its elite united and its peasantry crushed, the new Great Britain was ready to take on the world. The Anglo-Dutch-Habsburg alliance won great victories over France at Blenheim (1704), Ramillies (1706), Oudenarde (1708), and Malplaquet (1709), and pushed Louis XIV back beyond the Barrier Fortresses, including Ypres and Mons, whose names would become grimly familiar to British soldiers two hundred years later.

Soon, Parliament grew restive at the cost of European land warfare. "Rule, Britannia" was composed in 1740 not as a national anthem but as part of the campaign to change course seaward. In 1743, George II personally led the Pragmatic Army to victory over France, but it cost Britain £200,000 in subsidies to her allies. The following year, George Anson, the first Englishman since Drake to circumnavigate the globe, anchored safely home at Spithead, his hold stuffed with £500,000 in stolen Spanish gold. The math was plain.

The navy became Parliament's favorite child. Since it demanded technical skills, it accidentally became the most class-blind institution in Europe, another vehicle for England's unique trick of social mobility. It was even color-blind: John "Jack Punch" Perkins, of mixed race, born obscurely in Jamaica around 1750, died a rich post captain (the equal of a full colonel in the army). Well funded, manned by professional officers eager to make their careers, and *encouraged* (as Voltaire put it) by seeing Admiral Byng executed in 1757 for not being aggressive enough, the Royal Navy developed a cult of all-out attack.

There was one final piece in the makeup of this warlike new state. While harrying the Scottish Highlands after the Battle of Culloden in 1745, it had struck James Wolfe that "independent Highland companies might be of use, they are hardy, intrepid, accustomed to a rough Country and no great mischief if they fall." In 1759, he proved his point by using Highlanders as shock troops to capture Québec. By now, Catholic Irishmen were joining up, too, in such vast numbers that within two generations, around 40 percent of the entire British Army was Irish.

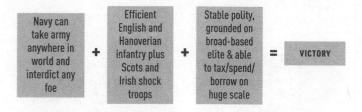

In the Seven Years' War (1756–63), this extraordinary, multinational, multilingual, socially mobile hybrid, Great Britain-and-Ireland-and-Hanover, mounted simultaneous, victorious offensives across the globe in a way no nation could emulate until the USA in 1944–45. And if that wasn't enough, Great Britain had an ace up its sleeve.

PART FOUR

Industrial Revolution
1763–1914

Where There's Muck, There's Brass

Britain had vast amounts of easily gettable coal, so it was the only major country already using it widely in homes and businesses. As the Royal Navy's oak-built ships and the ironmasters' charcoal burners devoured England's forests, entrepreneurs and industrialists finally cracked two great problems: how to get that heavy coal to markets far from mines, and how to use it to make workable iron.

England's unique fusion of businessmen and aristocrats was vital. In 1761, a visionary entrepreneur privately invested tens of millions in today's money to build the first great canal. This go-ahead investor was the Duke of Bridgwater, whose family had been landowners in the Northwest for centuries, and the canal was built to take coal from under his land to market in Manchester.

It was *under* his land: This was what mattered. Throughout history, growth had been limited because the land had to provide both food and fuel: Use too much for fuel, and people starved; use too much for food, and there wasn't enough fuel. This is known as the Malthusian Trap, and eighteenth-century England broke it. With mighty fossil energy being extracted from beneath the fields, agriculture could still thrive on the surface.

The brakes were off and the modern world was born, for good or ill. A medieval English peasant spent perhaps two hundred days per year actually working. By the late eighteenth century, dispossessed ex-peasants were working twelve-hour shifts three hundred days a year, in places like Arkwright's cotton mills. They needed fewer calories for this comparatively light, indoor work, and they needed to be ready according to the factory clock, not the seasons. So their days were chemically regulated by new, imported appetite suppressants, food substitutes, and pick-me-ups: rum, tobacco, tea, cocoa, coffee, and refined sugar.

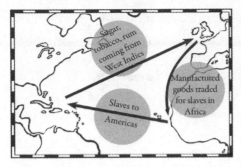

These were the product of another great dispossession. They were supplied by the richest of all colonial trades, tactfully known as the West India Interest. The raw material—African slaves—was invisible on the Middle Passage of a vastly profitable triangle. Britons simply saw manufactured goods leaving for Africa, and sugar, tobacco, or rum coming in from the West Indies.

> Whereas the cotton plantations of the American south were established on the soil of the continental United States, British slavery took place 3,000 miles away in the Caribbean.
>
> —David Olusoga

The Industrial Revolution was an effect, not the cause, of the new Great Britain's ruthless domestic modernization and empire building.

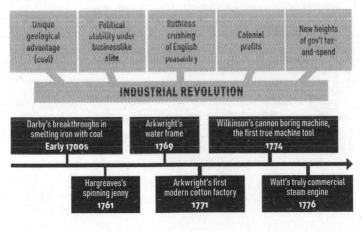

No human had ever seen gas burn the way it did in Priestley's experiments; no human had ever seen mountains of coal devoured like this; no human had ever stood beside a river of molten iron. Now people saw it, and were awestruck. Leonardo da Vinci had sketched machines impossible in his own day; two centuries later, the artisan-industrialists of Britain made such things reality.

The One Country That Could Beat Great Britain

The Seven Years' War left Great Britain with an astonishing empire, a vital head start in the Industrial Revolution, and the fatal notion that destiny was on its side.

> What lectures will be read to poor children on this era? Europe taught to tremble . . . the treasures of Peru diverted into the Thames, Asia subdued by the gigantic Clive! For in that age men were near seven feet high . . . Oh! I am out of breath with eloquence and prophecy.
>
> —Horace Walpole satirizes the megalomaniac atmosphere of 1762

Detail from *The East Offering her Riches to Britannia* (East India Company London Headquarters, 1778)

Yet an empire over which you actually rule is far more expensive than one of trade and influence. Paradoxically, the great victories of the Seven Years' War increased the bills. The hated window tax, based on the number of windows in your house, was repeatedly increased.

While Britain's property owners were hastily minimizing their tax exposure, its leaders forgot the basics of international negotiations. Pointless acts of imperial overreach, like forcing Spain to cede the Falkland Islands in 1771, made all of Europe fear there was no limit to British ambition. Disaster came when London tried to impose the new high-tax, high-spend Big State on the American colonies, and make them pay for their own defense. For it turned out there was one people that eighteenth-century Great Britain couldn't beat: the English.

Like the radicals of the English Civil War, America's Founding Fathers saw themselves as true Anglo-Saxons, fighting for their ancient rights against a foreign-style despotism.

> Our Saxon ancestors held their lands, as they did their personal property, in absolute dominion . . . America was not conquered by William the Norman.
>
> —Thomas Jefferson

> Liberty was better understood, and more fully enjoyed by our ancestors, before the coming in of the first Norman Tyrants.
>
> —James Otis

They were ethnically correct. The New England colonies were at least 70 percent English; the royal British Army facing them was over 70 percent non-English.

African: 2.3%
Scottish: 2.8%
Scots-Irish: 4%
Indigenous: 0.6%
Irish, Dutch, 2.9%
French, German
Unassigned: 16.9%

English: 70.5%

English: 29.8%
Scottish: 27.4%
Irish: 27.4%
American Colonials: 5.3%
Foreigners enlisted in Europe: 4.3%
Foreigners enlisted in America: 5.7%

New England colonies
approx. population 1776

British Army NCOs and privates
American War of Independence

Source: Peter Way, "Recruiting the British Army in the 18th century,"
University of Amsterdam, 2013

Foreign policy mistakes had united Europe's greatest maritime powers—France, Spain, and Holland—against Britain. The Royal Navy, fatally overstretched, for once failed at the Battle of the Chesapeake (1781). Besieged without hope at Yorktown, the British surrendered, and the New English went off to pursue life, liberty, and happiness in what Jefferson, Otis, and Adams believed was the true Old English way.

Stripped of America, and with a colossal national debt hanging over them, Tories and Whigs snarled blame at one another. In India, Britain's position was seriously threatened by defeats in the Second Anglo-Mysore War (1780–84). Any other country might have been ruined. But now, stimulated by all that government tax-and-spend, the Industrial Revolution truly blossomed.

The Northern Shift

For once, fate, in the shape of geology, was batting for the North. The ancient rocks beyond the Jurassic Divide might make for poor farmland, but they were packed with subterranean wealth.

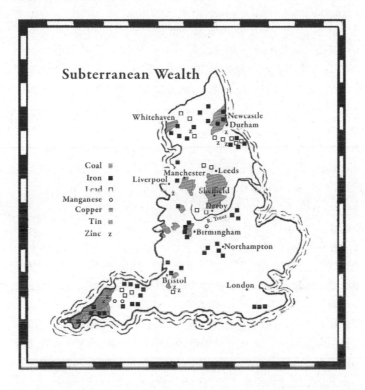

By 1800, the population of counties like Wiltshire had hardly changed since 1700, while that of northern, industrializing counties had grown enormously.

1750	Town	Population	1801	Town	Population
1	London	675,000	1	London	959,000
2	Bristol	45,000	2	Manchester	90,000
3	Birmingham	24,000	3	Liverpool	80,000
4	Liverpool	22,000	4	Birmingham	74,000
5	Manchester	18,000	5	Bristol	64,000
6	Leeds	16,000	6	Leeds	53,000

It was never enough to truly overcome the North-South divide. Relatively, Manchester, Liverpool, Leeds, and Birmingham all grew much faster than London; in absolute terms, London grew faster than them all combined. By 1800, it was easily the biggest city in the western hemisphere, with almost one million inhabitants, and one in eight English people lived there.

Yet the North was finally partaking more evenly of England's wealth, and this created a new sense of unity. Nobody could now believe, as rebellious Jacobites had still believed in 1715 and even in 1745, that the North of England would actually rise against London in favor of a French-backed invasion from Scotland. This was vital when the next war with France, newly energized by its revolution in 1789, pushed things to the limit.

New Money, New Country

In 1796, an attempted French invasion of Ireland was thwarted, but the following year, the navy was shaken by mutinies and the French landed briefly in Britain itself, at Fishguard in Wales. Panic led to a run on the banks: People demanded that their new-fangled banknotes be exchanged for gold, as the wording promised they could be. In desperation, the government passed the Bank Restriction Act (1797), which allowed the Bank of England to refuse them.

For the first time in European history, the citizens of a major state were told that they had to trust in paper money, to be redeemed at some unspecified later date. Hyperinflation could easily have been the result. Instead, Britain's political-commercial elite stepped up, in an event still studied by economists today.

> All over Britain, bankers and merchants declared that they would support public credit by accepting the Bank's notes.
>
> —Banque de France (2017)

Now the British government could print however much money it thought people would accept. Napoleon was always baffled and infuriated at how "perfidious Albion" could get away with this, when he still had to pay for everything in gold. The answer was simple: Britain had a far less narrow elite, who regarded the state as their very own, and hence trusted it. Jane Austen's *Pride and Prejudice* (set around this time) neatly dramatizes England's uniquely broad-based ruling class. People with Norman names (Fitzwilliam Darcy, Lady de Bourgh) still rule society. But Darcy's best friend is Bingley, whose family money has been *acquired by trade*.

This businesslike elite did what was necessary, even if it was deeply unpopular. A radical new tax was invented to back the radical new paper money.

January 12, 1799: It is now actually proposed to place A TAX ON INCOMES! ... It is a vile, Jacobin, jumped up Jack-in-office piece of impertinence—is a true Briton to have no privacy? Are the fruits of his labour and toil to be picked over, farthing by farthing, by the pimply minions of bureaucracy?

—Dr. John Knyveton

To control rebellious Ireland, a brand-new state was founded: In 1801, *Great Britain* became the *United Kingdom*. The new UK had nothing to do with domination by "the English" as a people or a nation. On the contrary, the ordinary English were more than ever just another people within the empire of their elite: At least a quarter of the inhabitants (the large majority of Irishmen, most Welshmen, and a large minority of Scotsmen) couldn't speak even basic English. The new state was thoroughly an elite construct.

Growth of the empire of the Southern English elite from the end of the French-speaking unity (1399) to the formation of the UK (1801). In each case, the rival elite was assimilated first.

The reason people could and did talk interchangeably about England, Britain, or the UK was that nobody who mattered, cared. And whatever you called it, it worked brilliantly.

Breaking Napoleon

Using the radical political tactic of the French Revolutionaries— the referendum—Napoleon made himself First Consul for Life (1802), then Emperor (1804). The sale of Louisiana to the Americans gave him gold aplenty to pay for a 250,000-strong *Armée d'Angleterre*, gathered at Boulogne.

Like the Spanish in 1588 and the Germans in 1940, Napoleon was faced with the British Navy. Nelson destroyed the Franco-Spanish fleet at Trafalgar in 1805, and the result was a cross-Channel standoff. Napoleon couldn't invade, but after his crushing victories against the Austrians, Prussians, and Russians in 1805–7, nobody dared put up an army against him, despite London's offer to pay £1.75 million for every 100,000 anti-French soldiers.

The navy ruled the waves so completely that even while still at war with Napoleon, Britain was able to worry about making the world a better place. In 1807, Parliament abolished the slave trade within the empire (though without freeing those already enslaved). Country after country fell into line, and the international suppression of the trade became a staple employment of the Royal Navy for the next half-century.

> If you were one of those slaves, on a slave ship, captured by the Royal Navy, intercepted at sea, and had the shackles broken off your wrists and your feet . . . then what had happened . . . was nothing short of a miracle
> —David Olusoga, BBC, November 29, 2016

The French dictator tried to bankrupt the moralizing, money-printing "nation of shopkeepers" by the Continental System, a Europe-wide embargo on British goods. When Portugal refused to comply, he invaded via Spain, sparking rebellion in Madrid. With Spain providing the vital ally and bridgehead in Europe, the newborn UK—militarily, it really was the *United* Kingdom—mobilized for all-out war. The Duke of Wellington whipped French general

Recruitment to British Army, July 1808 to June 1809, War Office figures

Scottish 1429
English & Welsh 7347
Irish 5621

after French general in the Peninsular Campaign. His control over Europe weakening, Napoleon lashed fatally out at the tsar in 1812. Because he was forced to leave 250,000 French troops in Spain, the *Grande Armée* that invaded Russia was half-composed of hapless conscripts from other European countries. Beaten on two fronts, he abdicated in 1814.

Even without him, Europe remained a toxic bear pit. Within six months, the UK found itself, incredibly, allied with France (and Austria) for a possible war against Russia and Prussia. Only the return of Napoleon reunited the Allies. After Wellington and the Prussians finally defeated him at Waterloo (1815), London was determined to wash its hands of the Continent.

Its exit strategy was to rebalance the European powers by handing the arch-militaristic Prussians the prosperous, peaceful German Rhineland. Then, having blithely kick-started the Prussian-ruled Germany which would become its nemesis, the UK bailed from Europe as gratefully as the USA in 1919.

The Empire of Progress

With the end of wartime tax-and-spend, the new industrial Britain experienced full depression for the first time, and with it came social unrest. The focus of agitation was the Corn Laws, which protected landowners by forbidding imports of grain until the price hit a certain level—set so high that it was never actually reached. The air grew heavy with various revolutions. In 1817, the year Jane Austen died, Mary Shelley invented modern science fiction and horror in one fell swoop, with *Frankenstein*. Two years later, sixty thousand people gathered in St. Peter's Square, Manchester, to hear the greatest speaker of the age, Henry "Orator" Hunt (a renegade member of the landowning class) lambast the Corn Laws. The 15th Hussars, who had charged the French at Waterloo, charged their fellow countrymen in the Peterloo Massacre. The following year, the men of the Cato Street Conspiracy planned to assassinate the entire cabinet in revenge.

Yet while Europe in the decades after Napoleon was dominated by absolutism and revolutions, Britain escaped both. The key, once again, was its uniquely broad-based elite.

> The English aristocracy has been adroit in more than one respect . . . what distinguishes it from all others is the ease with which it has opened its ranks.
>
> —Alexis de Tocqueville, 1838

There was bitter resistance to the final appeal of all laws against Catholics (1829), to the first great electoral Reform Act (1832) and to the abolition of slavery itself in the Empire (1833).

SLAVE EMANCIPATION; OR, "JOHN BULL GULLED OUT OF TWENTY MILLIONS." A corrupt politician picks £20 million for his slave-owning client from John Bull's pocket. This was a colossal sum in 1833—the British taxpayer didn't finally pay off the loan until 2015.

But however strong the opposition, it was all done through Parliament, and when Parliament made up its mind, that was the end of it. With the elite united, the rest of the country followed suit.

> The Chartist and Anti-Corn Law campaigns were . . . the most powerful systemic popular critique of British institutions since the American Revolution. They mobilised millions in their cause. Yet both looked to Parliament.
>
> —Angus Hawkins, *Victorian Political Culture*

There was clearly something special about England's political arrangements, and when the Houses of Parliament burned down in 1834, it was determined that this should be set in stone.

Left Radical classicism: Capitol, Washington, 1826. *Right* Royalist classicism: Buckingham Palace, 1834.

What did Britons want with either wild American democracy or that "monstrous architectural abortion" (as *Architectural Magazine* called Buckingham Palace in January 1836)? The competition to decide on the new buildings laid down that entries must be in the Gothic style. The idea was to take England back to its very own future, located roughly in the fifteenth century.

> A new and vigorous style upon the foundation of the glorious architecture of our own country and our own forefathers, in the place of one at once alien to our race and our religion.
>
> —Gilbert Scott, 1851

The new Houses of Parliament, begun 1840

Under the young Queen Victoria (ascended 1837), the new-look, Gothic-branded UK, easily the richest and most stable country in Europe, projected its image across the world.

Left: Trinity College, Toronto. *Right:* Christ Church, Simla, India.

Its thinkers developed a brand-new big idea: the religion of muscular, unstoppable *progress*. Soon, everybody would embrace the British Way, with a tough nudge from the Royal Navy and the Army where necessary. New lands were incorporated and ancient cultures forced to change.

> Be it so. This burning of widows is your custom; prepare the funeral pile. But my nation has also a custom. When men burn women alive we hang them.
>
> —General Sir Charles James Napier, putting down the practice of Suttee in India, 1843

Minor setbacks like the destruction of an entire army in Afghanistan in 1842 were shrugged off.

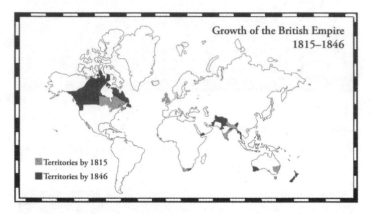

Growth of the British Empire 1815–1846

■ Territories by 1815
■ Territories by 1846

As the Empire grew unstoppably, its HQ offered people a living, and political liberties, which nowhere else in Europe could match. Since Ireland was now part of the UK, there was complete freedom of movement in the British Isles.

> More than 1 million have already immigrated . . . Their food consists of potatoes and potatoes only; whatever they earn beyond these needs they spend upon drink. What does such a race want with high wages?
>
> —Friedrich Engels, 1845

The UK had no border controls and no secret police: Other Europeans, fleeing poverty or oppression, flooded in as well. A militarily unassailable empire of prosperity and progress—the world had seen nothing like it since the great days of Rome, and it altered people's minds. The philosophy of Karl Marx, developed in England in these years, is really an extreme version of High Victorian liberalism: The fact of the worldwide British Empire created the fantasy of the worldwide Socialist Revolution.

The Last Challenge to London

In the very heart of empire, however, there was a problem: the old divide within England itself. At first, the Industrial Revolution had seemed to rebalance England more equally, but by the 1840s it had gone so far that the North was feeling almost like a different country again, though in a different way: not a backward, rural place but a hive of modernity, for good or ill.

Formerly the bastion of Catholicism, the North had by now expressed its difference from the Church of England South by

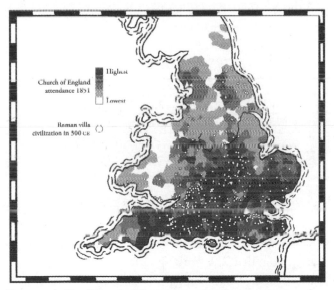

The strongholds of Church of England attendance in 1851 were very close to the mapped locations of Roman villa civilization in 300 CE.

thoroughly adopting Nonconformist Christianity and political Liberalism (politics and religion were as linked in Victorian England as in the modern Middle East). The Northern elite had their own brand of religion, their own *nonconformist dissenting academies*, teaching modern, practical subjects, and their own intermarrying industrial dynasties. They even had their very own economic theory. What we'd today call globalism—the credo of tariff-free international trade—was then internationally known as Manchesterism.

> Britain in effect contained two middle classes: by far the largest and wealthiest based on commerce and finance in London and the surrounding "home counties," the other on industry and manufacturing in the "north."
>
> —Ron Martin

As for the Northern poor, they, like the poor of London, lived in concentrations of urban misery so awful that they were physically shrinking.

> Urban-born men [in the UK] were shorter than rural-born men . . . the bulk of the decline in average heights was concentrated in urban areas between circa 1820 and circa 1860.
>
> —Floud and Harris, "Health, Height, and Welfare: Britain, 1700–1980"

The tensions in England were so clear that Marx and Engels (both living there) became convinced that class war was scientifically inevitable—Engels's studies of life in 1840s Manchester persuaded him that "the working-class has gradually become a race wholly apart from the English bourgeoisie." And it wasn't just career revolutionaries who saw conflict everywhere. The

"Condition of England Question" was widely discussed. The future prime minister, Benjamin Disraeli, in his popular novel *Sybil* (1845), believed that the key lay in uniting England's *two nations*, poor and rich, Saxon and Norman, North and South.

Just how real that divide was became clear in 1848. Harvests failed across Europe for the second year in a row. Governments everywhere, unable to pass the basic test of providing affordable carbohydrates for their masses, faced revolutions. In England, the crisis had a clear North-South character.

The Chartist demands seem perfectly reasonable today and are usually filed under the history of national political progress:

> The object of the Petitioners is to induce the House to pass measures for Universal Suffrage, Vote by ballot, Annual Parliaments, Equal Electoral Districts, Payment of Members and no Property Qualification.
>
> —Parliamentary Archives, April 10, 1848

This would have led to a massive transfer of power away from the South—which was what Chartism was really all about: Muscled-up by the Industrial Revolution, the North was refinding its own voice for the first time since the Civil War. It had allies among the poor of London, but not for nothing was its newspaper called the *Northern Star*. When their Great Petition failed to move Parliament, the Chartists made an extraordinary move: They proposed no less than a rival parliament in Manchester, now capital of the North.

> The mere assembling of such a Parliament marks a new epoch in the history of the world . . . two Parliaments in England, a Parliament at London, and a Parliament at Manchester.
>
> —Karl Marx, letter to the Chartist Congress, March 9, 1854

The Reverend Nathanial Woodard saw the danger to English unity (that is, to the rule of Southern England over all England) and stepped up to the crease.

Education, Education, Education

Woodard proposed to reeducate the fractious middle classes of Northern England into Southern English gentleman.

MR. WOODARD'S PUBLIC SCHOOLS FOR THE MIDDLE CLASSES.

> We in the south cannot realise the state of society. Dissent is not in any painfully obnoxious form here, nor are morals flagrant. To see it in the north, in the manufacturing districts, makes one shudder . . . We are determined to offer a good education, conducted on Church of England principles, to every shade of the middle classes . . . they are to be large public boarding schools . . . Our system of large public schools will quite alter the tone of the middle classes.
>
> —*Morning Chronicle*, November 18, 1851

It worked. Henceforth, the Northern elite sent their sons away to Gothic imitations (almost always south of the Trent) of truly ancient schools, where they were trained to be as like the old Southern elite as possible.

Left: Eton Chapel (1482). *Right:* Lancing Chapel (1868).

Soon, radicals like the Lancashire-based manufacturer, Richard Cobden, were despairing:

> Manufacturers and merchants as a rule seem only to desire riches that they may be enabled to prostrate themselves at the feet of feudalism ... We are a servile, aristocrat-loving people who regard the land with as much reverence as we still do the peerage.
>
> —Richard Cobden, 1863

Once again, the ruling order of England had pulled off its signature trick, inviting in new blood (so long as it had money and abandoned its own ways). Sports, often invented from scratch, became the great unifier of the old and new schools.

> A corps of men specially selected, brought up in a rigour of bodily hardship to which no other modern people have subjected their ruling class, trained by cold baths, cricket, and the history of Greece and Rome.
>
> —Philip Mason (aka Philip Woodruff)

Association Football (*soccer* to public schoolboys) was codified at Charterhouse in 1863. Cricket's bible, *Wisden*, was born the following year. The rules of Rugby's own in-school style of football (*rugger*) were laid down in the Pall Mall restaurant in

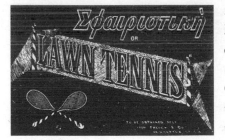

1871. The first book on Lawn Tennis (1874) even offered an alternative title in ancient Greek, to prove that this new sport was for the right sort.

Yet outside the real or fake Gothic quads, the English were getting jumbled together as never before, on railway platforms and in city shopping streets. A subtle new dress code was needed, so that the public school men could spot one another, while not too flagrantly inviting aggression or robbery. Aristocratic display was binned, replaced with modest-looking but expensive wear, which had to be changed at precisely the right places and times.

Even to get the smallest thing wrong could be disastrous. On a July morning in 1881, the Anglophile Count Ompteda (his ancestor had led the King's German Legion at Waterloo) found himself stared at in Piccadilly. He rushed home in confusion and checked in the mirror:

> That was it! I was wearing a *white* waistcoat, modestly but fatally visible under my frock-coat. And lo! it was the only white waistcoat in Piccadilly.

Once you had noted a man's correct waistcoat and suchlike, you could address him—and then, all would immediately become clear. From the 1870s, the accent that became known as Received Pronunciation, or RP, was the sole permissible one. It was, of course, a variant of Southern English.

> The accent most usually heard in everyday speech in the families of Southern English persons whose menfolk have been educated at the great public boarding schools.
> —Daniel Jones, the guru of RP, defines it (1916)

A new elite democracy was born, broader than ever, able to pick one another instantly out, whether in Mayfair or in Madras. Educated in the same (classical) subjects, singing the same (Anglican) hymns, dressed the same (correct) way, playing the same (fairly played) games, and talking in the same (RP) accent, the public school men threw up tennis courts, cricket pavilions, and rugby pitches from Cork to Calcutta, as surely as the Romans had thrown up forums, baths, and colonnades.

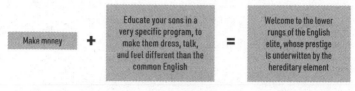

How to get into the elite of England, c. 1180–present day

The common people aped their hyper-confident ruling order. Cricket in particular became the national glue, a carefully regulated forum where ordinary Englishmen were allowed to send stone-hard balls hurtling at peers of the realm. Foreign visitors found it hard to believe. A visiting Russian aristocrat thought cricket looked fun, so he joined a scratch XI:

> He got terribly knocked about and afterwards expressed his conviction that pursuits of the mind were preferable.
>
> —*Daily News*, August 3, 1865

Mid-Victorian England seemed, at last, truly *one nation*. The Conservative Party (informally named in 1834) was notionally heir to the Royalists of the seventeenth century; the Liberal Party (informally named in 1839) was theoretically descended from the Parliamentarians. But there was so little ideology in either of them that W. E. Gladstone was able to leave the Tories to lead the Liberals, while the supposed High Church reactionaries of the Tory party chose a flamboyant Jewish writer, Benjamin Disraeli, to oppose him in the great parliamentary duels of the era. Not coincidentally, for the first time since Shakespeare,

England produced, in Charles Dickens, a writer who spoke to both high and low. United, it exercised an irresistible gravity within the UK. The elites of the other nations had long since adopted English as their first language, and now the mass of their common peoples followed suit, taking up the tongue of the Saxons after a thousand years and more of resistance. English was the only game in town—even, some English people were starting to think, in the world.

> Though Germans, French, and Russians may cling as hard as the Welsh and Irish to their ancient forms of speech, they are assuredly doomed to be extinguished by our own.
>
> —Henry Mayhew (founder of *Punch*), 1864

1800

Gaelic

Scots English

Scots English

Gaelic

Small elite set apart by having Latin, Greek, French. Favorite style: Classical

Welsh

English regional dialects

1880

National dialects of English

National dialects of English

Much larger elite set apart by speaking RP English. Celtic languages greatly diminished. Favorite style: Gothic

English regional dialects

How mighty the UK seemed! In the Crimean War (1853–56) it and France dealt Russia an epochal defeat on its own soil. The Indian Mutiny (1857) was crushed and free trade imposed on China in the Second Opium War (1856–60).

> The opening up of China is undoubtedly one of the most
> obvious causes of that wonderful, and to many inexplicable,
> prosperity which, amid the dangers of Europe and the
> convulsions of America, seems to settle in lieu of other
> sunshine upon these islands.
>
> —*The Times*, May 28, 1864

The country entered the 1860s triumphant, apparently able to spread its markets wider and wider, whatever the troubles of less fortunate lands.

The Inescapable Continent

It was an illusion. The UK was never a real hegemon. GDP peaked at 9.1 percent of the world total in 1870, but it was never greater than France and Germany combined (by comparison, the USA hit 40 percent in 1960). The British Empire depended on Europe being stable and politically agreeable, and its elite knew it. The remotest possibility of attack across the Channel was enough to cause a near-hysterical reaction. In 1859, a single new ironclad wooden warship (*La Gloire*) gave France a technological edge over the Royal Navy. Within a year, she was herself rendered obsolete by the all-iron HMS *Warrior* (1860) and the UK had started building an insanely expensive, never-used system of coastal forts.

Virtually indestructible, Palmerston's Follies (as they were known even before they were finished) can still be visited from Cork to Dover. Even at the height of its global power, the UK knew that what really mattered was Europe.

A single date, July 28, 1866, perfectly sums up the UK's position as a global power, but one inescapably tied to Europe. After a decade of failed attempts, a viable telegraph link to America sparked into life. At once, the stock exchanges of London and New York became a single information zone. The IT for globalization was in place.

Yet the very first piece of hard news transmitted across the Atlantic that day was of how Prussia had smashed Austria in the greatest European battle between 1815 and 1914. Four years later, in 1870, Prussia went one better and annihilated Napoleon III's France in six weeks. At first, some in England thought this might be a good thing: Paris had been challenging London as the world's great financial marketplace.

> With regards to money and capital it must be remembered that the plenteousness existing arises from London being again the great centre of finance of the world.
>
> —*The Gentleman's Magazine*, 1870

But England was soon swept by fear. The runaway bestseller of 1871 was *The Battle of Dorking*, a novel filled with convincing military details (the author was a serving lieutenant colonel), which foretold invasion and occupation by the new German Empire. Gladstone himself felt obliged to remind readers publicly that it was fiction.

Disraeli, the new Conservative PM (from 1874) saw that England absolutely had to reengage with Europe.

> The balance of power has been entirely destroyed, and the country which suffers most, and feels the effects of this great change most, is England.
>
> —Benjamin Disraeli

In 1875, he did the unthinkable, and forged an alliance with Russia to deter a new German strike on France. Three years later, he switched sides. At the Congress of Berlin (1878), in last-minute, late-night talks with Germany's Iron Chancellor, Otto von Bismarck, he dangled the prospect of a worldwide Anglo-German-Austrian alliance against Russia.

Bismarck was tempted. His ambassador in London reported on the warlike mood: Anti-Russian crowds known as "jingoes"— from the hit music-hall song of the day ("We don't want to fight, but by jingo if we do . . .")—were roaming the town, routing pacifist meetings, and even breaking Gladstone's windows.

EUROPE'S LATEST TREATY.

GREAT BRITAIN'S TRIUMPH.

New York Times, July 20 1878

The Iron Chancellor bit. Disraeli wrote to Queen Victoria (who adored him because he had created her Empress of India in 1876) that "before I went to bed, I had the satisfaction of knowing that St. Petersburg had surrendered."

The lesson of 1875–78 was clear: If the UK played up and played the game across the Channel, it could be the arbiter of Europe. The prestige of the Empire reached its climax. Leaders of faraway lands begged Queen Victoria to take their affairs in hand (in the case below, in vain).

> Dearest Madam,   *Cameroons River, Acqua Town, August 7, 1879.*
> WE your *servants* have *join* together and thoughts its better to write you a nice *loving* letter which will tell you about all our *wishes*. We *wish* to have your laws in our towns. We want to have every *fashion* altered, also we will do according to your Consul's *word*. Plenty wars here in our country. Plenty murder and plenty idol worshipers. Perhaps these *lines* of our writing will *look* to you as an *idle* tale.
> We have *spoken* to the English Consul plenty times about having an English Government here. We never have answer from you, so we wish to write you *ourselves*.
> When we heard about Calabar River, how they have all English *laws* in their towns, and how they have put away all their *superstitions*, oh, we shall be very glad to be like Calabar now.
>
>   We are, &c.
>   (Signed)   KING ACQUA.
>   PRINCE DIDO ACQUA.
>   PRINCE BLACK.
>   PRINCE JOE GARNER.
>   PRINCE LAWTON.

Disraeli, triumphant, seemed sure to win the 1880 general election, not least because he himself had given the vote to an extra million men in the Second Reform Act (1867).

Gaming Democracy

The Conservatives had not realized how much even a small dose of democracy had changed things. Gladstone had. His Midlothian Campaign is still the bible for electoral strategists: At almost seventy, he headed out from London on a marathon tour of until-then obscure Scottish constituencies, identified as targets by local research, making his campaign itself into the story.

> The campaign was effectively designed as a media event, with specific attention to the deadlines and operational requirements of the journalists covering it and crafted for maximum impact in the morning and evening papers.
>   —Paul Brighton, *Original Spin*, 2015

No member of the elite had ever paid such court to ordinary men, or to journalists. The British Empire, said Gladstone, should be a moral example, encouraging Europe to stay peaceful, but without "needless entanglements." The religion of progress dictated that the whole world would surely follow to a sunlit, low-tax upland of Christian peace and plenty!

With Gladstone grabbing the headlines, the world hung on the campaign, as it might today hang on a pivotal US election.

> From India and Central Asia to the populations of the Balkan Peninsula, from Stamboul to Rome and St Petersburg, all eyes are directed to the great electoral battle now raging.
>
> —*The Times*, February 3, 1880

To the horror of Victoria and Bismarck alike, Gladstone won a landslide, leaving the proposed UK-German-Austrian alliance against Russia dead in the water. Bismarck was stuck with Austria as his sole ally. Russia cozied vengefully up to France, which gleefully embraced it as the one power that could help it overturn the defeat of 1870. Almost immediately, Gladstone's retreat from Europe in 1880 created the lineup of 1914.

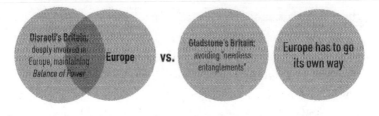

"The people's William" rammed home his victory by enfranchising many more males in the Third Reform Act (1884) and for the first time creating equal-number constituencies (1885).

Gladstone doubtless assumed that democracy would keep the Liberals in power forever. A radical new party hoped for even more. The earliest ancestor of the Labour Party, the Social Democratic Federation (1881) was founded, bankrolled, and run as a personal fief by H. J. Hyndman (said to have been outraged at not getting his cricketing blue at Cambridge). Members included star designer William Morris, Karl Marx's daughter Eleanor, and future Labour leader George Lansbury. Like every renegade member of the elite who has ever tried to win over the ordinary English, Hyndman proclaimed a lost golden age:

> Merrie England, in short ... for the benefit of the many, not the gain of the few.

But liberals and socialists both called it wrong. Mass voting immediately revealed the United Kingdom's deadliest enemy: its own ancient nations.

Doomed by Democracy

The UK had been founded by and for a united elite. Nobody had ever asked the peoples. From the moment they could use their votes, in 1885, the ordinary Irish, Scots, and Welsh used them to make nationalist demands, openly or implicitly.

The English, too, voted along ancient, tribal lines from the start. There were still regional complications, based around religion. The Southwest and East Anglia were traditionally nonconformist, hence anti-Tory. Lancashire had its very own micro-politics: Fear and loathing of the Catholic Irish in Liverpool (who elected an actual Irish Nationalist MP every year from 1885–1929) turned the Protestant English away from the Liberals. But the most important factor, down to the present day, was clear: The moment ordinary Southeasterners got the vote, they went, and stayed, Conservative.

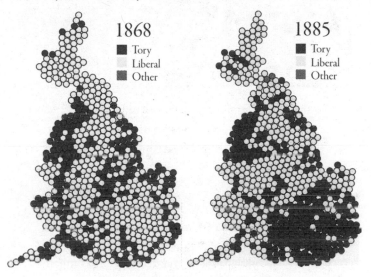

THE ENGLISH START TO VOTE TRIBALLY.
From 1885, Southern English voters formed a virtually impregnable Tory bloc in the Southeast. The Liberals only ever cracked it once, in 1906, so they more and more had to rely on an alliance of the Northern English + the Celts. This was later true, in spades, for Labour.

Gladstone could only stay in power by keeping the Celts onside. That meant the first Home Rule bill for Ireland, the first dedicated secretary of state for Scotland, and public support for the noisy, even violent Welsh campaign against paying taxes (tithes) to the Church of England.

Sometimes little ripples show deep currents. Rugby was the quintessential game of the UK's public school–educated elite. But even as the first Outer British coalition was forming, the Irish, Scots, and Welsh set up the International Rugby Football Union (1886), challenging England's claim to owning the game. Nine years later, the North of England broke clean away, adopting Rugby League.

The England XV for the first international against Scotland, 1871. This was Peak UK, with the elite as one. By 1886, people had started voting on national lines, and their elite sportsmen had begun to dispute Southern England's ownership of the rules.

The slow dissolution of the UK began just at the time when a firm, rational foreign policy was needful. For by 1887, it wasn't hard to see that a major war was coming in Europe, or what the sides would be.

> We have thus the certainty of a conflict sooner or later between Germany and France, and the extreme probability that this will either be precipitated by a new Russian advance in Eastern Europe, or immediately followed by such an advance. This advance will bring the Austrian armies into the field.
>
> —*Freeman's Journal*, December 19, 1887

Which side would the British Empire back? Its huge power and wealth, thrown into the scales, would clearly tip the balance. It was a tough choice: France and Russia were the great imperial competitors, but Germany was becoming the great industrial rival. Yet there was time enough to consider it. Never in the history of human conflict has so great a power been given so long to make so vital a decision.

The UK, however, was paralyzed by nationalist forces within. Gladstone was determined to regain power, but he could only do so with Irish help, so the Irish Question dominated Parliament from 1886–95. He also promised the Scots and Welsh religious disestablishment (that is, devolution, Victorian-style): anything to trump the fortress-like Tory bloc in the South of England. Small wonder that governments tried desperately to avoid life-or-death foreign policy choices.

> Whatever happens will be for the worst and therefore it is in our interest that as little should happen as possible.
>
> Lord Salisbury, 1887

The Empire vs. English Nationalism

Why didn't the Conservatives just go nationalist themselves, get shot of the smaller nations, and rule England (from the South, naturally) forever? The reason was simple: The southern elite had never been nationalists, and weren't about to start. As their favorite poet, Kipling, put it: "What should they know of England who only England know?"

When they said *England* they didn't actually mean the whole country at all. They meant Imperial HQ, a network of exclusive southern spaces: the great public schools, Oxbridge, country houses, the right parts of London, and the Home Counties, Lords, Henley, Cowes, the Inns of Court, Parliament, the Guards, St James's, and so on. Their England was a South of the mind, a vision as unconnected to any real place as the RP accent in which they all spoke.

> We swept round a corner of the Downs. At our feet lay the green and golden carpet of the Sussex Weald. Suddenly out of the hidden lane right across our bows came the South Down hounds, homing after cubbing... We were silent. We had all seen a holy thing. We had seen England. None of us will ever be able to communicate what we saw: none of us will ever forget it.
>
> —S. B. P. Mais, 1922

Britain's imperial elite cared nothing for nationalism. Sir Nicolas Roderick O'Conor, British ambassador to its great rival, Russia, was a Catholic Irishman. But being descended from the highest aristocracy of old Gaelic Ireland, he was perfectly at home in Imperial HQ circles where a mere English doctor or lawyer would barely have been greeted.

The rulers of empire mocked the doubters of empire as *Little Englanders*. They were not going to risk their global destiny to please voters. Yet those voters now had power, and needed a story about why they should keep backing the imperial elite. So from 1885 the Conservative Party went populist, claiming to be the party that would defend the rights of ordinary people against overtaxation, foreign competition, immigrants, and do-gooding Liberal licensing laws. But it always carefully hid appeals to the English within a wider patriotism of the Union, the Crown, the Empire—becoming in the process the Conservative *and Unionist* party.

Ireland, Scotland, and Wales all got openly or

THE ALIEN PAUPER QUESTION.
FOREIGN PRODUCE—"MADE IN GERMANY."

implicitly nationalist politicians. England never did, because its leaders weren't nationalists. The job of the new English voters was to salute the Union Jack so that their rulers could get on with running a quarter of the world. Kipling told it straight:

> The poor little street-bred people that vapour and fume and brag,
> They are lifting their heads in the stillness to yelp at the English Flag...
> What is the Flag of England? Ye have but my breath to dare,
> Ye have but my waves to conquer. Go forth, for it is there!

And that was exactly what was happening. The elite were leaving the *poor little street-bred people* behind, and *going forth*. Or at least, their money was.

Globalization and Redivision

The developed world was in depression from 1873–96. Almost everywhere became protectionist. The UK didn't. Its ruling class was uniquely plugged-in to emerging world markets, where returns were better than in the UK. Who wanted barriers between markets? Not they.

> No other major economy has ever held such a large proportion of its assets overseas. More British capital was invested in the Americas than in Britain itself between 1865 and 1914.
> —Niall Ferguson

> Never before or since has one nation committed so much of its national income and savings to capital formation abroad.
> —Michael Edelstein

As the workshop of the world became the development banker of the world, London and its hinterland began to decouple and take flight on wings of invisible earnings.

1881	Town	Population	1901	Town	Population
1	London	3,814,600	1	London	6,339,500
2	Liverpool	552,400	2	Liverpool	702,200
3	Birmingham	400,800	3	Manchester	543,900
4	Manchester	341,500	4	Birmingham	522,200
5	Leeds	309,100	5	Leeds	429,000
6	Sheffield	284,400	6	Sheffield	409,100

The brief near-equality of Northern and Southern England was over. And things were getting worse. The Second Industrial Revolution had dawned. While rivals (notably, Germany and the USA) were retooling for new products electrical, chemical, and automotive, the UK was falling behind. From 1896, the Royal Navy itself was clad in Krupp of Germany's patent armor-plate, merely produced under license by British firms. The balance of payments depended more and more on the extraction and export of coal. Like oil today, this low-tech industry was massively profitable—while the coal seams lasted and everybody used coal.

Until c. 1870

By late 1890s

United Kingdom
Centered on unified England–investing in itself, workshop of the world, arbiter of Europe, unchallenged in Empire

London & hinterland
Financial services, investing capital abroad

Outer Britain
Based on low-skilled export

Two different economies were developing: the global, information-based financial sector in the Southeast of England; low-skilled jobs in Outer Britain with built-in shelf lives.

Sinks the Fire

In 1896, Victoria overtook George III as the longest-reigning monarch in English history. As Britons prepared for the celebrations (which she had requested be put off until 1897, when she would reach the full sixty years), they could tell themselves that the Empire was the greatest ever.

What they were reading, however suggested that they knew the great days were over. The runaway bestseller of 1896–97 was E. E. Williams's *Made in Germany*. Using as its title the official import mark introduced ten years before, it told English readers that Germany wasn't just an ordinary commercial rival, but had entered into "a deliberate and deadly rivalry with her, and was battling with might and main for the extinction of her supremacy." Readers who preferred (pure) fiction could, even as they celebrated the Queen Empress, thrill at two stories which appeared that very year: one telling of Surrey being laid waste by unstoppable alien technology, the other of London being infected by a terrible, sexual plague from Europe.

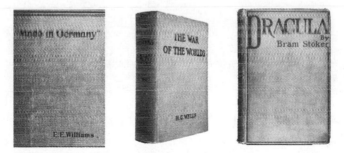

1896–97: Over in Vienna, Sigmund Freud was just developing his theory of repression while the English devoured books that spoke of downfall, destruction, and decay.

The "Poet of Empire" himself, Kipling, struck an unmistakably fate-laden note in his Jubilee offering:

> Far-called, our navies melt away;
> On dune and headland sinks the fire:
> Lo, all our pomp of yesterday
> Is one with Nineveh and Tyre!
> —"Recessional" by Rudyard Kipling, 1897

Rational voices pointed out that there were real grounds for the relative decline—and real solutions.

> Let our manufacturers do as the German manufacturers do, and bring their sons up to be better manufacturers than themselves, instead of bringing them up to be gentlemen who do nothing but hunt and shoot.
> —J. W. Logan, MP, House of Commons, 1897

But that would have meant real change. Luckily, the poet Henry Newbolt had another answer: If everyone just behaved like brave boarding schoolboys, brought up in the ways of cricket, all would be well, dodgy military hardware or not:

> The Gatling's jammed and the Colonel dead,
> And the regiment blind with dust and smoke . . .
> But the voice of a schoolboy rallies the ranks:
> "Play up! play up! and play the game!"

Admiral Nelson and the Duke of Wellington had placed their trust in trained firepower; nervous late Victorians were invited to place theirs in the superpower of their public school elite.

The Gentleman Capitalists

No lectures on the need for technical education, or for investment at home, could stop that elite from transforming themselves into gentleman capitalists—because they could.

In the great rivals, America and Germany, men were not exposed to the same temptation. America had no aristocracy, and worshipped money quite undisguisedly. Germany still had a real, hereditary aristocracy which was almost impossible to enter. So one way or another, Americans and Germans who made millions stayed commoners and concerned themselves openly with their trades.

Only England offered the irresistible lure of a genuine, hereditary aristocracy which was nevertheless open to new money. Like Saxon yeomen assimilating to their Norman overlords in the twelfth century, English industrialists and tradesmen of the nineteenth century denied their own backgrounds and became country house–living gentlemen.

> The more an occupation or a source of income allowed for a life-style which was similar to that of the landed classes, the higher the prestige . . . A "gentlemanly capitalist" did not despise the market economy, but he did hold production in low regard.
>
> —Martin Daunton, *State and Market in Victorian Britain*

Unrivaled access to markets via city, telegraph, and penny post across Empire **+** Opportunity to assimilate with the landed elite **=** CULT OF GENTLEMAN CAPITALIST WHO INVESTS RATHER THAN PRODUCES

This created a uniquely English divide, physical and cultural, between the owners of industry and the source of their wealth—which is exactly what the rich of the world found so

attractive. They all longed to dress, talk, and play like English gentlemen, hanging out with genuine aristocrats, untroubled by work, Socialists, or anarchists, in the peasant-free British countryside. The vision has remained unchanged, still entrancing American billionaires, Russian oligarchs, and suchlike—as well as newly rich English. Wealthy Late Victorian Germans didn't just borrow the word "sport," and the names of individual games, from England: This magazine (right) also taught them "English Chat."

Americans, having no trouble at all with English Chat, were particularly attracted. With safe, luxurious transatlantic journeys now possible, the UK and US elites were soon more than just business partners.

[Watson reads out from a newspaper] "One by one the management of the noble houses of Great Britain is passing into the hands of our fair cousins from across the Atlantic . . . the Californian heiress is not the only gainer by an alliance which will enable her to make the easy and common transition from a Republican lady to a British peeress."
"Anything else?" asked Holmes, yawning.
—Conan Doyle, *The Adventure of the Noble Bachelor*, 1892

This sense that the US elite was more or less family created the military *special relationship*. There had been serious tension in 1895–97 over America's determination to rule the South American roost—yet in 1898, at Manila Bay, without any orders whatever from London, the Royal Navy's commander on the spot instinctively backed the US Navy in the face of a powerful German squadron which seemed inexplicably bent on muscling in. It was noted with surprise and gratitude in the USA.

THANKSGIVING DAY AT MANILA.

Observed by British as Well as Americans—Banquet to Officers.

This was lucky. For it was about to become clear just how vulnerable the British Empire was.

A Degenerating Race?

In 1899, suspecting that the British in South Africa were thinking of seizing their madly lucrative diamond fields (they were), the Boer Republics struck first. The army was humiliated and decimated in Black Week (December 1899). All Europe gloated.

German cartoon mocking the catastrophic inability of the army to deliver in 1899. The image of British generals as donkeys was born here, not in World War I.

Patriots flocked to recruiting stations, but the menfolk of the UK, the most urban and industrial in Europe, were often just not physically up to soldiering. The army turned thousands away before, in desperation, dropping its 5'6" height barrier to 5'0".

The idea of a sort of British racial superpower was kept desperately up, but adverts like this told, to put it mildly, a somewhat inaccurate picture of the fighting.

Longing for a hero, the press seized on Colonel Robert Baden-Powell, besieged in an obscure railway junction called Mafeking (though not so besieged as to stop his plucky missives from getting out). When the town was relieved in May 1900 a new word, *maffeking*, was coined to describe the manic celebrations.

The new century began with the bitter Khaki Election of 1900, its agenda and tone set by the Boer war, with smears and conspiracy theories on both sides. The Conservatives sponsored a campaign of yellow journalism to link the terms *liberal*, *Little Englander*, *pro-Boer*, and *traitor*, while eighty-three trade-union officers (including Labour Party founder Keir Hardie) signed a resolution declaring that "the Capitalists, who bought or hired the Press both in South Africa and in England to clamour for war, are largely Jews." In the end, the Southern heartland was solid as ever and the wartime patriotic appeal also worked in the Outer UK, so the Conservatives smashed it.

On January 22, 1901, Queen Victoria died and King Edward VII took over. The war against a few Boer farmers was finally won in 1902, partly by using the new tactic of concentration camps against the civilian population, which was loudly opposed by some in Britain. Victory cost the British Empire fifty thousand dead and left a deep sense of unease. The Committee on Physical Deterioration (1903) investigated why Britain's manhood was so unmanly. Go-ahead types happily mixed sociology and biology in think pieces on the degenerating race.

> [In the East End] the streets were filled with a new and different race of people, short of stature, and of wretched or beer-sodden appearance.
>
> —Jack London, *The People of the Abyss*, 1903

> The multiplication of the Feeble-Minded, which is proceeding now at an artificial rate, unchecked by any of the old restraints of nature, and actually fostered by civilised conditions, is a very terrible danger to the race.
>
> —Churchill to Asquith, December 1910

It was by now obvious that the kaiser's mighty new battle fleet had only one possible target. The Royal Navy responded with the game-changing battleship *Dreadnought* (1906). That same year, the *Daily Mail* serialized William Le Queux's novel, *The Invasion of 1910*, complete with news vendors dressed in Prussian uniforms, dummy maps, and a foreword by Lord Roberts, former commander-in-chief, who was campaigning for conscription.

At the 1906 election, the Liberals cracked the Tory bloc of Southern England for the first and only time by offering nervous voters a handy sidestep: The problem was Tory corruption, jingoism, and incompetence. All would be well if the UK just changed its management, stuck to Free Trade, and adopted a "friendly and unprovocative" foreign policy. This happy vision won them a landslide, partly thanks to a secret pact with the new Labour Party, which won twenty-nine seats, none south of the Trent except three in East London.

Unfortunately, Germany's Grand Admiral von Tirpitz saw the new friendly and unprovocative foreign policy as a sign of weakness, so he upped the ante and launched his own clones of *Dreadnought*. The Tory battlecry resounded—"We want eight and we won't wait!"—and the Liberal chancellor, Lloyd George, was bounced into delivering battleships (which he didn't want) as well as Old-Age Pensions (which he did). In revenge, his People's Budget of 1909 proposed unheard-of levels of taxation on the wealthy, and he publicly spun things as a battle between the national interest and Tory privilege. The Conservatives fought back, presenting themselves as defenders of the Union against Germany, radicalism, and Home Rule.

Class war and the threat of real war on Liberal and Tory campaign posters (1910)

Wars and Rumors of Wars

In 1910, democracy finally turned the UK on its head. There were two bitter general elections, and in both, the Conservatives won a majority in England, thanks to that great southeastern bloc. But the Liberal English opposition, concentrated north of the Trent, was backed by Wales, Scotland, and Ireland. Southern England was the prisoner of the UK—and its jailers were considering how to lock the door and throw away the key. The victorious Outer British coalition was now proposing more than just Home Rule for Ireland. For the first time since the Tripartite Indenture of 1405, England was threatened with division, as part of a grand plan for a federal UK: "Home Rule All Round."

The man with this drastic vision was none other than Winston Churchill, at this time one of the Liberal leaders:

> There would be no difficulty in applying the federal system to [Scotland or Wales], as well as to Ireland.

Well and good, the Celts could all enjoy nationhood within the UK. But what of the English?

> When they came to England a very real difficulty arose. England was so great and populous If there were, as there very likely might be, a divergence of feeling and policy between the English Parliament and the Imperial Parliament, the quarrel between these two tremendously powerful bodies might tear the State in halves.

There certainly was a *divergence of feeling*. England had returned a Tory majority in seven out of the eight elections since the Third Reform Act. Scotland and Wales had been Liberal every time, and the Irish had always voted Nationalist. With England so different, and so much the largest, how could the four nations ever work as a federation? There was only one answer.

> They would have to face the task of dividing England into several great self-governing areas . . . Lancashire . . . Yorkshire . . . the Midlands . . . London . . . four great areas in England which might well have a conscious political entity, an effective political machinery, bestowed upon them.

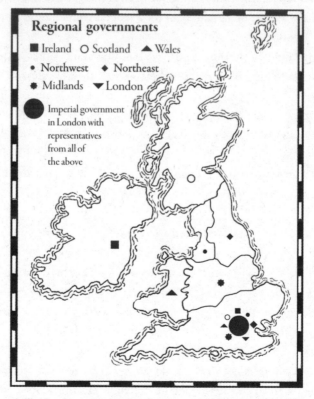

Churchill's idea for an Imperial Parliament, 1912. The South was not to get institutions of its own: To Churchill it was, implicitly, England itself.

THE SHORTEST HISTORY OF ENGLAND

| Outer UK Alliance wants federal UK, so England must be divided up because it is too big and too Tory. | The Party of the South wants United Kingdom as heart of Empire, so English nationalism is submerged in the Union. |

1910–14: No place for the English. On the eve of the Great War, the Liberals loved Small Nations and the Tories loved Empire, but English Nationalism was anathema to both.

Despite their majority in England, the United Kingdom's parliamentary arithmetic meant that the Conservatives had no way to stop Home Rule All Round—unless they took the fight beyond Parliament. Bonar Law, their leader, declared that there were "things stronger than parliamentary majorities"; if loyalist Irishmen would stand against Home Rule, there was "no length of resistance" he wouldn't back (July 29, 1913). When British Army officers at the Curragh Barracks in Ireland indeed seemed to be on the verge of mutiny, Churchill hit back for the Liberals in even more ominous tones: Home Rule would go through, by force if need be, for there were "worse things than bloodshed, even on an extended scale" (March 14, 1914).

As the political class recklessly bandied near–civil war talk, the industrial Outer UK was in a state of near insurrection. Parts of South Wales, Red Clydeside, and Liverpool had to be placed under semi-martial law in 1911. The following year, the first national miners' strike, by almost one million men, seemed about to tear the country apart. The 1914 Triple Alliance of miners, railwaymen, and transport workers deliberately sounded like one of the military leagues in Europe.

With the UK falling apart, the Liberals didn't dare tell their ramshackle alliance of nationalist Celts and Nonconformist Englishmen (who had strong pacifist traditions) about the most important thing of all. Churchill, Lloyd George, and the foreign secretary, Sir Edward Grey, were by now certain that war was coming, and that, once again, the country would have to intervene in Europe in order to save itself.

Almost incredibly, even as generals planned the British Expeditionary Force, and admirals disposed their dreadnoughts jointly with the French Navy, the public, and even most members of the Liberal cabinet itself, were assured that no such plans existed. Any talk of an upcoming fight was just Tory warmongering. When Lloyd George spoke too openly at the Guildhall in 1912, he personally begged the editor of the *Manchester Guardian* the next day not to tell its Northern readers what he'd said about the "German business."

And so, on August 4, 1914, the deadlock of UK politics in the democratic era plunged it, with almost no open preparation, into a war that had been clearly foreseeable, and foreseen, since 1887.

PART FIVE

Farewell the Eagles and Trumpets
1914–Present

The Great War

Luckily, the British Empire was still genuinely mighty. Australia and New Zealand had been straining at the leash to have a crack at the Germans in the Pacific since the 1890s, so they declared war the moment they heard about it, without even being asked.

And suddenly, the UK itself was united. Now that ships and guns needed building as fast as could be, industrial Outer Britain was no longer the Cinderella of the economy. Investment, which for years had been aimed abroad, was repatriated. The war rebalanced the economy and plastered over its cracks.

But only plastered over. The bitterness of the prewar disputes wasn't forgotten, even when it came to arms production. No one in England had heard the word *Bolshevik* yet: This was pure, homegrown industrial conflict.

> Among employers and employees the words "after the war" are constantly uttered . . . The conviction that the greatest war in the history of the world will be followed by an economic struggle on an equally large scale is extraordinarily widespread.
>
> —*Economic Journal*, March 1916

And even though they fought and died together, the men of the UK existed in different cultural worlds. At one place on the front in 1915, ordinary Tommies challenged their officers to a game of what both sides called *football*:

> To these [Tommies], Rugby Football—the greatest of all manly games—was a mere name. Their attitude when the officers appeared upon the field was one of indulgent superiority—the

sort of superiority that a brawny pitman exhibits when his Platoon Commander steps down into a trench to lend a hand with the digging. But in five minutes their mouths were agape with scandalised astonishment . . . the exhibition of savage and promiscuous brutality to which their superiors now treated them shocked the assembled spectators to the roots of their sensitive souls. Howls of virtuous indignation burst forth.

—John Hay Beith, 1915

Still, as long as it lasted, the men of the UK—including, for the first eighteen months, the Irish—pulled together. Unfortunately for many of them, field marshals Kitchener and Haig found their plans overtaken by events. The Liberal government's refusal to acknowledge that a war was coming had left the British Army tiny compared to European forces. The idea had always been to slowly build it up and train it, then strike at the vital moment. The trouble was, that moment came too soon. By late 1915, the French army was severely mauled, the tsar had lost rich territories the size of England, and the zeppelins were bombing London. With Germany and Austria winning, Kitchener and Haig had no choice but to take the offensive in 1916.

At the Somme (July–November 1916) the new, huge, but often barely trained volunteer army went over the top, led—as the myth of "British pluck" demanded—by a ridiculously high proportion of young ex-public school officers (17 percent of them died during the war, as opposed to 12 percent of ordinary soldiers). Casualties were appalling and the gain negligible— yet morale didn't collapse, lessons were learned fast, and the German Army was shaken as never before. Meanwhile, the kaiser's fleet was neutralized by sheer numbers after the indecisive battle of Jutland (May–June 1916) and an unbreakable naval blockade began to choke the enemy.

The *Englanders* were now Berlin's enemy number one. So the German Navy opened unrestricted U-boat warfare to break the vital trade with America. In 1917, this finally brought the New World in to settle the affairs of the Old. General Ludendorff threw in everything he had to win the war before the Americans could arrive in strength. The men of the UK and the Empire rose to Haig's desperate "backs to the wall" order. The army which every Prussian general had despised in 1914 delivered the "black day of the German Army" (General Lundendorff) at the Battle of Amiens in August, leading to the military, social, and moral collapse of the Second Reich. As other empires crumbled, the UK—and the British Empire—held (though only just, in Ireland).

Things Fall Apart

It looked like victory. The "Prussian Beast" was conquered, the Empire greater than ever. In reality, the United Kingdom

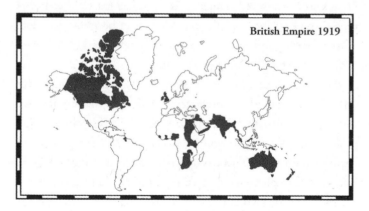

British Empire 1919

was not only far poorer, with huge war debts (mainly to America, for guns and food); it was also still riven by the internal fractures that had brought it close to civil war in 1913–14. These immediately reopened after the war. After two years of increasingly desperate mutual brutality in the War of Independence (1919–21), the Irish Free State took twenty-six of Ireland's thirty-two counties out of the Union.

This revealed the deep strangeness of the UK in the democratic age. It had been constructed from 1536 to 1801 by a political elite based in the South of England, as the center of Empire. So it might seem obvious that losing part of the UK would be a terrific blow to them—and indeed, they had tried to cling on to Ireland. Yet the moment Ireland left, the Party of the South was actually much stronger. The first normal postwar election showed why. In 1910, winning 344 MPs wouldn't have given the Conservatives an overall majority; in 1922, with ninety-two Southern Irish seats gone, it was comfortable enough.

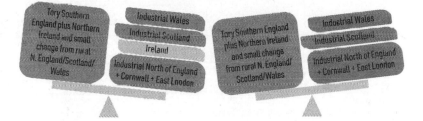

The smaller the UK, the more powerful the Southern English

This new electoral balance made the North-South political divide clearer still. Before the war, faced with three Celtic nations who were inherently hostile, the Conservatives had to contest seriously in the North of England. In the new, smaller UK, all they had to do was keep the Southern heartland happy.

The Gagging of the North

Coincidentally or not, the Southern elite now unleashed a great play to remake all of England in its own image. Or rather, its own voice. The report on *The Teaching of English in England*, led by Sir Henry "play up and play the game" Newbolt, insisted that every child in England be taught RP—if need be, as if it were literally a second language.

> Children who speak a dialect should, as often happens, become bi-lingual, speaking standard English too.
>
> —*Newbolt Report*, 1921

The new BBC, founded in 1922, adopted RP and by 1926, 2.25 million licenced radios were pumping out the accent of the public schools across the land. Yet again, the ambitious of England were essentially told: *Come, talk like us—and set yourself apart from your own folk.* Since RP was basically a Southern accent, it was relatively easy for Southerners to pick up; in the North, you had to lose your whole born way of speaking if you wanted to be more than a comic turn.

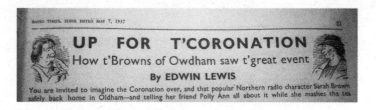

RADIO TIMES, ISSUE DATED MAY 7, 1937 21

UP FOR T'CORONATION
How t'Browns of Owdham saw t'great event
By EDWIN LEWIS
You are invited to imagine the Coronation over, and that popular Northern radio character Sarah Brown safely back home in Oldham—and telling her friend Polly Ann all about it while she mashes the tea

The BBC-led drive for RP pulled together two great strands of English history: the dominance of the South and a cultural divide based on what language you used in public.

The North-South Divide Gets Ideology

At the 1924 election, former Southern Liberal voters went Tory, and stayed there; former Northern Liberal voters went with Labour, and stayed there. This finally locked down the political North-South divide.

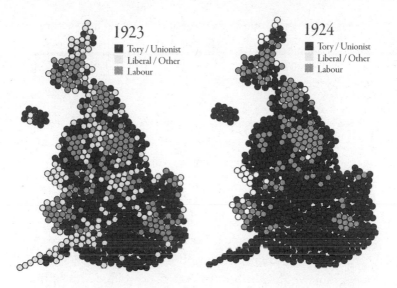

The Liberal Party was English, with an ancestry going back beyond the Union of 1707. Although it had come to be identified with Outer Britain during the struggles of the nineteenth century, it never completely lost traction in the South—until now. The Labour Party was a very different animal. It was born of the United Kingdom, its first five leaders were Scotsmen, and for the first two decades of its existence it had zero impact south of the Trent except in the poor quarters of London's vast city-state.

The Conservatives were no longer facing off against a genuine rival English party. The opposition now was the Party of Outer Britain (Northern English + Celts) aka Labour. This hardened the age-old suspicion among Southerners that the North was somehow not properly English. Essentially the battle lines were the same as in 1461, 1642, or 1848 (or, for that matter, as when Northern thanes and Welsh princelings had united against the Godwins of Wessex under Edward the Confessor).

The ancient struggle was now window-dressed with fashionable, twentieth-century ideologies. Labour, the new incarnation of the Outer British Alliance, claimed its members were all somehow instinctively peace-loving, communitarian, and internationalist. This self-image remains central to many Scots, Welsh, and Northern English.

> Men live by their generosities, by their loyalties; not by their interests, and their self-regarding impulses . . . that is the aim of the Socialist inspiration that gives us power in our Labour Movement.
>
> —Ramsay MacDonald, Labour leader, 1924

Meanwhile, the latest version of the Party of the South claimed to represent a "deep ethnic England." This vision is still widespread among those who love Barbour coats, the Cotswolds, and suchlike.

> The preservation of the individuality of the Englishman is essential to the preservation of the type of the race . . . To me, England is the country, and the country is England . . . The sounds of England, the tinkle of hammer on anvil in the country smithy, the corncrake on a dewy morning, the sound of the scythe against the whetstone . . .
>
> —Stanley Baldwin, Conservative leader, 1924

Northern England allegedly (like Scotland and Wales) multicultural, internationalist, communitarian

Southern England supposedly the timeless, rural fortress of a deep, national, ethnic idyl

The North-South divide locked down in 1924 and was recast in classic early 20th-century ideologies: internationalist fantasy vs. nationalist mythology.

A Tale of Two Economies

However you framed it, the Southern English were in control, so they made their own economy their priority. During the war, the gold standard (the idea that each currency was worth a fixed amount of actual bullion) had been abandoned, allowing the Bank of England to print as much sterling as it thought people would believe in. But now, people preferred to believe in America, which still anchored the dollar to gold. The City (the modern financial district of London, which is traditionally a separate administrative entity from London) was determined to compete again, so in 1925, the gold standard was readopted, with the pound-dollar rate fixed at the 1914 level, almost five dollars to the pound, as if nothing had really changed. The realistic rate would have been more like 3.5 dollars to the pound. Allowing the City to live in the past was a body blow to industrial Britain.

> Returning to the gold standard then raised export prices to impossible levels. Investment collapsed, diversification faltered, and the merchant networks that had coordinated Northern manufacturing withered.
> —*UK North-South Divide*, Jesus College, Cambridge 2015

Unemployment in the North soared away. The two different economies in England, South and North, were now in direct confrontation: What was good for one was bad for the other.

Only One Winner

In the General Strike (1926) millions of trade unionists backed the miners as they fought vainly to defend their wages. The strike was quickly broken in the South, but in the coalfields it dragged on for grim months until it was finally defeated.

Before World War I, English industry was linked, by its need for power, to the coalfields. Now came total electrification (the Central Electricity Board was founded in 1925) and modern telephone communications, so factories could locate anywhere. CEOs chose to open their new businesses—or at least, their new HQs—away from the grime and industrial strife of the North, close to the social, financial, and international hub of the City.

Left: Hoover Building, London, 1932. *Right*: Lever Bros. had been one of the great Merseyside industrial concerns. But in 1929, the HQ moved to London.

The Great Depression (1929–c. 1935), in which the American stock market crashed and froze the world's great source of loan capital, was the final blow to the North.

> Little could be done to overcome the prejudice of industrialists against the impoverished and uncongenial character of the depressed regions . . . such as to deter even the most active entrepreneur.
>
> —Panel of Ministers on the Depressed Areas, 1930–31

Intermission: Enter the Good Guys

In 1928, *The Jazz Singer* premiered in London and the moving pictures started talking. It amazed everyone in the world, but in England it had a peculiar impact because here the actors weren't dubbed. America was addressing the ordinary English directly, in their very own language—and it wasn't RP.

What's more, those American voices were unconsciously telling a profoundly English tale. The ancient English cultural divide had, it turned out, crossed the Atlantic with them. From *Robin Hood* and *Mr. Smith Goes to Washington* via *Casablanca* up to *Rambo* and *Star Trek*, the bad guys of American mass culture, whether they are corrupt elites, Nazis, evil masterminds, Russians, or aliens, always use the half-French language of the English elite. The good guys speak in language Harold's men might almost have understood.

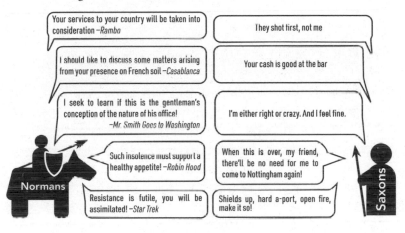

After nine hundred years of being second-class, the ordinary English found a world again where the heroes talked their talk. No wonder that, to the horror of their elites, both of the left and the right, they lapped up American culture from the word go.

North or South?

Meanwhile, back in the real England, the North-South divide became a public talking point. In 1933, bestselling author J. B. Priestley made his *English Journey*. He found an Olde England that had great charm—"the cathedrals and the colleges and the Cotswolds"—but was strictly for tourists. When it came to real lives, he divided non-London England into two: the old North/ Midlands, dying on its feet; and the new light-industrial region northwest of London, all too modern.

On the North & Midlands:
Nineteenth-century England, the industrial England of coal, iron, steel, cotton, wool, railways ... sooty dismal little towns, and still sootier grim fortress-like cities. This England makes up the larger part of the Midlands and the North ... it is not being added to and has no new life poured into it.

On the new region to the NW of London:
America, I supposed, was its real birthplace. This is the England of arterial and by-pass roads, filling stations and factories that look like exhibition buildings, of giant cinemas and dance-halls and cafes, bungalows with tiny garages ... as near to a classless society as we have yet got. Unfortunately, it is a bit too cheap.

—J. B. Priestley, *An English Journey*, 1933

According to theories of class, this new, light-industrial Northern Home Counties/Southern Midlands—literally, Middle England—should have felt it had common interests with the industrial North. But it turned out that transforming this region from rural to urban-industrial made no difference to the North-South divide.

Voters—male and female—in this new Middle England were faced with a choice of two very different political tribes: that great bloc of Tory Southern England, or the Outer British alliance of Northern England + the Celts. The question that really mattered was which tribe they felt was broadly theirs. Modern political jargon calls this *valence voting*.

Most people ... are mainly valence voters. Their broad
judgments about parties and politicians matter more than
their views on most specific policies.

—Peter Kellner, May 27, 2020

George Orwell was in no doubt about it. When he went northward in 1937, researching *The Road to Wigan Pier*, it all felt safe
and familiar until after Birmingham:

As you travel northward your eye, accustomed to the
South or East, does not notice much difference ... In
Coventry you might as well be in Finsbury Park ... When
you go to the industrial North you are conscious, quite
apart from the unfamiliar scenery, of entering a strange
country ... Labyrinthine slums and dark back kitchens with
sickly, ageing people creeping round and round them like
blackbeetles ... your "educated" accent stamps you rather
as a foreigner than as one of the local gentry.

In a grotty Northern boardinghouse, Orwell the old Etonian
was thrown together with "a little, black-haired sharp-nosed
Cockney." The class divide could hardly have been more
extreme, yet "he caught my eye and suddenly divined that I was
a fellow-Southerner."

"The filthy bloody bastards," he said, feelingly.

The Cockney felt more in common with the Etonian than with
the Northerners. And the English of the new Middle England,
industrialized and almost classless or not, felt more in common
with Southerners than with Northerners and Celts. So they
only abandoned the Conservative Party three times: when it

lost the plot in the face of massive social changes (1945 and 1964–66) and when it self-destructed (1997–2005). Otherwise, they broadly voted like Southerners.

The Ministry of Labour itself recognized the North-South split in England. Indeed, it seemed unconsciously to doubt whether the North was really English at all, for its two sections, as it called them, filed the North along with the Celts.

The UK according to the Ministry of Labour's official divisions, 1937

England (and Wales) was socially divided along simple geographical lines ... in fact involving simply one line: the line that divided the North from the South ... I find the divide to be staggering.

—Danny Dorling, 2007

With England so split, it could no longer provide the gravity to hold even the rump UK together. Northern Ireland became a sectarian, paramilitary substate with its own de facto prime minister-for-life; the Scottish National Party was founded in 1934; in 1936, Plaid Cymru (born 1925) carried out its first arson attack, on an RAF base in Wales.

This divided kingdom now faced the greatest test of all.

(Just) Before The Deluge

As Nazi Germany armed up, the Conservatives couldn't decide whether to prepare for a land war in Europe, or defend the Island Fortress. Most chose the latter: New planes and battleships were ordered from 1935, despite the opposition of Labour and the Liberals, who were convinced that international cooperation could avoid war altogether. Hitler was meanwhile

appeased by being given whatever he wanted in Europe: "Good man," cabled Roosevelt to Neville Chamberlain, when the PM returned in triumph from Munich, waving Hitler's promises in his hand, having just forced the Czechs (who had a very decent army and highly defensible, mountainous borders) into handing a large slice of their country to the Reich.

Churchill was one of the few to see that Britain's fate was, as ever, tied to Europe's.

> Silent, mournful, abandoned, broken, Czechoslovakia recedes into the darkness . . . I fear we shall find that we have deeply compromised, and perhaps fatally endangered, the safety and even the independence of Great Britain.
>
> —Winston Churchill, House of Commons, October 5, 1938

Yet the delay meant that by September 1939, ten thousand Jewish children had been spirited to safety in the Kindertransport and the RAF was ready with new and far more planes, backed by radar, to combat a Luftwaffe that would have massively outgunned it in 1938.

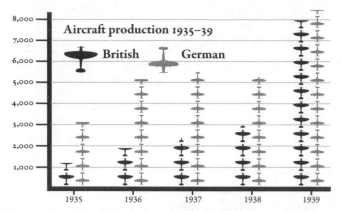

Aircraft production 1935–39

British   German

The myth of the Island Fortress pushed the army, which had defeated the Germans in 1918, to the back of the queue for funds. When it was belatedly sent to France, it found itself almost without operational plans, facing Panzer divisions, which had been Germany's number one priority for years.

> Britain went to war without a single effective armoured division or a coherent doctrine of armoured warfare.
>
> —Brian Bond

On May 7, 1940, as the unequal sides lined up, Leo Amery, Churchill's MP warm-up man, quoted Oliver Cromwell, demanding that Chamberlain "go in the name of God." But first, he called for the political chasm in England to be overcome.

> The time has come when the organisation, the power and influence of the Trades Union Congress cannot be left outside . . . The time has come, in other words, for a real National Government.

For the second time in twenty-five years, the United Kingdom was held together by war.

The Second World War

After the fall of France in June 1940, the British Empire stood alone for a year against a Nazi Germany that even had Stalin's Russia as an ally. With America still unwilling to take its place in history, the survival of Western civilization was in the balance.

Churchill's eloquence inspired the nation. The army was saved by the miracle of Dunkirk. The Royal Navy's power meant that Hitler could only invade if his Luftwaffe could dominate the skies over the Channel.

"The Battle of Britain is rapidly approaching its climax. Between now and October, when the mists of Fall settle over the chalk cliffs of England's Channel coast, the fate of Great Britain and of the world, as we have known it, may be decided." *New York Times*, August 17, 1940

The RAF won, and the world was saved. What counted now was morale and production. The interests of the financial South again took a back seat. The factories, shipyards, steelworks, and mines of the Midlands and Outer Britain were now the vanguard; the long-depressed rural peripheries were now vital to feeding the country; rationing now gave the poorest a better diet than they'd ever had. When people look back wistfully to the unity of early World War II, they aren't deluded.

And united, Britain was strong. Hitler had expected his Italian allies to run the Mediterranean, but the navy and the army routed them by land and by sea in early 1941. Furious, Hitler attacked his supposed ally, Russia, in June 1941. One of the main reasons he gave his generals was that this was the best way to beat the *Englanders*.

> "The possibility of Russian intervention in the war was sustaining the English," he went on. "They would only give up this contest if the last continental hope were demolished."
>
> —Ian Kershaw, *Nemesis*

Few expected Russia to survive. Churchill used the breather to pursue his personal mission: roping in New England. His unbreakable self-confidence, his own Anglo-American lineage, and the victories over Italy enabled him to tread a delicate line, persuading Roosevelt of the urgent need to help without seeming a hopeless case. Still, it took the Japanese bombing of Pearl Harbor to finally tip Washington into the war (December 1941).

ACT II: THE END OF THE BEGINNING

Official reconstruction of El Alamein. As this famous photograph shows, the army remained convinced that every two dozen soldiers needed a member of the officer class to lead them (in the German army, the ratio was about 100:1). Proportionally, even more ex-public school boys were killed in World War II than in World War I.

As the USA readied itself, the UK still had a year of holding the fort. The Navy's relief of Malta (August 1942), the British Empire's last great land victory at Alamein (October–November 1942), and the winning of the Battle of the Atlantic against the U-boats (May 1943) belong in the annals of world history: If any had been lost, so might the war.

The vast power of the New World mobilized at last. Two million male Americans appeared, looking and talking like those New English demigods from the movies, pockets full of dollars.

> I took round the House of Commons an American sergeant-major, and I asked him his pay. I found out that he obtained considerably more than is received by a Member of Parliament.
>
> —Colonel Cazalet (Chippenham),
> House of Commons, November 19, 1942

> We were invaded by our allies instead. The old power of British traditions, the magic of British uniforms and the authority of British upper-class voices, the power of British ceremony, began to crumble from within at this point.
>
> —Peter Hitchens

By the end of 1943, there could be little doubt about the eventual outcome.

ACT III: A BRIDGE TOO FAR

Ordinary Britons, in uniform and out, seemed understandably to feel that they'd already done their bit. During the slog up through Italy (1943–44) *stickiness* (military code for *unwillingness to attack when ordered*) and even outright desertion became such a problem that several generals asked for the death penalty back. At home, the Beveridge Report (1942), sketching the outlines of the welfare state, was a national bestseller. Strikes became widespread. And really, since there was (unlike in 1917–18) no real danger of losing, Britain's leaders might have eased off a bit and looked to the postwar future. But Churchill and his chiefs were determined to stay in the Big Three, so the pedal was kept pressed hard to the floor.

Game-changing technological advances like the world's most advanced early computers, built at the Bletchley Park code-breaking center by Alan Turing and his colleagues, were shared with America as if Britain expected they'd work together forever.

> The August 1943 Québec agreement between Winston Churchill and Franklin D. Roosevelt asserted collaboration but proved a fire-sale of British nuclear research.
>
> —Max Hastings

Britain agreed that it should build only fighters and bombers, leaving all transport planes to the Americans. This preserved British military clout, but left America ready to sweep the peace-time aviation world with aircraft like the Douglas DC-3.

And perhaps Britain's economic future wasn't the only casualty. After the heroics of D-Day and Normandy (where front-line units suffered Somme-like casualties), the outcome of the war was just a matter of time—yet the army's chief, Montgomery, insisted on the ill-fated airborne assault on Arnhem (September 17–25, 1944). There has to be a suspicion his elite soldiers were sacrificed to show the Americans that the British Empire still had what it took.

Arnhem: "Just prior to the Operation's commencement, [Maj-Gen] Urquhart met [Lt-Gen] Browning to inform him he believed the operation would be 'a suicide mission.'"
—Dan Snow, *History Hit*

> Montgomery refused to acknowledge what almost all other senior British officers had understood. Britain was now very much the junior partner in the alliance ... one could argue that September 1944 was the origin of that disastrous cliché that lingers even today about the country punching above its weight.
>
> —Antony Beevor

After a grim six months, with V1s and unstoppable V2 rockets plaguing London almost to the very end, the war in Europe was finally won in May 1945. A British force was sent to help finish Japan, but America's A-bombs meant that it never had to fight.

(Not) Facing the Future

After Victory in Europe Day, Churchill wanted a referendum to extend the National Government. Labour leader Clement Attlee (deputy PM since 1942) insisted on a general election.

> I could not consent to the introduction into our national life
> of a device so alien to all our traditions as the referendum.
>
> —Clement Attlee to Winston Churchill, May 1945

Churchill made the huge mistake of claiming that his longtime deputy, Major Attlee (educated at an elite school and Oxford University) "would have to fall back on some kind of Gestapo" if he won. It was clearly absurd, and seemed to plunge England back into the vicious party-politicking of the 1930s. Most Britons were broadly satisfied with the centralized, state-run way things had been done during the war, and now Attlee looked like the small-c conservative choice to take things forward.

Vitally, he also sounded like it. For the first time, the Party of Outer Britain was led into battle by a proven, national leader from the Southern elite itself. Attlee's RP tones, beamed by radio to firesides across the land, helped Labour win its first majority of English seats.

With the Party of Outer Britain triumphant at last in England too, a united UK seemed ready to face the future. Unfortunately, its leaderships were also united in their delusions.

Buddy, Can You Spare a Dime?

Leaders of the right assumed the Empire would be maintained. Leaders of the left expected that they could exert worldwide moral leadership. Both assumed that America would go on acting as if Britain was, strategically and financially, all but a part of the United States. A comedown, perhaps, but it meant Britain still mattered. As Attlee told his cabinet:

> It may be that we must regard ourselves in future not as a
> European power looking towards the East, but as the eastern
> extension of a western block centred on North America.

The world according to Attlee, 1945: The UK is the eastern arm of a
US-centered Anglosphere.

The economist John Maynard Keynes saw that as the greatest debtor nation in history, the UK now faced a "financial
Dunkirk," but he was initially confident that he could persuade
the Americans to bail London out. Unfortunately, the Americans themselves bought the fantasy that Britain, though cur-
rently broke, was still a world power which might become a
trade rival again. So in 1945 they lent billions, but at market
rates and on the condition that the Empire be opened up to
American business and finance—aka *world trade*—within two
years.

> One of [Keynes's] colleagues commented bitterly: "A visitor
> from Mars might well be pardoned for thinking that we
> were the representatives of a vanquished people discussing
> the economic penalties of defeat."
>
> —Niall Ferguson

Then, to London's utter shock, the US McMahon Act (1946)
declared all nuclear research in America to be *restricted data*
despite the clear wartime understanding that it was a shared

project. Even as the welfare state was created, and industries nationalized, at huge expense, Britain was left to fend for itself.

It couldn't. In 1946, defense spending actually rose beyond its wartime peak, to a mind-boggling 44 percent of GDP: The huge American Loan of 1945 was devoured by the twin demands of the New Jerusalem and the British Empire, leaving nothing in the coffers to replace destroyed houses, modernize crumbling infrastructure, or stimulate business.

By 1947, the UK was virtually begging America to take over its chunk of vanquished Germany and its role in the Eastern Mediterranean. Even bread was rationed, which had never happened during the war. The Empire was collapsing: In August the British exited India, leaving hundreds of thousands to be hacked to death as the hastily agreed Partition bore modern India and Pakistan.

Losing India was one thing, but losing the allegiance of the "White Dominions" was unthinkable. So London tried to keep their hearts and minds (and bank accounts) British with the Citizenship Act (1948): Every "citizen of the United Kingdom and Colonies" was now a "British subject." The result was unexpected. Serving the Empire in arms had given non-white colonial folk ideas, and the war had left a massive oversupply of transport shipping, making long-distance travel far cheaper. Five weeks before the act was passed, the *Empire Windrush* docked at Tilbury, filled with West Indians who had set off for the motherland on their own initiative.

> Even before the *Windrush* had left Jamaica, the prime minister, Clement Attlee, had examined the possibility of preventing its embarkation or diverting the ship and the migrants on board to East Africa.
>
> —David Olusoga

> For many West Indians . . . the shock was not the
> imperialism of the British but the lack of it—these British
> failed to recognise the West Indians as fellow, equal
> subjects of the Empire, as the official version of Empire
> required.
>
> —David Edgerton

Over the next twenty years, half a million more West Indians
followed, and as many people again from the former Raj, multicultural England, because the elite refused to let go of Empire.
They could only keep up the fantasy because America now
changed its mind.

Free Dollars!

Washington belatedly realized that the British Empire was fin-
ished. Faced with a new global rival in the Soviet Union, the
US had a simple choice: Take over the whole shebang—in
Germany, Greece, Turkey, Africa, the Middle East, Singapore,
and Malaya—or prop Britain up as a crumple zone and proxy.
It chose the latter. In 1948, London was assigned more Marshall
Aid—not a loan, this time, but an outright gift—even than
war-wrecked Germany.

This was a priceless opportunity. Export rivals were out cold. Long-established trade links meant that in practice, British firms still had more or less exclusive access to India, Australasia, and large parts of Africa.

> Marshall Aid dollars presented [Britain with] a last chance to modernise herself as an industrial power before her old trade rivals could recover from defeat and occupation.
>
> —Corelli Barnett

Top Left: The De Havilland Comet (1952) was the first jet airliner. *Top Right*: Jaguar's C-Type won Le Mans in 1951 and 1953. *Bottom Left*: Rover's 1949 gas-turbine JET-1 was amazingly bold. *Bottom Right*: The fastest manned thing on Earth in 1956 was the Fairey Delta.

Britain had the men, the machines, and the (American) money, too. Unfortunately, it lacked the one thing any country needs: good governance.

In the 1950s, two-party, North-South English politics finally locked down. The divide was magnified by the First Past the Post voting method, which exaggerated the power of local majorities. If MPs had been awarded according to the national vote, the Liberals could have offered the second-biggest party a coalition after every general election from 1950, barring only (by a whisker, in both cases) 1955 and 2019. That way, England might have gotten a truly national politics. Instead, it was stuck with two tribal parties, each rooted in a culturally and economically different part of the country.

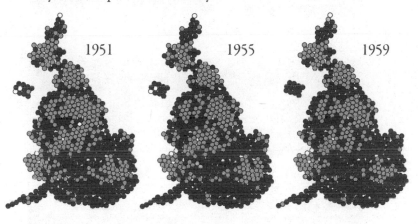

■ Tory / Unionist   ▨ Labour   Liberal / Other

Added to this fatal domestic cycle was a hopeless diplomatic one. Sending the army to Korea and building the A-bomb (exploded under Churchill in 1952, having been green-lit by Attlee) were parts of a desperate bid to keep the Americans onside.

> We are still more important to America than any other of her allies; we are the only country in Europe on whose resistance to genuine aggression she can really count.
>
> —Fabian Society pamphlet,
> John Freeman and Denis Healey, 1951

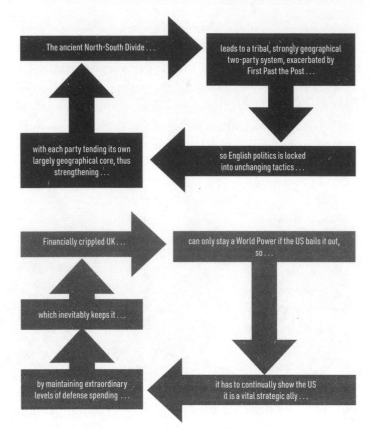

The ancient North-South Divide . . .

leads to a tribal, strongly geographical two-party system, exacerbated by First Past the Post . . .

with each party tending its own largely geographical core, thus strengthening . . .

so English politics is locked into unchanging tactics . . .

Financially crippled UK . . .

can only stay a World Power if the US bails it out, so . . .

which inevitably keeps it . . .

by maintaining extraordinary levels of defense spending . . .

it has to continually show the US it is a vital strategic ally . . .

Vicious circles at home and abroad

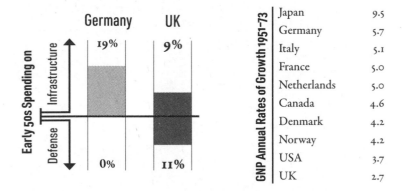

Early 50s Spending on

Infrastructure

Defense

	Germany	UK
Infrastructure	19%	9%
Defense	0%	11%

GNP Annual Rates of Growth 1951–73	
Japan	9.5
Germany	5.7
Italy	5.1
France	5.0
Netherlands	5.0
Canada	4.6
Denmark	4.2
Norway	4.2
USA	3.7
UK	2.7

BUILDING THE NEW WELSH AUTOBAHN

To Shorten the Route Through the Heart of Industrial South Wales

Of all the priorities in the nation's economic programme, road development has been the most neglected in the post-war years, and indeed so pressing has been (and is) the need for houses, so necessary the construction of new generating stations, that the roads have commanded little or no attention. London, in particular, can point to no major improvements, save perhaps the reorientation of Parliament Square to meet the needs of Festival of Britain traffic.

THE DAM BUSTERS ARE BACK ...with VULCANS of course!

In 1953, eight years after beating the Germans, the UK was only starting to build modern roads like theirs, and didn't know what else to call them. But at least it had the Dam Busters, now with A-bombs!

And so, the war having been won, the peace was lost.

U, Non-U, or American?

Still, all that defense money sustained the cultural rule of the South. Under National Service (1945–63) all young men were called up, and about 4 percent picked for the *potential officer stream.*

> Men from the South of England were most likely to be commissioned . . . Accents mattered, in the Army . . . A public school education was the single most important asset . . . a boy born into a modest background in 1935 stood a better chance of becoming a cabinet minister than a second lieutenant in the Grenadier Guards.
>
> —Richard Vinen

National Service gave the elite a new way to make the old offer to England's yeomanry: *Abandon your native culture and clamber onto our lowest rungs!*

The sublieutenant above, graduating as an officer in 1953, was only a grammar-school boy, from a line of modest Bedfordshire farmers-cum-businessmen. But his accent was near-RP, he was Church of England, tall, good at tennis, and a cousin to a well-known navy captain, so he was made an officer. After two years cruising the Mediterranean, he emerged with tastes and ambitions utterly foreign to his parents.[*]

In 1954, a British linguist explained English class and accent in a half-joking article for an obscure Finnish journal. It went viral, 1950s-style, and is still remembered.

> The question "can a non-U speaker become a U-speaker" is one noticeably of paramount importance for many Englishmen . . . The answer is that an adult could never attain complete success . . . There is one method of effecting change in your voice, provided the speaker is young enough. This is, to send him first to a preparatory school, then to a good public school.
>
> —Alan Ross

Knowing this, the middle classes scorned the grammar schools, never mind the new comprehensive schools (begun 1954), to make sure that even if they weren't *U*, their children would be.

> Middle-class parents, including left-wing ones, saved to send their sons to fee-paying schools . . . the public schools—133 of them, many of which before the war had been close to bankruptcy—emerged stronger than ever.
>
> —Anthony Sampson, *The Anatomy of Britain* (1962)

While the truly *U* ran the place and the would-be *U* tried to get in, the ordinary English frankly didn't give a damn. They

---

[*] He was the author's father, much missed. The cousin was Boutwood of the Curacoa.

just wanted to be Americans. The demand for Hollywood films was so great that movie imports became a balance-of-payments problem. All British popular musicians tried to look and sound like Americans.

> English readers have not to be conducted across the Atlantic now to observe the American style of urban life: it can be discovered in the nearest town. It is now the great invader.
> —J. B. Priestley and Jacquetta Hawkes, 1955

The elite despised them for it, yet they too were desperate trans-Atlanticists, especially after the catastrophic failure of a last attempt to go it without the Americans in the Suez Crisis (1956). Britain set out to force regime change on Egypt, in cahoots with

France and Israel, but Washington publicly refused its backing, leading to a deeply humiliating climb-down.

The UK's place at the "top table" (as its diplomats lovingly called it) was at mortal risk. Only the H-bomb could save it. The crash-project succeeded in 1957, at Christmas Island in the Pacific, in the process exposing thousands of servicemen to massive levels of radiation.

The US was impressed, and in 1958 allowed Britain the unique privilege of buying US nuclear weapons. The home-built Blue Streak system was aborted after vast expense, to be replaced with America's Polaris in 1962. It was the first clear sign that the industrial edge had gone. Over the next few years, the state-owned airline, BOAC, bought Boeing 707s from Illinois, not Comets from Hatfield; the RAF abandoned the homegrown TSR-2 in favor of US aircraft; and Germany overtook as the second-largest car manufacturer.

Meanwhile, the southward economic drift resumed after WWII, to the point where it became a problem for the South itself. In 1962, the Conservative PM Harold Macmillan's team admitted they needed "to prevent two nations developing geographically, a poor north and a rich and overcrowded south." But nothing was done, because there was a payback to being America's prime ally. The Federal Reserve quietly propped up the pound, allowing the UK to keep on importing food, energy, and raw materials beyond its real means. This enabled the English to remain deluded, and let them enjoy a brief golden age of social mobility.

The Swinging Sixties (by the Grace of the Federal Reserve)

1964: the Tories are in power, but anything old seems on the way out. *Left*: Leicestershire firefighters set about destroying Garendon Hall, which the family couldn't afford to keep up. *Right*: Even Etonians want to be like those cool lads from Liverpool who had conquered America by sounding half-American.

The baby boomers were taking over. For the working classes, employment was full. The middle classes had the new, free "plate-glass universities," and because so few people went to university at all, a degree in anything practically guaranteed a professional career. The average house could be bought with four years' average salary. For the wealthy, though, income tax was very high and few had yet worked out how to avoid it. The old rich virtually gave away their useless country houses, or demolished them to avoid upkeep. What you were born with seemed hardly to matter. England was ready to embrace modernity.

The Conservative Party wasn't. In 1963, an "Etonian magic circle" (as one failed Tory hopeful bitterly called it) announced, to widespread astonishment, that the UK's new PM was a tweedy aristocrat, the 15th Earl of Home. At the 1964 election, he faced off against the first would-be PM to understand the power of television images, sound bites, and popular beat combos.

Harold Wilson (here six months before the election) knew how valuable it was to be seen on TV with The Beatles. Alec Douglas-Home (right) had no idea, and just tried to be decent.

With the Conservatives hopelessly off the social pace, Labour was able to rebrand as the almost non-political Party of Modernity, playing down policy and hymning the "white heat of technology." Now Liverpool accents were suddenly cool— the Fab Four were touring England even as the election took place—Wilson's gentle Yorkshire brogue, softened by many years at Oxford, seemed positively attractive, even to younger Southerners, compared with Douglas-Home's patrician drawl.

In the elections of 1964 and 1966, London broke more for Labour than anywhere else, helping it to win (just) a majority of English seats for only the second time. America declared it the "Swinging City," and when England won the World Cup in 1966, barely a St. George's flag was to be seen: The English were still happy to be British.

Behind the scenes, the lost opportunities of the 1950s were coming home to roost. The productivity edge over France and Germany was gone, never to return. Worse, the national figures masked the old split. The South had always been far ahead in the service sector; now, it had overtaken in manufacturing as well.

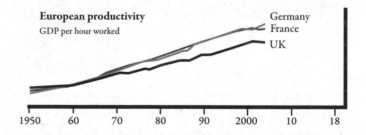

By the mid-1960s, the "south and east" of Britain had emerged as the country's major geographical concentration of manufacturing.

—Ron Martin, 1988

Then Wilson broke the unwritten pact with America. He slashed defense spending so drastically that the UK could no longer afford to defend its last imperial outposts. If Britain wasn't up to playing international military sidekick, why should the US subsidize it? The Fed pulled the plug and in 1967, Wilson had to devalue sterling for the first time since 1949, infamously claiming that this made no difference to "the pound in your pocket." Immediately, the endgame of the UK started.

The Birth of Populism

Even as Northern Ireland turned murderous, the UK's central institution, Parliament, was challenged on its most basic idea: that the people elect representatives, but that those representatives are then free—indeed obliged—to make their own choices.

> Your representative owes you, not his industry only, but his judgment; and he betrays, instead of serving you, if he sacrifices it to your opinion.
>
> —Edmund Burke, Speech to the electors of Bristol, 1774

And that's how MPs acted until 1968. They didn't consult before suspending capital punishment (1965), decriminalizing homosexuality (1967), or legalizing abortion (1967). Voters might well (almost certainly, in the case of the death penalty) have thought differently, but they weren't asked. It was up to MPs.

This was the British way until, in 1968, a leading Conservative went over Parliament's head to speak directly to electors about another thing they'd never been asked about: immigration.

The ordinary English didn't get the classical allusion, but they got the picture: Astonishingly and gratifyingly, a paid-up member of the elite was addressing them directly for once. Many leapt on Powell's words. The looming extinction of the ancient London Docklands had nothing whatever to do with immigration, yet thousands of dockers—supposedly natural Labour voters—marched on Parliament crying "We want Enoch!"

And then there was Europe. Both leaderships planned to take the UK in, but both knew ordinary Britons were uneasy, so both 1970 manifestos promised muscular negotiations before any commitment. Neither, of course, proposed that deeply un-British thing—a referendum.

Since the Conservatives won the 1970 election (Southern voters returned to default, which was all it took), it fell to them, under PM Edward Heath, to introduce the European Communities Act in 1972. Labour treated it as a party-political opportunity, and opposed. Thirty-nine Tory MPs were ready to destroy their own government to keep Britain out, but enough Labour MPs were ready to defy the whip and save a Tory PM, to get Britain in. Europe was the one thing that crossed over the two-tribe party war.

The Seventies

The high hopes of the 1960s were over. Old taboos had been broken down but no new codes of conduct were ready to replace them. Football terraces became battle zones. Alcohol and drug consumption rose dramatically. Graphic violence— almost always WWII-themed—and soft porn went main-stream. Men like Jimmy Savile and Gary Glitter discovered that if they just got on the telly, they could do whatever they liked.

No sooner was the UK in the European Economic Community (EEC) than it was engulfed by a great miners' strike (1972), the oil price shock, the Three-Day Week, and another miners'

strike (1973–74). At times the strikes were openly a political challenge from the North: one Labour MP spoke of another Ulster in the Yorkshire coalfield. Labour, certain as ever of its Northern English/Celtic core, still faced its eternal struggle to gain Southern votes, so it now made a tactical move that changed everything. It weaponized Europe. In the two elections of 1974, Wilson first implied, then promised, that EEC membership would be decided by the first-ever national referendum. It was enough to get Powell onside: "Enoch puts the boot in!" cried the *Sun*. In 1974, there was no rational link whatever between disliking immigration and disliking the EEC, but Powell and his followers didn't need one: Theirs was a generalized discontent. Appealing to that was enough— just—to get Wilson home. The price was undermining forever the ancient principle that MPs decided things.

1974 revealed the absurdity latent since Gladstone's day: The Outer British alliance could only win the UK by dooming the UK.

When it came to the actual referendum, the parliamentary elite were largely united and most voters still accepted that the parliamentary elite knew best. Only the hard left and the Powellites wanted out (and were quite happy to work together).

It was the Labour left led by Tony Benn who were most fiercely for leaving. They used many of the same arguments right-wing Brexiteers use today.

—Dominic Sandbrook, *Seasons in the Sun*

If we came out now ... we should have to say: "Now we have broken one treaty, we want you to give us another on a different basis—as a free trade area." Such a course of action would deal Britain's reputation a severe blow ... If the pro-European cause is to triumph, every person who believes in it must go in to the polls and vote "Yes."

—Margaret Thatcher, *Daily Telegraph*, June 4, 1975

So the English voted—even more heavily than the Scots and Welsh—to stay in.

YES 67.23%

NO 32.77%

The South at Bay Again

Being in the EEC couldn't stop the rot. Emigration was higher than immigration. The population of London kept falling, leaving whole streets near-derelict. Inflation hit 26 percent. In Northern Ireland, the army could only limit things to "an acceptable level of violence," while the IRA seemed able to bomb English cities at will. The UK had to be bailed out by the IMF, and saw itself derided as the "sick man of Europe."

Britain is a tragedy ... sunk to begging, borrowing, stealing.

—Henry Kissinger, 1975

Labour, its tiny majority whittled away in by-elections, clung desperately on, promising outright devolution referendums for

the Scots and Welsh, more MPs for Ulster, and disproportion-
ate public spending for all three under the Barnett formula.

As in 1910, the Conservatives could only look powerlessly
on at national decline and division, despite having a majority
in England. Uncoincidentally, politics hit similar levels of
bitterness. In letters to the *Daily Telegraph*, General Sir Walter
Walker proposed that patriotic civilians be recruited against
"the Communist Trojan horse in our midst, with its fellow
travellers wriggling their maggoty way inside its belly."
Popular culture echoed the sense of national decay and
looming conflict. In the 1950s and 60s, the English had sung
about peace, love, and hope, like Americans. Now, the punks
just wanted to "get pissed, destroy"—and they sang in
authentic, non-RP Southern English accents.

The Sex Pistols: A truly Southern English popular music?

With the dead lying unburied and the rubbish piling up during
1978's strike-bound Winter of Discontent, the UK went back
to the future. At the time, Margaret Thatcher's 1979 victory felt
like a revolution, but it was merely a reset to default.

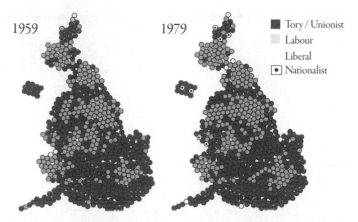

1959   1979

■ Tory / Unionist
■ Labour
Liberal
⊙ Nationalist

So much for the '60s and '70s. The small but ultimately vital difference: By 1979 there were nationalist MPs in Scotland and Wales.

On the political map, 1979 looked just like 1959, but that just showed how stuck English politics was. Outside Parliament, things were very different: Unemployment was huge and intractable; social discipline had broken down.

The 1981 Brixton riots and the Toxteth riots in Liverpool were both sparked by confrontations between the police and black youths; in both, white youths soon joined in.

Yet even as Thatcher fought her early battles, Southern culture was back: Almost overnight, everything old and posh was cool. Like *U* and *non-U* in 1954, the *Sloane Ranger Handbook* (1980) explained, as a Norman might have explained to an ambitious English freeman in 1170, that if you displayed the right culture

in public, you might just be accepted into the elite. The suburban English began to sport things they'd never heard of before—Hunter Wellingtons and Barbour coats—as the signs of their allegiance.

It might have stopped at fashion. Two years into her premiership, Thatcher's poll ratings were abysmal. Then, encouraged by her defense cuts, Argentina's military junta, desperate for some popular success, invaded the Falkland Islands. The UN, the Commonwealth, and the EEC all backed Britain. Nobody expected a fight, even after the Navy was mobilized. But with neither government ready to back down, it became a real little war.

Unsurprisingly, since the UK spent 4.71 percent of its GDP on defense in 1981 (compared to West Germany's 2.63 percent), its armed forces still worked. Military victory did what military victory does: It transformed the status of the winning leader. To many, it seemed the cure for decades of hopeless decline. After the 1983 elections, Thatcher's English MPs outnumbered Labour's by well over two-to-one. The Party of the South could now do exactly as it liked.

Loadsamoney

One thing it wanted was to settle a very old fight, once and for all. Since the Industrial Revolution, coal and coal-fueled industry had given the North the means to resist the hegemony of the South. The miners were considered (not least, by themselves) to have destroyed the last Tory government in 1972–74. It was time to finish things.

In 1984, two hundred thousand miners struck against pit closure plans. They were led by Arthur Scargill, a Yorkshire demagogue who had just moved the National Union of Mineworkers' (NUM) headquarters from London to his own power base, Sheffield. Only 1 percent of his strikers worked in the South (in Kent), so the battle line was clear: Thatcher's "enemy within" was the North of England (plus, of course, its Celtic allies).

The struggle was so bitter that when, in the middle of it, the IRA narrowly missed killing Thatcher in the Brighton bombing, some Britons openly wished they'd succeeded. But the government won out: With the miners defeated and the northern pits closed, the South was fully ascendant, as it had been before the Industrial Revolution, and ready for a future that needed not raw materials, but education and skills.

By 1986, the South had regained 449,000 jobs, the North only 83,000. Meanwhile, Thatcher's "right to buy" program (1980 onward), which allowed council tenants to buy their homes cheaply, added to the old cultural rift, because it was far more popular in the South (where tenants could often see expensive properties very nearby) than in the North (where there was often little sign of potential gain).

And that was before the South really took off. On October 27, 1986, the City was transformed in "the Big Bang." Electronic trading was introduced, the carve-up between jobbers and brokers abolished, and foreign firms allowed into the stock exchange. London's natural advantages now shone through. The North-South divide again became a public talking point, as it had been in the 1930s. Home supporters at London clubs might greet Northern fans with chants of "you're all on the dole!"

The *Loadsamoney* TV satire became (to the dismay of its creator) the icon of the newly rich, newly property-owning Southeasterner.

After her third election triumph in 1987, Thatcher seemed unassailable and declared her intention to "go on and on." But what did she have left to do? The North was routed and the booming South in full control. Swinging her legendary handbag, she had won a large reduction in Britain's payments to the EEC. Britain was America's most important partner, and the Cold War was palpably nearing an end—she herself had first identified Russia's new leader, Gorbachev, as "a man we can do business with."

True Thatcherism

The reason Thatcher felt she still had a mission was that she wasn't really a British Conservative at all. Her most important influence wasn't Disraeli, or Salisbury, or Churchill, but an aged Austrian economist, Friedrich von Hayek, adored by the American right.

> The most powerful critique of socialist planning and the socialist state which I read at this time [the late 1940s], and to which I have returned so often since [is] F. A. Hayek's *The Road to Serfdom*.
>
> —Margaret Thatcher

> The Conservative Party of Britain . . . had long resisted free market ideas and favored expansive government, especially one that would maintain established privileges . . . Hayek thus perceived "true conservatism" to be liberty's adversary.
>
> —Institute of Economic Affairs

When Thatcher made her Bruges Speech (1988), the deeply conservative German Chancellor Helmut Kohl and other EEC leaders were astonished to hear the entire European project denounced as a quasi-socialist plot: "We have not successfully rolled back the frontiers of the state in Britain, only to see them re-imposed at a European level." No established body, even if it was an ancient, private institution, was now safe from her.

> Margaret Thatcher's government is virtually proposing to abolish the Bar of England as it has existed for nearly 1,000 years, to bring her country's legal profession much more into line with the American model.
>
> —*Los Angeles Times*, April 2, 1989

> Her messianic, hectoring intolerance proved her undoing.
>
> —David Cannadine

Even as boom turned to bust in 1989–90, she insisted on introducing the poll tax, which forced councils to charge everybody exactly the same, rich or poor. The plan was that Labour councils

would have to slash expenditure and roll themselves back, or become hated by their own voters. Soundly Hayekian it might have been, but vast numbers of Britons found it plainly unfair. Mass civil disobedience resulted, climaxing with central London's biggest riots in living memory.

Thatcher's ratings slumped; her cabinet lined up against her; previously loyal MPs, whose voters were learning the dread words *negative equity* for the first time, thought of their futures; and she jumped before she was pushed, in November 1990.

Desperate to regain the popular touch, her party plumped for the grammar-school boy from Brixton, John Major. Nobody gave him much chance at the 1992 election. After all, no modern party had ever won four times in a row, let alone with rising unemployment, interest rates at over 10 percent and the housing market collapsing.

Major was rescued by the oldest factor of all in English politics: the North-South split, which the opposition managed to remind everybody about. A week before the vote, Labour's very Welsh-sounding leader, who had promised an immediate Scottish Parliament and a Welsh assembly, allowed himself to be seen live on national TV, seeming to hail victory before eleven thousand chanting supporters in Sheffield, where, eight years before, Scargill had led the last violent confrontation with the South.

The pictures and sounds from Sheffield in 1992 set alarm bells ringing deep in Southern English hearts. Whether on purpose or not, the English flag is behind those of Wales and St. Patrick, never mind the Union Jack itself.

Wavering Southerners saw another incarnation of the Celts + Northerners alliance ranged against them, and the Conservatives won an unprecedented fourth term. It proved fatal both to their party and to the UK.

The Anglosphere Warriors Spoil the Party

John Major's administration should have been a triumph. In 1992, the English were still living in the 1980s, and deep in recession. By 1997, they were sending emails and making mobile-phone calls, in a booming land.

The long uptick which began in 1993 was another free gift from America: In the Third Industrial Revolution, the mother tongue of the internet and globalization was English, so the service economy of the South was automatically ahead of the curve. When Oasis and Blur dueled for the crown of Britpop, Hirst, Emin, and others invented Britart, and Philip Pullman revitalized Britlit, a world audience took note.

1995: the year Amazon and eBay were founded. In the age of the English-language Internet, British culture from pop battles to Pullman's blockbusters could play around the globe in a whole new way.

The boom was firmly concentrated in the South. Oasis vs. Blur (Tough Northerners vs. Art-School Southerners) was the fun version of the divide: In less amusing reality, the North once again seemed recovery-proof. The Conservatives saw no reason to worry about that. In fact, they saw no reason to worry about anything. With no apparent need to ever fear electoral defeat, they could let the North go hang, embrace blatant personal enrichment (which became known as *sleaze*), and, most importantly, indulge their ideological fantasies.

Thatcher's continuity army—the zealots whom moderate Tory grandee Douglas Hurd had described in 1990 as like "some demented Marxist sect"—now determined to save her legacy from their despised, traditionalist comrades. Their dream had a name: America. With the fall of the Soviet Union (1991), American political gurus proclaimed the "end of history" and the "remaking of the world order." In the first Gulf War (1991), Britain had rediscovered its sort-of-imperial role as Washington's military wingman. English-speaking globalization was bringing London and New York ever closer. Surely the future was mighty free-market America, not feeble crypto-socialist Europe.

The Anglosphere warriors of the 1990s still believed in the United Kingdom. Northern Irishman Col. Tim Collins's biblical speech on the eve of battle against Saddam ("we are bringing about his rightful destruction") was said to hang in Bush's Oval Office. It made him the poster boy for the buzz-think which claimed that America's hegemony was built on supposed Ulster Scots frontier values: The US was really just the British Empire 2.0, so clearly the UK should be in on it.

OLD TORY ELITE
Pro-EU, often guarded toward America, politically gradualist, support capitalism but also see role for Big State and international law

NEW TORY ELITE
Anti-EU, pro Anglosphere (i.e., pro-US), want radical change toward Small State and "buccaneering capitalism" free from international controls

The split within the Conservative Party, 1992–2019

The rebellion that ultimately decided the fate of the UK began with the parliamentary ratification of the Maastricht Treaty (1993), which turned the EC into the EU. The Anglo-sphere Warriors harried their own PM almost to destruction, abetted by a Labour Party which (as in 1972) treated Europe not as a national issue, but as a party-political opportunity. Major, showing unexpected toughness, just managed to see them all off.

Vengeful associates of his enemies founded pressure groups like the UK Independence Party (UKIP; 1993), the European Research Group (1993), and the Referendum Party (1994), but they mistook their own obsession for the national mood. In fact, polls clearly show that the years 1989-94 were the longest and strongest period of pro-European public opinion. The anti-EU movement wasn't born out of pent-up public anger, but from the ideology of the rebel Tory elite; not as a mass movement, but as the vehicle of a small number of obsessive, wealthy individuals. Ordinary voters were baffled.

Speak of England

With the Party of the South tearing itself apart, there was a chance again, at last, for the Outer British Alliance. Labour's director of communications, Peter Mandelson, knew a man who might have been created for the especial purpose of leading the Outer British while at the same time reassuring the South-erners: Anthony Charles Lynton Blair.

> The MP to do the business would be the family man who was born in Scotland, represented a Northern seat but had (in Mandelson's phrase) "southern appeal."
>
> —Charlie Whelan, *Guardian*, January 6, 1999

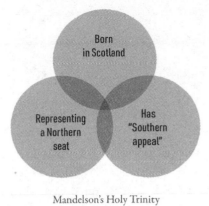

Mandelson's Holy Trinity

Desperate after nearly two decades in the wilderness, Labour allowed Blair to demolish its traditions. One thing didn't change, because the electoral math said it couldn't: Labour still had to be the Outer British Party. Like Gladstone and Asquith, Wilson, Callaghan, and Kinnock before him, Blair kept the Celts onside by promising devolution. The vow was made in both his 1994 and 1995 conference speeches.

He didn't say *England* or *English* a single time in either speech. He couldn't. As Churchill had seen in 1912, the UK might cope with Celtic nationalism, but English nationalism would surely destroy it. So while Blair offered semi-independence to Wales and Scotland, his Northern English troops had to be content, as their grandfathers had been, with hymns to the greatness of *Britain*.

Then, suddenly, almost as if they had been listening, the English called time on this fudge that had been going on ever since the start of mass voting. At the 1996 European Football Championships, spontaneously, they became *England* fans for the first time. First they dumped the Union Jack in favor of the Cross of St. George for the game against Scotland—and then they kept it. As they waved it, they chanted a strange ditty that had almost failed to make the cut because it wasn't triumphal enough.

> The FA hated Three Lions when they first heard it. "What's all this about, *We're gonna throw it away?*" The players were the same at first.
>
> —Ian Broudie of The Lightning Seeds

The song didn't sing of the joy of soccer, or the hope of victory, but of how after "so many jokes, so many sneers" over "thirty years of hurt," a despised people with a glorious, dreamlike past yearned to bring home something that had always belonged to them but had somehow been taken away: "Football's coming home." Without realizing it, the writers had nailed the deep, half-understood feeling of the ordinary English that their "rightful inheritance was once stolen, we don't quite know how, by people from elsewhere" (Roger Scruton).

Blair's antennae twitched. At the 1996 conference, he talked of "seventeen years of hurt," declared "Labour's coming home" and finally, guardedly, mentioned the dreaded E-word. He took his script straight from Churchill in 1912. For the Welsh and Scots, devolution was for whole nations, but for the English, the only permitted devolution was division: "If, in time, the regions of England want a greater say . . . then that can come too."

And so the Outer British alliance, "regions of England" and all, was mustered under a leader who sounded, to doubtful Southern voters, like a member of their own tribe.

Cool Britannia: The Last Redoubt

In 1997, for only the third time, Labour won a majority of English seats; for the first time, the Conservatives were completely wiped out in Scotland and Wales. Blair immediately nailed his status with his "People's Princess" speech, flawlessly channeling popular emotion at the funeral of Princess Diana. His approval rating hit an impossible 93 percent.

The Celtic nationalists won their devolution referendums and settled down to savor their new powers. As best friend of US President Bill Clinton, and assiduously copied by Germany's Chancellor Schröder, Blair was able to play the linkman between Europe and America as Churchill had only dreamed of doing. This helped him to cajole the warring tribes of Northern Ireland into the Good Friday Agreement (1998), his undying memorial.

Labour victory may have felt like revolution after years of Tory rule, but the real tone of Cool Britannia was liberal conservatism. The two greatest cultural exports of Blair's heyday were enabled by Hollywood but very different from anything born in the USA. The world was entranced by J. R. R. Tolkien's 1950s fantasy about the defense of preindustrial England (the Shire), led by a young member of the rural gentry and a white-bearded wizard; and even more by J. K. Rowling's dream about the defense of an ancient boarding school (Hogwarts), led by a young member of the hereditary elite and a white-bearded wizard. Hogwarts was founded by and for a special caste, yet it was open to a few ordinary folk able, determined, and thick-skinned enough to succeed in adopting its arcane culture, dog Latin and all: The only major figure not born into the hereditary elite married into it. Under the magical gloss, this was a hymn to social mobility through a very specific kind of education, as practiced in England since approximately 1170.

Real school shop, Eton, and imaginary school shop, Harry Potter world

Readers got the point: *Harry Potter* transformed the fortunes of England's real boarding schools.

As the millennium approached, the UK looked healthier than at any time since the 1870s: a voluntary union of peoples at peace with itself and in love with its own past, under a One Nation leader who bestrode the world and the media, the nearest thing to Disraeli since Disraeli himself.

There was just one specter at Cool Britannia's feast: England.

The Trouble with England

There remains an embarrassing obstacle to national oneness: the North-South divide.

Blake Morrison, *Independent*, October 23, 2011

English fans now all flew the cross of St. George, but that was sport. When it got real, the old battle line of Northern English + Celts vs. Southern English was as clear as ever. Even in 1997, outside the global city-state of London, Labour only won an absolute majority in Scotland, Wales, and the North of England. In the Midlands, the combined Tory-Liberal vote was larger, and through the whole of the South except London, the Conservatives were the largest party. In the Southeast they actually had an absolute majority of their own.

New Labour's first victory in 1997 saw Conservative southern England beaten back to its core. The map of that core is very similar to a map of the areas most attached to the Church of England in the 1851 census. It is also very similar to a map of market density in England in 1230, or of Roman villa civilization c. 300. Blair had hailed a "new dawn," but there was nothing new about it.

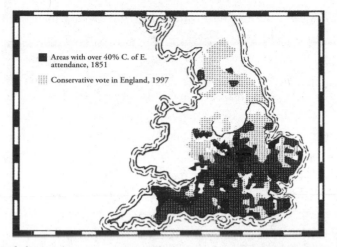

Areas with over 40% C. of E. attendance, 1851

Conservative vote in England, 1997

While Cool Britannia partied, the Southern English, the largest and richest single bloc in the UK, were left sulking in their tents, more than ever convinced they were the only true England. Meanwhile, the Northern English soon began demanding that Blair deliver.

By the turn of the millennium, Blair was coming under open pressure from his own ranks, so he and his chancellor, Gordon Brown, hit on a radical plan. Instead of trying to cajole investment away from the Southeast, they would go all-out with the flow. The City was positively encouraged to boom wildly under Brown's self-proclaimed "light touch" (i.e., virtually nonexistent) regulation—so that it could bankroll Outer Britain.

> New Labour made a Faustian bargain with the City . . . using the government's rake-off to expand the size of the state's presence in the UK's old industrial heartlands.
> —Larry Elliott, *The Guardian*

England's economy, long split, became completely bizarre: a heavily state-dependent North funded by a wheeler-dealer, global London. At the same time, England divided anew, with the latest, and greatest ever, project to assimilate ambitious ordinary people into the lowest rungs of the ruling order.

The UK's elite education system—boarding school, followed by at least three years at a university that provided campus residence as well as tuition—had always been unique (only America had copied it to any extent at all). The middle classes had been invited in on the university stage of this educational game in the 1960s. In 1992, many more institutions had been allowed to call themselves *universities*, and they all tried to offer cheap versions of the old model. By 2000, 25 percent (and rising fast) of the population were going away to *uni* and a critical mass had built. Any teenager with ambition now thought it was just natural to leave your home, family, friends, and region behind you, and spend your formative years in a monoculture of other ambitious and uprooted young people. No other developed country did this.

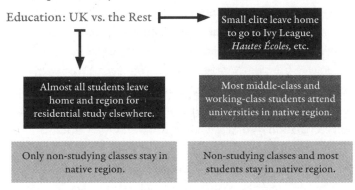

Millions imbibed a whole set of values unlike those of their parents or schoolmates: individual choice in all things, internationalism, and political liberalism. To the real elites, these were tools in a globalized world. For the majority of students, they were of no more practical use than a Range Rover to a suburban commuter. It was like learning French in medieval England: a sign of your ambition to join the elite. A new word, *chav*, expressed contempt for the class that the new university students had left behind, culturally and geographically. In 2004, with university attendance pushing 30 percent, it was declared "word of the year" by the publishers of the Oxford Dictionary. The BBC got in on the laughing-at-the-plebs act with the hit satirical sketch show *Little Britain*.

> Whereas wealthy media executives once sought to investigate poverty or arouse anger against it . . . now they commission programmes that laugh at it.
>
> —Nick Cohen, 2008

For once, poor Northerners and Southerners were united, because under New Labour small towns beyond commuting distance in the South took a double hit. They didn't partake of the London boom, but didn't qualify for Brown's public sector jobs bonanza either, because they weren't Labour tribal lands. The peripheries of the South began to feel as economically barren, as politically impotent, and as culturally despised as the North had so often felt.

A series of hapless Conservative leaders aimed patriotic rhetoric at this remaining southeastern core:

> Talk about Europe and they call you extreme . . . Talk about asylum and they call you racist. Talk about your nation and they call you *Little Englanders*.
>
> —William Hague, Leader of the Opposition, 2001

This was toxic in booming, global London, which during these years became a fortress for Labour.

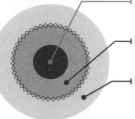

LONDON: booming, sucking in global elite and poor migrant workers. *Labour or Liberal.*

INNER SOUTH: prosperous Home Counties within reach of London boom. *Tory or Liberal.*

SOUTHERN PERIPHERY: left out of both London boom and New Labour job creation. Radicalized 1997–2005. *Tory or . . . ?*

In 1992, the South was still united and in control of the UK. In the 2000s it began to divide, as London went one way and the southern periphery went another.

Uniting the English (by Mistake)

Blair's nemesis was his love for playing America's imperial help-meet, irrespective of its president. Having already taken part in the bombing of Serbia (1999) and the occupation of Afghanistan (from 2002), he followed George W. Bush into the strategic disaster of the Second Gulf War (2003), backing himself up with a "dodgy dossier" of alleged intelligence.

As his popularity crashed and burned, England began resetting to its ancient default. In the 2005 election, the North-South political divide showed up more starkly than ever: The Conservatives couldn't break out of their Deep South heartlands, but they piled up such vast majorities inside it that under proportional representation, they would have won the whole of England. With the core rock-solid, they chose a new leader to *detoxify* them for more liberally inclined Southerners.

In 2007, a top social geographer published a map which showed that despite the swinging sixties, the terrible seventies, the Thatcherite eighties, Cool Britannia, and New Labour's siphoning of City profits northward, things had changed little since . . . well . . .

The line that separates upland from lowland Britain, the hills from the most fertile farmland, areas invaded by Vikings from those first colonized by Saxons . . . the only line within another European country that is comparable to the North-South divide is that which used to separate East and West Germany.

—Danny Dorling, 2007

Beneath the surface, though, the effects of Blair's second great mistake were starting to unite the English. In 2004, he had given the new EU *accession states* from the former Warsaw Pact immediate access to the UK jobs market, assuming that other EU leaders would follow his moral example. They didn't. In 2002, twelve times as many Poles had gone to Germany, looking for work, as to Britain; by 2006, Britain was easily their most popular destination.

One of the largest mass population movements since the second world war . . . radically transformed the terrain of British politics.

—Nicholas Watt and Patrick Wintour, *The Guardian*, 2015

Earlier mass migrations could be made into flattering stories about saving people in peril (Ugandan Asians in the 1970s, Somalis in the 1990s), or explained by old imperial links (cricket-loving West Indians, Pakistanis, and Indians). Everyone knew the Poles were only here for the money. Fine, as long as the economy was booming. But when the global financial crisis of 2008 stopped things in their tracks, nobody had a convincing tale about why the Poles should still be here, competing for now-scarce work.

The English attitude to this new mass immigration wasn't about racism or cultural differences. The Poles were football-loving, beer-drinking, white Christians; their grandfathers had flown Hurricanes and fought side-by-side with British troops in WWII; Poland was a very keen member of NATO. But like everybody in history, the ordinary English needed a clear reason to welcome newcomers who spoke a different language and competed for things they regarded as theirs by right.

Emily Thornberry MP
@EmilyThornberry

Image from #Rochester

A senior Labour MP's mocking tweet of this southeastern White Van Man's home seemed to sum up the scorn of the political class for the Poor White English.

At the 2009 European elections, the anti-immigration British National Party (BNP) shocked Labour by taking two seats in the North. Nigel Farage's UKIP tore far more dramatically into the South. It was the first true challenge to the Tories there since 1906. The 2010 general election seemed to restore near-normality, but it was in fact the last straw. For it yet again delivered that fatal paradigm whereby Tory control of the core South gave them a comfortable majority of MPs in England—but left them outgunned within the UK. Cameron had to form the first ever Lib-Tory coalition, which was regarded as deeply unnatural by his own hardliners. The Southern English hadn't seen their party win a UK majority since 1992. Fed up with their votes being rendered impotent, they were ready for a serious tribal revolt.

This Southern alliance embraced *austerity* as the cure for the Great Crash, turning off the public spending tap. Since this had primarily been used to pump money into the Outer UK, the impact was greatest there.

The long-planned opening ceremony of the London Olympics (2012) tried to express the idea of a UK at ease with itself. Really, though, it was an elegy. Together, New Labour and the coalition had accidentally created a new constellation that gave the Southern and Northern English real things in common.

NORTHERN ENGLISH suffering under austerity, dislike whole Southern (London) elite and immigration

+

SOUTHERN ENGLISH dislike liberal, young, multicultural London and immigration

=

ARMY OF ANGRY ENGLISH VOTERS BRIDGING NORTH-SOUTH DIVIDE

The new army of English voters-in-waiting created by Cool Britannia, EU immigration, austerity . . .

Two Englands, One Party

But would the angry English, North and South, ever vote as one? In the second decade of the new millennium, their allegiances were as tribal as ever.

> The Labour north and Conservative south make England look ever more like two nations . . . cultural and political identities are ever more distinct.
>
> —*Economist*, September 18, 2013

Even the protest vote was split North/South: The only place where both the BNP and UKIP were at peak strength was Essex, which became the "capital of Brexit" (Danny Dorling).

Farage showed the way. His UKIP had hit a glass ceiling because the EU wasn't a burning issue to enough people. Immigration, though, was another story. In 2012, the BNP destroyed itself in faction-fighting, and he went after its voters. The new hybrid BNP/UKIP piggybacked its niche obsession onto the mass worry, and crossed the old divide.

Voters who think EU is most important issue. Natural home = UKIP **+** Voters who think immigration/race is most important issue. Natural home = BNP **=** NEW UKIP/BNP HYBRID LINKS ANTI-EU AND ANTI-IMMIGRATION FEELING

> UKIP's surge . . . has relatively little to do with the public's hostility to Europe, an issue which never makes the top 10 of their daily concerns.
>
> —*Financial Times*, March 2013

Daniel Hannan, the Tory MEP whom the *Financial Times* would later call the "brains behind Brexit," saw that Farage had cracked it. The anti-Europeans, who had been plotting vainly for two decades, had their English foot-folk at last. Hannan proposed a UKIP/Tory pact—and entirely rewrote his anti-EU story.

The original 1990s version was all about an ideological crusade for unfettered capitalism. It hadn't played to voters then and it wouldn't play to Farage's New Model Army: Most of them just wanted stable communities who spoke English, with less competition for jobs, affordable housing, and doctor's appointments. So the script was changed. Leaving the EU was no longer about all the British going boldly off aboard the *USS Free Enterprise*. Instead, it was last-ditch cultural class war between the English and the elite collaborators of a European occupation.

In the 1990s, the anti-EU rebels had hymned freebooting, ocean-spanning *British* capitalism; now, they went after a defensively minded working-class audience, and they changed their story to one of *English* resistance.

14 October 1066: England's Nakba. Harold Godwinson, the last Anglo-Saxon king, fell in battle, opening the door to occupation and feudalism.

—Daniel Hannan on Twitter, October 14, 2015

"The English," Hannan writes, had brought Liberty with them from "deep in the German woods" until, with the Conquest, "Englishness became, almost by definition, a badge of poverty and subjugation." Within living memory, he claims, Royal Navy sailors "assumed that, being upper-class, the admiral was likely to be more sympathetic to the French." The EU was just the latest continental dictatorship to be inflicted by a collaborating elite on the hapless English.

Instinctively freedom-loving ordinary folk. Like their own culture and speak plain English.

Instinctively centralizing descendants (often literally) of Normans. Like multiculturalism and speak Frenchified jargon.

Cultural class war, according to Daniel Hannan

Like all effective rabble-rousing, it worked because it had a germ of truth. The daily, lived experience of the ordinary English, generation to generation, was that they were ruled by an elite who spoke differently.

Almost 1,000 years after the Normans took power in England, the language of power (parliament, government, civil service, police, court, judge) the military (army, navy, soldier, battle, campaign) and finance (interest, rent, money, tax, mortgage, asset, property, inheritance) retains a strong French cast . . . Anglo-Saxon-derived words still make up the lexis of the everyday.

—James Meek, *The Guardian*

In 2013, an extraordinary study, published by the London School of Economics, showed just how alive that history was. Researchers put the names of students in the ancient and modern records of Oxford and Cambridge through algorithms that tracked *status persistence*. It turned out that nothing—not the Black Death, not the Reformation, not the Industrial Revolution, not two world wars—had seriously disrupted the elite since records began, in the late 1100s. The *Daily Mail* boiled it down:

> 1,000 years after William the Conqueror invaded, you still need a Norman name like Darcy or Percy to get ahead.

Small wonder that when the rebel elite told their new tale of why the EU was evil, the ordinary English, feeling under siege by change, immigration, and austerity, were ready to believe it.

Exit Scotland, Enter Boris

Like Communists sneaking into the Labour Party, well-funded activists targeted Conservative constituency associations (which often had small, and aged, memberships), in areas where UKIP was strongest. Thus radicalized, the associations put pressure on their MPs. The prime minister, David Cameron, was soon running scared of the "mad swivel-eyed loons," as a source close to him called them. He promised a referendum if he was reelected, and set in motion the transformation of the Conservative and Unionist Party.

The Scots had only just reaffirmed their allegiance to the Union in the 2014 referendum, and the Scottish National Party held a paltry six seats. Yet in the 2015 election campaign, for the first time since 1745, English nationalism—disguised, but only just—was deployed against the other founding member of

Great Britain. The Scots were portrayed as virtually an enemy nation, with their Northern English/London allies mere gullible traitors.

Traditional Conservatives were worried. Others thought it a splendid tactic.

> Boris Johnson, London mayor, told the *FT* this week that criticisms of the Tory campaign's focus on Mr. Miliband and the SNP were "namby-pamby."
>
> —*Financial Times*, April 23, 2015

It worked so well that it changed everything. The United Kingdom was handed its death warrant as Scotland went almost completely nationalist. The Outer British alliance that Gladstone had created in 1885, and that gave birth to the Labour

2015

■ Tory / Unionist
▨ Labour
▧ Liberal
◉ Nationalist

Party, lay in ruins. The South of England was now completely in the ascendant, and the prospect of limitless dominion concentrated the minds of big Tory beasts on their own, personal futures. This decided the Brexit referendum.

The biggest beast was Alexander Boris de Pfeffel Johnson, who had by now perfected the popular comedy figure Boris (aka "Bonking Boris")—a music-hall "Merrie Monarch" replete with entitlement, yet always playing to the gallery as he shrugged off sackings, lies, and mishaps with grimaces and winks. London, despite its huge anti-Tory majority, had twice chosen him as its mayor, and by 2012 he was widely tipped as the next Tory leader.

But to oust the victorious Cameron, Johnson needed a cause. The "swivel-eyed loons" had found their cheerleader at last: Like nobody else, Boris could put a jolly gloss on their ugly tale of Brexit as cultural class war. In the referendum campaign (2016), every time a Remain expert pointed out the logical consequences of leaving the EU, the Leave team rejoiced, for all experts were by definition members of that half-foreign elite.

> People in this country have had enough of experts.
>
> —Michael Gove, Justice Secretary, 2016

Boris sound bites, on the other hand, might almost have been understood by a despairing Anglo-Saxon after the Conquest:

> We can see the sunlit meadows beyond. I believe we would be mad not to take this once in a lifetime chance to walk through that door.
>
> —Boris Johnson, May 9, 2016
> [Only *chance* isn't from pre-Conquest English]

Boris told the ordinary English, who were sick of being taken for granted (if not publicly mocked as chavs), that they were the salt of the earth. All their ills were due to Europe and its collaborators. He might have been quoting the first manifesto of anti-European English nationalism, published almost half a millennium earlier:

> Then shall these great yearly exactions cease. Then shall we have enough and more than shall suffice us; which shall be the best hospital that ever was founded for us.
>
> —*A Supplication for the Beggars,* 1528–29

Not for the first time, the English were invited to give their Europe-loving, freedom-stealing, fancy-foreign-speaking elite a good kicking, by a paid-up member of that very elite. And not for the first time, they did.

Reduced to Absurdity

After almost three years of parliamentary deadlock about what Brexit actually meant, Johnson became PM and purged the Conservative Party of dissent. The politics of the UK were now reduced to absurdity. Since 1885, there had been many alliances of Outer Britain against the South of England, but never had it been so obvious that this was a straight fight between the Tory block and a tactical, even cynical, league of convenience among the Ulster Unionists, the Scottish nationalists, Labour, and the Liberals—who all wanted different things.

In the 2019 election, the Conservatives finally embraced the destiny manifest since 1885 and became the English National Party in all but name. Boris toured beyond the Trent, promising that if Northerners would help "get Brexit done," they would be "leveled-up" as equally English, at long last.

> Boris Johnson says it's his government's job to end the north-south divide.
>
> —*Newcastle Chronicle*, October 2019

The Southern English intuitively grasped what was going on, and approved: Clear majorities of Tory voters said that Brexit was worth destroying both the Conservative Party and the UK.

> Brexit has read the rites over British conservatism.
>
> —*Financial Times*, September 4, 2019

This new English nationalism did what nationalism does: It convinced people whose lives were actually very different that they had common interests. Northerners, whose old Scottish allies had in any case deserted them, were persuaded, often for the first time ever, to vote with the South.

As Churchill saw and said in 1912, an England united under the Tories would inevitably destroy the UK now that the Celts were awake again. And so it came to pass: In the election of December 2019, that unique, multinational construct, which had bestridden the world in 1879 but had been tottering since the dawn of mass voting, was finally given a bullet in the head.

The UK, that construct founded in 1801 to control Ireland, and that should really have died in 1921 when most of Ireland tore itself away, is actually dead already. We haven't noticed only because its politics was blast-frozen where it stood by COVID-19 almost immediately after the 2019 election. When the thaws comes, the UK falls. So the next act in this strange, eventful history is clear: The English will emerge, blinking, from their long submersion within the empires of their elites, to find themselves alone in the big, bad world—and as divided as they were thirteen hundred years ago, when Bede first described the North-South split within them.

NORTHERN REVOLT

Daily Mirror headline, October 16, 2020

After the death of Elizabeth II, will they have any use for the royal family, whose younger members often seem more interested in US-based global celebrity culture than in the sort of duty-before-all-else ethos of the queen? With the Empire gone and the UK too, what would they represent? There hasn't been a solely English monarchy since 1536. King Charles III will have to reinvent the family's role completely—or perhaps some patriotic Little England genealogist will dig out a descendant of the last truly English king, Ethelred the Unready...

Ourselves, Alone

But seriously: What will England be like? If anyone doubts the thousand-year-old chasm between the English and their educated elites, here is the Cambridge professor of Economic Geography with some radical thinking about the North-South divide—in what is basically French:More so, indeed. For while other countries are riven by geography and history, none has that thousand-year-old chasm of culture that separates the ordinary English from their elites. If anyone doubts how profound this twofold divide still is, here's the Cambridge Professor of Economic Geography writing about the North and South, in what is basically French:

> The geography of spatial imbalance has frequently been characterized as a "North-South Divide"... the broad divergence between these two major areas is incontrovertible... Enhanced decentralisation of the UK's centralised governance system in England could provide the greater freedoms, flexibilities, resources and fiscal capacity required...
>
> Ron Martin, et al., *Spatially Rebalancing the UK Economy*, 2015

Only one noun is from Anglo-Saxon: *freedoms*. No wonder the ordinary English fell for Boris Johnson.

Our book-learned folk, North and South, need to start speaking English, and fast. For great events are in the wings. The new English National Party (formerly known as the Conservative and Unionist Party) is so abhorrent to almost everybody under twenty-four—and to most people under fifty—that at the last election, they preferred even the train wreck that was the opposition.

> Labour would have won almost every seat in England if under-24s were the only voters . . . if only 25–49 year-olds could vote: LAB: 310 seats (43%) CON: 240 (34%).
>
> —*Daily Mail*, January 1, 2020

But the task for the former League of Outer Britain is colossal. If it is to seriously compete within a lonely England, it will have to reinvent itself completely in order to become the party of an all-English center, appealing to people who see that they must now try to make an honest living in the world, not hope to live off the economic and psychological dregs of Empire.

Yet is there really an all-English center at all? Can England's very own—but much older and deeper—version of the Mason-Dixon line ever really be overcome? Was Churchill right in 1912 when, with his extraordinary feel for the long waves of history, he saw that Home Rule for England would have to mean dividing England into "several great self-governing areas"? Is it time to look history in the eye and stop pretending that England has ever really been a single nation, and will only ever work as some kind of federation?

One thing is certain: The new elite will not go easily. Their dream of being sidekicks in a world-dominating Anglosphere may be a moth-eaten 1990s fantasy, but the field, at present, is theirs. When Brexit goes wrong, it's a fair bet what they will do. Like the "demented Marxist sect" that Conservative grandee Douglas Hurd said they were, they will cling to power by hiking up their cultural class war (it is one sadly familiar to readers in the US, too) between the supposed will of the people and the allegedly treacherous old elite. That, after all, is how they won their coup.

We shall see. And we shall see soon. The Empires of England are fading into history. The battle for England is about to begin.

The Very Shortest History of England

What we now call England is naturally divided: Geology, climate, and geography all favor the Southeast.

The Roman Empire made this area an integral part of European culture. Then it was settled by seaborn Germanic tribes. Spreading out, they soon divided into what they called *suðan* and *norðan*. They were all almost conquered by Scandinavians, but a southwestern royal dynasty defeated the invaders and claimed (shakily) to rule all of what now became known as *Engla-londe*.

The country was then overwhelmed, first from Denmark and then, conclusively, from France. For the next three centuries, the colonial elite were united by speaking French. They developed a defense against royal absolutism, called *Parliament*. They then began speaking English and starting to think like rival English warlords. The unity of the country was threatened by rebellions and civil war. A new dynasty reimposed order by creating a European Renaissance elite of education. For the next five hundred years, the English ruling class all had ancient Greek, Latin, and (of course) French.

It took over 150 years for this new elite, centered on the Southeast, to defeat and assimilate the Northern elite. At times, the common people of England were enlisted in the fight, by being sold a fantasy of lost freedoms. At one point this got out of control, and the elite became so fragmented that the king himself was beheaded. The elite reunified, naturally under Southern control, and chose new kings for England, first from Holland, then from Germany. Finally they assimilated the other elites of the British Isles, creating *Great Britain*, then the *United Kingdom*.

A new ruling class emerged, whose badge was classical European culture. They conquered a vast world empire and finally dispossessed the common people of England of their traditional lands and way of life.

There now occurred an industrial revolution: The North, being full of useful minerals, flourished unusually for about a century. At the height of this, the religious-political representatives of the North challenged the supremacy of the South, but the Southerners successfully co-opted their leaders into an even wider elite who all spoke English the same, southern way. At this point, the Empire, whose headquarters were in Southern England, ruled a quarter of the world.

Then the elite began to cede power to the common people, who immediately began to vote on ancient, tribal lines. For over a century, the question was whether Southern England could continue to dominate against tactical alliances between northern England and the non-English nations.

Crippled by its own nationalities, the UK drifted until it was forced to intervene again in Europe to save itself. Two vast wars were won in a single generation, but they left the country (now shorn of Ireland) a military, economic, and cultural satrap of the USA. Attempts were made to link it to Europe more strongly, but these always met powerful opposition.

The Empire disappeared. The original, Celtic colonies got semi-federal institutions. The Southern and Northern English factions still believed that they could rule the whole of England, and hence the UK, until their tribal warfare drove the Scots to declare for independence. The Party of the South for once persuaded the North to back it, by claiming that the Free Trade block of Europe was actually a hostile superstate, so the English must pull together. But almost immediately, the COVID-19 crisis came and the North-South divide reopened as if automatically.

The English, as split as ever and soon to be alone in the world for the first time in centuries, should think very clearly about what is past, and passing, and to come.

Acknowledgments

My original publisher, Ben Yarde-Buller, and editor, Matt Baylis, have been tough and thoughtful in equal measure. No writer could ask for more; every writer should wish for such help. James Nunn's artwork is far more than decoration. In the preparation of this, the US edition, with its full references in place, Anna Bliss and the team at The Experiment were heroic and exact.

Dr. Jeremy Knight, FSA, is the ultimate begetter of this book, having generously employed me as an archaeological site supervisor and researcher in the 1980s. More recently, insights were freely given by: Dr. Kieran O'Conor, Dr. Stefan Szymanski, Dr. Peter Thompson, Professor Richard Percival, Professor Karen Leeder, John Holme, and John McTernan. My eldest son, Owain, and his partner, Marton, helped greatly with the research. My brothers and sisters listened kindly. Dr. Karoline von Oppen, being married to me, lived with it all patiently for three years.

Notes

PART ONE

"Having called to him the merchants . . .": Caesar, chapter 12.

"the maritime portion": Ibid.

"country of the Belgae": Ibid.

"It was in the fruitful plains of the Southeast . . .": Trevelyan, p. 24.

"*comes litoris Saxonici*": Seeck (ed.)

"443 CE This year sent the Britons to Rome & bade them assistance . . .": Giles.

"the king's Welsh horse": vol. 1, pp. 20–27, 89–123.

"The practice of furnished burials . . .": "Redating Early England," *Current Archaeology*, November 6, 2013.

"Offa's Dyke is the largest…": *The United Kingdom's World Heritage: Review of the Tentative List of the United Kingdom of Great Britain and Northern Ireland*, Independent Expert Panel Report to the Department for Culture, Media, and Sport, March 2011.

"The traditional symbolic dividing line . . .": Ruddick.

"king of all the provinces which are generally called by the name of the South English": Hudson.

"the collective oath of loyalty sworn . . .": Wickham, p. 458.

"I remembered how the knowledge of Latin . . .": Cook, pp. 69–70.

"Athelstan, the great conqueror . . .": Holland, p. 6.

"Among the Danes . . .": Baker, p. 49.

"From the moment of Emma's marriage . . .": Green, John R., p. 100.

"A great mound of earth . . .": Morris, *Castle*, p. 8.

"what followed makes *Game of Thrones* look like a game of musical chairs": Snow, January 5, 2019, 4:33 PM.

"scenting the booty that the conquest of England offered": Vitalis, p. 465.

"The second half of the eleventh century . . .": Keen, p. 24.

"The first of the four, piercing the king's shield . . .": Barlow, p. 33.

"The First New England": Green, Caitlin R., May 19, 2015.

"A small armed group speaking a language . . .": Bartlett, p. 1.

"miserable provincials . . . so feeble that they failed after the first battle . . .": *William of Malmesbury's Chronicle of the Kings of England*.

PART TWO

"all were intent on other matters": *William of Malmesbury's Chronicle of the Kings of England*.

"God chose the Normans to exterminate the English nation": Henry of Huntingdon, p. 208.

"*Dunc parlat Kenut mult sagement . . .*"; "Then Gnut spoke very sagely . . .": Gaimar, lines 4301–4.

"In 1154, the English monks . . .": McCrum et al., p. 73.

"French literature begins . . .": Short, p. 229.

"Many historians have remarked on the openness . . .": Sayer, p. 1402.

"The difference between French and English . . .": Holt, pp. 14–15.

"What miserable drones and traitors have I nourished . . .": Reis.

"Philip sent a warning message to John: Look to yourself; the devil is loose.": New World Encyclopedia.

"The road from Bouvines . . .": Holt, p. 100.

"Throughout the document it is implied . . .": Churchill, *A History of the English-Speaking Peoples, Vol. I*, p. 256.

Magna Carta's clauses: The Magna Carta Project.

"*Icy comence la chartre le Rey Johan done a Renemede*": British Library.

"Foul as it is, Hell itself is made fouler by the presence of John": Rochford.

"*Et se nul v nus viegnent encunt . . .*": Brody, p. 25.

"most radical scheme of reform undertaken before the arrest and execution of King Charles I": UK Parliament, "The Provisions of Oxford."

"In France, the manor lost; the peasant won . . .": Morier, p. 323.

"a legacy of division that has lasted from his day to our own": Morris, *The Norman Conquest*, pp. 263–64.

"*Sire, grauntez vous a tenir et garder . . .*": Hoyt, p. 356.

"The English archers took one step forwards . . .": Froissart, p. 27.

"When a peasant leaves the manor or dies without heirs . . .": Tawney, p. 78, 81.

"[They] do withdraw themselves from serving great men . . .": The National Archives.

"Chyldren in school, against the usage and manner of all other nacions . . .": Hansen and Nielsen, p. 346.

"In a short time there were fiue thousand gotten togither . . .": Holinshed, pp. 716, 737–39.

"[Richard] went up by himself to the insurgents . . .": Richard II quoted in Thierry, p. 291.

"It seemeth a great wonder how English . . .": Hansen and Nielsen, 347.

"Now, in the year of oure Lord…": Ibid., 346–47.

"*Londoun, and of xvii shires lyying aboute*"; "*destroie thaym*": Davies, John, pp. 12, 4.

"*smoot of the lordis heddis*": Davies, John, p. 21.

"for himself and his successors": Livingston, pp. 145–68.

"Henry V's use of English marks . . .": Fisher, p. 22.

"The return of the garrisons and armies from overseas . . .": Trevelyan.

"The said captain rode about . . .": Davies, p. 66.

"King Henry's *fals cowncell* had led England to disaster . . . '*the hyghe and myghty prynce*'": Stowe.

"Thenne kyng Harry, with Margarete his quene . . .": Bric, p. 378.

"Some Northern merchants, becalmed off the Kent coast . . .": Caxton, p. 2.

"The war saw the complete breakdown . . .": West.

"By the time the two armies met . . .": Goodwin.

"The realm of England was first inhabited of the Britons . . .": Fortescue, pp. 38–39.

"Neither the countryside nor the people…": de Commynes, p. 394.

"Backwards travels our gaze . . .": Powell, Enoch, 1961.

"common opinion of the people" and the "publique voice": Titulus Regius.

"The catte [Catesby], the ratte [Ratcliff], and Lovell our dogge rulyth all England under the hogge": Boffey, p. 428.

"curious terms which could not be understood of common people"; "satisfy every man": Caxton.

"the English was so rude and broad . . .": Caxton.

"This book is not for every rude and uncunning . . .": Caxton.

"We intend that he shall shortly with God's grace . . .": Henry VII's letter, p. 2.

"had spent the night in Spain": Carroll.

PART THREE

"The king, or the Lord of the Manor . . .": Fairlie.

"A family able to keep two cows . . .": Shaw-Taylor, p. 509.

"Noble man and gentleman . . . and certain Abbots . . .": More, pp. 38–39.

"ate the bread from poor fatherless children": Tawney and Power, p. 4.

"Then shall these great yearly exactions cease . . .": Fish, p. 216.

"a banner to go and conquer England": Hill, "Tyndale and His Successors."

"The king is, in this world, without law . . .": Tyndale, p. 32.

"from fear of his subjects": Froude, p. 228.

"England is an Empire, and so hath . . .": quoted in Goodman, p. 296.

"so that no more mention shall we made of him never.": Fideler and Meyer, p. 25.

"Tyndale [Reformer and translator of the Bible into English] associates himself . . .": Hill, "Tyndale and His Successors."

"the Word of God [he cried to Parliament] is disputed, rhymed, sung . . .": quoted in Anderson, p. 344.

"Blessed Virgin and holy company of Heaven": quoted in Gairdner and Brodie, p. 320.

"This largely state-sponsored destruction . . .": Tate Museum.

"cause the said Slave to work by beating, chaining or otherwise . . .": Davies, C. S. L., p. 534.

"Our holy and festival days are very well reduced . . .": Harrison, p. 36.

"One of these cursed boys, putting down his hose . . .": Hampton, p. 116.

"I can not tell how naturally the Mother loveth the Child . . .": Foxe.

"would not open windows into men's souls.": Elizabeth I quoted in Ratcliffe.

"The Kynge of Englande can neither change laws without the consent . . .": Fortescue, pp. 25–40.

"north of the Trent men know no other Prince but only a Percy or a Neville": Kim.

"good southern as we of Middlesex or Surrey do": Puttenham, p. 229.

"[Writers must not use] the terms of northern men . . .": Ibid.

"[Successful and thrifty commoners] . . . setting their sons to the schools . . .": Harrison, pp. 117–18.

"There are at this day great numbers . . .": Hakluyt.

"servant of crime": Pope Pius V.

"And therefore I am come amongst you . . .": cited in Somerset, p. 591.

"She cheerfully received not only rich gifts . . .": cited in Knight, p. 111.

"small Latin and less Greek": Jonson.

"English has the odd facility . . .": Watson.

"The moment was of supreme importance . . .": Rowse, p. 5.

"A nation that was almost begotten and born under her . . .": cited in Walker, Julia, p. 25.

"without any Bloodshed, tumults or uproars . . .": cited in Richards, p. 518.

"Wherefore We have thought good to discontinue . . .": cited in Wormald, p. 178.

"whore-houses, called the stews . . ."; "the King hath no prerogative but . . .": Proclamations.
"they must not look for more Parliaments in haste": cited in Thrush.
"The arrival of the first twenty or more Africans . . .": Riches, *Irish Journal*, p. 6.
"those vast & unpeopled countries of America . . .": Bradford, pp. 32–33.
"a capital enemy to this Kingdom and Commonwealth.": Vaughan, p. 249.
"and these our humble desires being granted by your Majesty . . .": cited in May, p. 127.
"In this Kingdom the Laws are jointly made . . .": Charles I, pp. 23–26.
"The North and West were regarded by parliamentarians . . .": Hill, *The World Turned Upside Down*, p. 73.
"Out instantly all you can! . . .": Cromwell, p. 129.
"It is now a time to speak . . .": Ibid, p. 176.
"true English hearts": Ibid.
"harlots with golden tresses": Tombs, p. 234.
"the time before the Conquest": Online Library of Liberty.
"O what mighty Delusion . . .": Wistanley and the Diggers, pp. 8, 11.
"The People of England . . . shall from henceforth be Governed . . .": Firth and Rait (eds.), p. 122.
"We shall with ease cast down . . .": Wistanley, p. 107.
"At all places of Garrison . . .": Taylor, p. 20.
"Great joy all yesterday at London . . .": Pepys, p. 13.
"Really, the Law is scarcely expressible properly in English": North, p. 13.
"It is Modish to Ape the French . . .": Behn.
"The King of Great Britain . . . is determined to declare himself a Catholic . . .": Churchill, *A History of the English-Speaking Peoples, Vol. II*, p. 210.
"This our expedition is intended for no other design . . .": Orange.
"The Dutch army, composed of men . . ." Macaulay, pp. 372–73.
"Dutch Blue Guards took up all the posts . . .": Jonathan Israel cited in Shah, p. 26.
"The Ministry distinguished with the name of Tory . . .": *The Gentleman's Magazine*, pp. 397–98.
"polity programmed for commerce and war": Simms, p. 71.
"A tour thro' the whole island of Great Britain": Defoe, p. 21.
"It is not my intention to detain . . .": Gibbon, p. 207.
"all [court] proceedings shall be in the English tongue and language only . . .": cited in Melinkoff, p. 133.
"To cheat plain honesty by force of might . . .": John Clare cited in Haughton et al., p. 160.
"Warkworth meadow was common to the inhabitants . . .'": Neeson, p. 278.
"I have no particular tenderness of peasants . . .": Priestley, *The English*, p. 136.
"independent Highland companies might be of use . . .": Wright, pp. 168–69.

PART FOUR

"Whereas the cotton plantations of the American south . . .": Olusoga, *The Guardian*, July 11, 2015.
"What lectures will be read to poor children on this era? . . .": Walpole, p. 199.
"Our Saxon ancestors held their lands . . .": Jefferson, pp. 138–39.
"Liberty was better understood . . .": Otis, p. 31.
"All over Britain, bankers and merchants declared . . .": Antipa and Chamley, p. 13.
"perfidious Albion": Wheeldon.
"January 12, 1799: It is now actually proposed to place A TAXON INCOMES! . . .": Knyveton cited in Sabine, p. 31.

"If you were one of those slaves . . .": Olusoga, BBC.

"The English aristocracy has been adroit . . .": de Tocqueville, p. 59.

"The Chartist and Anti-Corn Law campaigns were . . ." : Hawkins, p. 372.

"monstrous architectural abortion": *Architectural Magazine*, p, 10.

"A new and vigorous style...": Scott, p. 69.

"Be it so. This burning of windows . . .": Napier, p. 35.

"More than 1 million have already immigrated . . .": Engels, pp. 90–91.

"Britain in effect contained two middle classes . . .": Martin.

"Urban-born men [in the UK] were shorter than rural-born men . . .": Floud and Harris, p. 105.

"the working-class has gradually become a race wholly apart . . .": Engels, p. 124.

"The object of the Petitioners is to induce the House . . .": UK Parliament, "1848 Chartist Petition."

"The mere assembling of such a Parliament marks a new epoch . . .": Marx.

"Manufacturers and merchants as a rule seem only to desire . . .": Richard Cobden cited in Morley, p. 482, 346.

"A corps of men specially selected . . .": Woodruff, p. 15.

"That was it! I was wearing a white waistcoat . . .": Ludwig Ompteda, p. 269.

"The accent most usually heard in everyday speech . . .": Daniel Jones cited in Durkin, p. 302.

"Though Germans, French, and Russians may cling as hard . . .": Mayhew, p. 559

"The opening up of China is undoubtedly . . ." *The London and China Telegraph*, p. 299.

"With regards to money and capital . . .": *The Gentleman's Magazine*, p. 763.

"The balance of power has been entirely destroyed . . .": Disraeli cited in Buckle, p. 134.

"before I went to bed, I had the satisfaction of knowing that St. Petersburg had surrendered.": Disraeli cited in Seton-Watson, p. 448.

"The campaign was effectively designed as a media event . . .": Brighton.

"From India and Central Asia to the populations of the Balkan Peninsula . . .": *The Times* Digital Archive, "Germany."

"merrie England, in short . . . for the benefit of the many, not the gain of the few": Hyndman, p. 9.

"We have thus the certainty of a conflict . . .": *The Times* Digital Archive, "The European Situation."

"Whatever happens will be for the worst . . .": Salisbury, p. 343.

"What should they know of England who only England know?": Kipling, "The English Flag," p. 89.

"We swept round a corner of the Downs . . .": Mais, pp. 311–12.

"The poor little street-bred people . . .": Kipling, "The English Flag," p. 89.

"No other major economy . . .": Ferguson, "Why we ruled the world."

"Never before or since has one nation committed so much . . .": Edelstein.

"a deliberate and deadly rivalry with her . . .": Williams, p. 8.

"Far-called, our navies melt away...": Kipling, "Recessional," p. 219.

"Let our manufacturers do as the German manufacturers do . . .": Logan.

"The Gatling's jammed and the Colonel dead . . .": Newbolt, "Vitaï Lampada."

"The more an occupation or a source of income allowed . . .": Daunton, p. 148.

[Watson reads out from a newspaper] "One by one the management . . .": Doyle, pp. 180–81.

"the Capitalists, who bought or hired the Press . . .": Ogden, p. 83.

"[In the East End] the streets were filled . . .": London, pp. 6–7.

"The multiplication of the Feeble-Minded . . .": Churchill, Letter to Asquith, December 1910.

"friendly and unprovocative": cited in Dale (ed.), p. 29.

"There would be no difficulty in applying . . .": Churchill quoted in *Westminster Gazette*.

"When they came to England a very real difficulty arose . . .": Ibid.

"They would have to face the task . . .": Ibid.

"things stronger than parliamentary majorities"; "no length of resistance": Bonar Law cited in Powell, David, p. 54.

"worse things than bloodshed, even on an extended scale": Churchill quoted in Lustick, p. 214.

"O God, Who art the Father of all . . .": prayer cited in Gill.

"German business": Lloyd George cited in Gilbert, p. 869.

PART FIVE

"Among employers and employees the words 'after the war' . . .": *The Economic Journal*, p. 34.

"To these [Tommies], Rugby Football . . .": Hay, pp. 82–83.

"Children who speak a dialect . . .": Newbolt, p. 67.

"Men live by their generosities . . .": MacDonald.

"The preservation of the individuality of the Englishman . . .": Baldwin.

"Returning to the gold standard . . .": Williamson, p. 8.

"Little could be done to overcome . . .": Garside, p. 247.

"the cathedrals and the colleges and the Cotswolds": Priestley, *English Journey*.

"19th-century England, the industrial England of coal . . .": Ibid.

"Most people . . . are mainly valence voters . . .": Kellner.

"As you travel northward your eye . . .": Orwell.

"a little, black-haired sharp-nosed Cockney"; "yet he caught my eye . . .": Ibid.

"'The filthy bloody bastards,' he said, feelingly.": Ibid.

"England (and Wales) was socially divided . . .": Dorling, "Distressed times and areas," pp. 44, 62.

"Britain went to war without a single . . .": Bond, p. 180.

"go in the name of God": Amery.

"The time has come when the organization . . .": Ibid., cols. 1149–50.

"The possibility of Russian intervention . . .": Kershaw.

"I took round the House of Commons . . .": Cazalet.

"We were invaded by our allies instead . . .": Hitchens, pp. xiv–xv.

"The August 1943 Quebec agreement . . .": Hastings.

"Montgomery refused to acknowledge what . . .": Beevor.

"I could not consent to the introduction . . .": Attlee quoted in Peat.

"would have to fall back on some kind of Gestapo": Churchill, *His Complete Speeches*.

"It may be that we must regard ourselves in future . . .": Attlee, UK Parliament.

"financial Dunkirk": Keynes, p. 410.

"One of [Keynes's] colleagues commented bitterly . . .": Ferguson, *Empire*.

"Even before the Windrush had left Jamaica . . .": Olusoga, *The Guardian*, April 22, 2018.

"For many West Indians . . . the shock was not the imperialism . . .": Edgerton.

"Marshall Aid dollars presented . . .": Barnett.

"We are still more important to America . . .": Freeman and Healey, p. 12.

"Men from the South of England . . .": Vinen, *National Service*.

"The question 'can a non-U speaker become . . .": Ross, pp. 47–48.

"Middle-class parents, including left-wing ones . . .": Sampson.

"English readers have not been conducted across the Atlantic . . .": Priestley and Hawkes, p. xi.

"to prevent two nations developing geographically . . .": Macmillan quoted in *The Economist*, September 15, 2012.

"white heat of technology": Wilson quoted in Ratcliffe.

"By the mid-1960s, the 'south and east' of Britain . . .": Martin.

"Your representative owes you, not his industry only . . .": Burke.

"We must be mad, literally mad as a nation . . .": Powell, Enoch, 1968.

"If the present system of election . . .": Mount.

"It was the Labour left led by Tony Benn . . .": Sandbrook.

"If we came out now . . . we should have to say . . .": Thatcher, "The Choice Before Us."

"an acceptable level of violence": Maudling.

"Britain is a tragedy . . .": Kissinger quoted in Vinen, *Thatcher's Britain*.

"the Communist Trojan horse in our midst . . .": Sir Walter Walker quoted in Ferguson, *The Square and the Tower*, p. 277.

"get pissed, destroy": Sex Pistols.

"The most powerful critique of socialist . . .": Thatcher quoted in Powell, James.

"The Conservative Party of Britain . . .": Miller, pp. 181–82.

"We have not successfully rolled back the frontiers . . .": Thatcher, "The Bruges Speech."

"Margaret Thatcher's government . . .": Bresler.

"Her messianic, hectoring intolerance . . .": Cannadine, p. 41.

"The MP to do the business would be the family man . . .": Whelan.

"The FA hated Three Lions . . .": Broudie.

"so many jokes, so many sneers . . . football's coming home": Lightning Seeds, et al.

"rightful inheritance was once stolen . . .": Scruton.

"seventeen years of hurt"; "Labour's coming home": Blair, 1996.

"if, in time, the regions of England . . .": Blair, 1995.

"There remains an embarrassing obstacle . . .": Morrison.

"New Labour made a Faustian bargain . . .": Elliott.

"Whereas wealthy media executives . . .": Cohen.

"Talk about Europe and they call you extreme . . .": Hague.

"The line that separates upland from lowland Britain . . .": Dorling, "Persistent North-South Divides," pp. 24–26.

"One of the largest mass population movements . . .": Watt and Wintour.

"The Labour north and Conservative south . . .": *The Economist*, April 20, 2013.

"UKIP's surge . . . has relatively little to do with the public's hostility. . .": Pickard.

"14 October 1066: England's Nakba . . .": Hannan, Twitter.

"The English . . . deep in the German woods. . . more sympathetic to the French.": Hannan, *Inventing Freedom*.

"Almost 1,000 years after the Normans took power. . .": Meek.

"1,000 years after William the Conqueror invaded . . .": Doughty.

"Boris Johnson, London mayor, told the FT . . .": Parker, et al.

"People in this country have had enough of experts": Gove quoted in *The Spectator*.

"We can see the sunlit meadows beyond . . .": Johnson.

"Then shall these great yearly exactions cease . . .": Fish, p. 216.

"Boris Johnson says it's his government's job . . .": Walker, Jonathan.

"Brexit has read the rites over British conservatism": Stephens.

"The geography of spatial imbalance . . .": Martin, et al.

"Labour would have won almost every seat in England . . .": *Daily Mail*.

Selected Bibliography

"1647: The Putney Debates," Online Library of Liberty (OLL), Liberty Fund Network.

"1848 Chartist Petition," UK Parliament, parliament.uk.

Amery, Leo. House of Commons. UK Parliament Hansard Archives, Vol. 360, Column 1146. May 7, 1940.

"An Impartial Examination of the Conduct of the Whigs and Tories, from the Revolution Down to the Present Times," *The Gentleman's Magazine*, Vol. 33, 1763.

Anderson, Christopher. *The Annals of the English Bible*. New York: Robert Carter & Brothers, 1852.

"Another China Debate," *The London and China Telegraph*, June 4, 1864.

Antipa, P., and C. Chamley, "Monetary and Fiscal Policy in England during the French Wars (1793–1821)." Banque de France Working Papers, No. 627, 2017.

Attlee, Clement. UK Parliament Hansard Archives, Mr. Clement Attlee: speeches 1946.

Baker, Derek (ed.), *England in the Early Middle Ages*. Dallas: Academia, 1993.

Baldwin, Stanley. "What England Means to Me," speech to the Royal Society of St. George, May 6, 1924.

Barlow, Frank (ed. and trans.). *The Carmen de Hastingae Proelio of Guy Bishop of Amiens*. Oxford: Clarendon Press, 1999.

Barnett, Correlli. "The Wasting of Britain's Marshall Aid," BBC History, March 3, 2011.

Bartlett, Robert. *England Under the Norman and Angevin Kings, 1075–1225, New Oxford History of England*, John M. Roberts (ed.). Oxford University Press, 2000.

Beevor, Antony. *Arnhem: The Battle for the Bridges, 1944*. New York: Viking Components, 2018.

Behn, Aphra. *The Works of Aphra Behn: Seneca Unmasqued and Other Prose Translations* (Janet Todd, ed.). Routledge, 2016.

Blair, Tony. From 1996 party conference speech, quoted in "Blair: In his own words," *BBC News*, updated Mary 11, 2007.

———. From 1995 leader's speech, Brighton. British Political Speech, Speech Archive.

Boffey, Julia. Quote cited in "London Books and London Readers," in *Cultural Reformations: Medieval and Renaissance in Literary History* (Brian Cummings and James Simpson, eds.). Oxford, 2010.

Bond, Brian. *British Military Policy Between the Two World Wars*. Oxford University Press, 1980.

Bradford, William. *Of Plymouth Plantation: 1620–1647*. New York: Modern Library, 1981.

Bresler, Fenton. "Thatcher vs. the British Legal System," *Los Angeles Times*, April 2, 1989.

Brie, Friedrich W. D. (ed.). *The Brut, or The Chronicles of England, Vol. 2*. London: Oxford University Press, 1906, 1908.

Brighton, Paul. *Original Spin: Downing Street and the Press in Victorian Britain*. Bloomsbury, 2005.

Broudie, Ian, interviewed by Dave Simpson, "The Lightning Seeds' Ian Broudie," *The Guardian*, June 11, 2014.

Buckle, George Earle, in succession to W. F. Monypenny. *The Life of Benjamin Disraeli: Earl of Beaconsfield.* New York: Macmillan, 1920.

Burke, Edmund. Speech to the Electors of Bristol, November 3, 1774. *The Works of the Right Honourable Edmund Burke.* London: Henry G. Bohn, 1854–56.

Caesar, Julius. *Gallic War, Book 4,* W. A. McDevitte and W. S. Bohn (trans.). New York: Harper & Brothers, 1869.

Cannadine, David. *In Churchill's Shadow: Confronting the Past in Modern Britain.* London: Oxford University Press, 2003.

Carroll, Leslie. *Notorious Royal Marriages.* New York: New American Library, 2010.

"Case of Proclamations," England and Wales High Court (King's Bench Division), November 1, 1610.

Caxton, William. *Caxton's Eneydos, 1490,* M. T. Culley and F. J. Furnivall (eds.). London, 1890.

Cazalet, Colonel. House of Commons, UK Parliament Hansard Archives, Vol. 385, Column 560. November 19, 1942.

Charles I. *His Majesties Answer to the XIX Propositions of Both Houses of Parliament.* Oxford, 1642.

Churchill, Winston S. *A History of the English-Speaking Peoples, Vol. I.* London: Bloomsbury, 2015.

———. Address in Dundee, quoted in *Westminster Gazette,* September 13, 1912.

———. Churchill, Winston and Robert Rhodes James (ed.). *Winston S. Churchill: His Complete Speeches, 1897–1963.* New York: Chelsea House, 1974.

———. Letter from Churchill to Asquith, December 1910. *The Asquith Papers,* miscellaneous letters to Asquith or his private secretaries, 1909–1910, MS. Asquith 12.

———. The Secret Treaty of Dover, cited in *Winston S. Churchill: A History of the English-Speaking Peoples, Vol. II.* London: Bloomsbury, 2015.

———. "Winston Churchill's Remarkable Speech," *San Jose Mercury-News,* Vol. LXXXIII, No. 122, October 30, 1912.

Cohen, Nick. "History Shows How Poverty Helps the Right," *The Guardian,* October 11, 2008.

de Commines, Philip. *The Memoirs of Philip de Commines, Lord of Argenton, Vol. 1,* Andrew R. Scoble (ed.). London, 1877.

Cook, Albert S. *Asser's Life of King Alfred.* Boston: Ginn & Co., 1906.

Cromwell, Thomas. *Oliver Cromwell's Letters and Speeches with Elucidations by Thomas Carlyle.* London: Chapman and Hall, 1865.

Dale, Iain (ed.). Sir Henry Campbell-Bannerman's election address, "Liberal Party General Election Manifesto 1906," in *Liberal Party General Election Manifestos: 1900–1997.* London and New York: Routledge, 2000.

Davies, C. S. L. "Slavery and Protector Somerset; the Vagrancy Act of 1547," *The Economic History Review* 19, no. 3. 1996.

Davies, John S. *An English Chronicle of the Reigns of Richard II, Henry IV, Henry V, and Henry VI.* London: The Camden Society, 1856.

Daniel Defoe. *A Tour thro' the Whole Island of Great Britain, Vol. 3.* London: 2001.

Daunton, Martin J. *State and Market in Victorian Britain: War, Welfare, and Capitalism.* Woodbridge, Broydell & Brewer, 2008.

"Dilution of Skilled Labor, The," *The Economic Journal* 26, no. 101, March 1916.

Dorling, Danny. "Distressed Times and Areas: Poverty, Polarisation and Politics in England, 1918–1971," *Geographies of England: The North–South Divide, Material and Imagined,* Alan R. H. Baker and Mark Billinge (eds.). Cambridge University Press, 2004.

———. "Persistent North-South Divides," *The Economic Geography of the UK,* Neil M. Coe and Andrew Jones (eds.). London: SAGE Publications, 2010.

Doughty, Steve. "So Much for Social Mobility . . . ," *Daily Mail,* October 29, 2013.

Doyle, Conan. *The Adventures of Sherlock Holmes.* Saint-Petersburg: Palmyra, 2017.

Durkin, Philip (ed.). *The Oxford Handbook of Lexicography*. Oxford University Press, 2016.

Edelstein, Michael. "Foreign Investment, Accumulation and Empire 1860–1914," *The Cambridge Economic History of Britain*, Roderick Floud and Paul Johnson (eds.). Cambridge University Press, 2004.

Edgerton, David. *The Rise and Fall of the British Nation: A Twentieth-Century History*. London: Allen Lane, 2018.

Elliott, Larry. "Margaret Thatcher Was Loved and Hated—Both for Sound Economic Reasons," *The Guardian*, April 14, 2013.

Engels, Friedrich. *The Condition of the Working-Class in England in 1844*. New York: Cosimo Classics, 2008.

"England's Two Nations: Divided Kingdom," *The Economist*, April 20, 2013.

"European Situation, The," *The Times*, December 19, 1887.

Fairlie, Simon. "A Short History of Enclosure in Britain," *The Land*, Summer 2009.

Ferguson, Niall. *Empire: How Britain Made the Modern World*. London: Penguin, 2004.

———. *The Square and the Tower: Networks and Power, from the Freemasons to Facebook*. New York: Penguin, 2018.

———. "Why We Ruled the World," *The Times*, January 6, 2003.

Fideler, Paul, and Thomas Meyer. *Political Thought and the Tudor Commonwealth: Deep Structure, Discourse and Disguise*. London and New York: Routledge, 2003.

Firth, C. H., and R. S. Rait (eds.). "May 1649: An Act Declaring and Constituting the People of England to be a Commonwealth and Free-State," *Acts and Ordinances of the Interregnum, 1642–1660*. London: 1911.

Fish, Simon. "A Supplication for the Beggars," in *The Thought & Culture of the English Renaissance*, ed. by Elizabeth Nugent. Cambridge University Press: 1956.

Fisher, John H. *The Emergence of Standard English*. Lexington: University Press of Kentucky, 1996.

Floud, Roderick and Bernard Harris (eds.). "Health, Height and Welfare: Britain, 1700–1980," *Health and Welfare During Industrialization*. University of Chicago Press: 1997.

Fortescue, John. *A Learned Commendation of the Politique Lawes of Englande*, Robert Mulcaster (trans.), 1599.

Foxe, John. "The Oration of Q. Mary in the Guild Hall," *The Acts and Monuments* (TAMO), 1570 edition.

Freeman, John, and Denis Healey. "Rearmament—How Far?" London: The Fabian Society, 1951.

Freeman's Journal, December 19, 1887.

Froissart, John. *The Chronicles of Froissart*, John Bourchier (trans.), Lord Berners and G. C. Macaulay (eds.). New York: Harvard Classics, 1910.

Froude, James Anthony. *The Divorce of Catherine of Aragon*. New York: Charles Scribner's Sons, 1891.

Galmai, Gemel, *L'Divore des Englers*, Alexander Bell (ed.), Anglo-Norman Text Society, 14–16. Oxford, 1960.

Gairdner, James, and R. H. Brodie (eds). "Henry VIII's Will," *Letters and Papers, Foreign and Domestic, Henry VIII, Vol. 21, Part 2*. London, 1910.

Garside, W. R. *British Unemployment 1919–1939: A Study in Public Policy*. Cambridge University Press, 1990.

"Germany," *The Times*, February 3, 1880.

Gibbon, Edward. *The Decline and Fall of The Roman Empire, Vol 1*. London: 1825.

Gilbert, Bentley B. "Pacifist to Interventionist: David Lloyd George in 1911 and 1914. Was Belgium an Issue?" *The Historical Journal* 28, no. 4, 1985.

Giles, J. A. (ed.), *The Anglo-Saxon Chronicle*. London: G. Bell and Sons Ltd., 1914.

Gill, Peter. "National Coal Strike," petergill7.co.uk.

Goodman, Ellen. "Act in Restraint of Appeals," *The Origins of the Western Legal Tradition: From Thales to the Tudors*. Sydney: Federation Press, 1995.

Goodwin, George. "The Battle of Towton," *History Today* 61, no. 5, May 5, 2011.

"The Great Divide: Economically, Socially and Politically, the North Is Becoming Another Country," *The Economist*, September 15, 2012.

Green, Caitlin R. "The Medieval 'New England': A Forgotten Anglo-Saxon Colony on the North-Eastern Black Sea Coast," caitlingreen.org, May 19, 2015.

Green, John R. *The Conquest of England*. London: Macmillan & Co., 1899.

Hague, William. "Hague's 'foreign land' speech," *The Guardian*, March 4, 2001.

Hakluyt, Richard. *The Principal Navigations, Voyages, Traffiques, and Discoveries of the English Nation Made by Sea or Overland to the Remote & Farthest Distant Quarters of the Earth at Any Time within the Compasse of These 1600 Yeares*. New York: E. P. Dutton & Co., 1927.

Hampton, Christopher (ed.). *A Radical Reader: The Struggle for Change in England, 1381–1914*. Penguin, 1984.

Hannan, Daniel. "14 October 1066: England's Nakba," Twitter, @DanielJHannan, October 14, 2015.

———. *Inventing Freedom: How the English-Speaking Peoples Made the Modern World*. New York: Broadside Books, 2013.

Hansen, Erik, and Hans Frede Nielsen. "John of Trevisa's 'On the Languages of Britain,'" *Irregularities in Modern English*. Odense, 2007.

Harrison, William. *The Description of England: The Classic Contemporary Account of Tudor Social Life*, Georges Edelen (ed.). Washington, DC: The Folger Shakespeare Library and Dover Publications: 1994.

Hastings, Max. "Trinity by Frank Close review—Klaus Fuchs: 'the Most Dangerous Spy in History,'" *The Times*, July 28, 2019.

Haughton, Hugh, Adam Phillips, and Geoffrey Summerfield (eds). *John Clare in Context*. Cambridge University Press, 1994.

Hawkins, Angus. *Victorian Political Culture*. Oxford University Press, 2015.

Hay, Ian. *All In It. "K(1)" Carries On*. Boston and New York: Houghton Mifflin Company, 1917.

"Henry VII's Letter to John Morton Concerning William Weston's Voyage to the New Found Land," E. T. Jones and M. Condon (eds.), 2011.

Henry of Huntingdon, *Henrici Archidiaconi Huntendunensis Historia Anglorum*, Thomas Arnold (ed.). London: 1879.

Hill, Christopher. *The World Turned Upside Down: Radical Ideas During the English Revolution*. London and New York: Penguin, 1991.

———. "Tyndale and His Successors," The Tyndale Society.

Hitchens, Peter. *The Abolition of Britain*. London: Quartet Books, 1999.

Holinshed, Raphael. *Chronicles of England, Scotland and Ireland, Vol. 2*. London: 1807.

Holland, Tom. *Athelstan: The Making of England*. London: Penguin, 2016.

Holt, James C. *Colonial England 1066–1215*. London: Rio Grande, 1997.

———. *The Northerners: A Study in the Reign of King John*. Oxford, 1961.

Hoyt, Robert S. "The Coronation Oath of 1308," *The English Historical Review, Vol. 71*, 1956.

Hudson, Alison. "Early Anglo-Saxon kingdoms," British Library.

Hyndman, H. M. *England for All*. London, Glibert & Rivington, 1881.

"Investor, By a City Authority, The," *The Gentleman's Magazine*, 1870.

Jefferson, Thomas. *The Writings of Thomas Jefferson, Vol. 1*, H. A. Washington (ed.). Cambridge: 2011.

Jobson, Adrian. "The Provisions of Oxford," in *The First English Revolution*. London: Bloomsbury, 2012.

Johnson, Boris. "Boris Johnson's Speech on the EU Referendum: Full Text," *Conservative Home*, May 9, 2016.

Jonson, Ben. "To the Memory of My Beloved the Author, Mr. William Shakespeare."

Keen, Maurice. *Chivalry*. New Haven/London: Yale University Press, 2005.

Kellner, Peter. "Dominic Cummings Turns a Problem into a Crisis for Boris Johnson." May 27, 2020.

Kershaw, Ian. *Hitler: 1936–1945: Nemesis*. New York and London: W. W. Norton, 2001.

Keynes, John Maynard. *The Collected Writings of John Maynard Keynes, Vol. 24*, Donald Moggridge (ed.). Cambridge University Press, 1979.

Kipling, Joseph Rudyard. "The English Flag," *Verse*. Garden City, NY: The Country Life Press, 1922.

———. "Recessional," *Collected Verse of Rudyard Kipling*. Garden City, New York: Doubleday, Page & Company, 1916.

Kim, Jaecheol. "The North in Shakespeare's *Richard III*," *Studies in Philology* 116, no. 3, 2019.

Knight, Charles. *The Popular History of England, Vol. 3*. London: Bradbury and Evans, 1856.

Liebermann, Felix (ed.). *Die Gesetze der Angelsachsen*, 4 vols. in 3 books. Halle, 1903–16.

Lightning Seeds, David Baddiel, and Frank Skinner. "Three Lions," *The Beautiful Game*, May 20, 1996.

Livingston, Michael. "Owain Glyndŵr's Grand Design: 'The Tripartite Indenture' and the Vision of a New Wales," *Proceedings of the Harvard Celtic Colloquium, Vol. 33*. Department of Celtic Languages & Literatures, Harvard University, 2013.

Logan, John William. Speech to House of Commons, UK Parliament Hansard Archives, Vol. 45, Column 638, January 27, 1897.

London, Jack. *The People of the Abyss*. New York: Macmillan, 1903.

Ludwig Ompteda, Freiherr von. *Bilder aus dem Leben in England*. Breslau: S. Schottlaender, 1881.

Lustick, Ian S. *Unsettled States, Disputed Lands*. Ithaca and London: Cornell University Press, 1993.

Macaulay, Thomas Babington. *The History of England from The Accession of James II, Vol II*. New York: Harper and Brothers, 1850.

MacDonald, J. Ramsay. Labour Leader's speech, London, 1924. British Political Speech, Speech Archive.

"Magna Carta translated into Anglo Norman French," Magna Carta Collection, British Library.

Mais, S. P. B. *Oh! To Be in England*. London: Grant Richards Ltd., 1922.

Martin, Ron. "The Political Economy of Britain's North-South Divide," *Transactions of the Institute of British Geographers* 13, no. 4, 1988.

———, Andy Pike, Pete Tyler, and Ben Gardiner. "Spatially Rebalancing the UK Economy: The Need for a New Policy Model," *Regional Studies*, 2015.

Marx, Karl. "Letter to the Labour Parliament," *People's Paper*, March 18, 1854.

Maudling, Reginald. "Acceptable Level of Violence," quoted in CAIN Web Service: A Glossary of Terms Related to the Conflict, Martin Melaugh and Brendan Lynn (eds.).

May, Thomas. "The Nineteen Propositions," *The History of the Parliament of England, Which Began November the Third, 1640*. London, 1812.

Mayhew, Henry. *German Life and Manners as Seen in Saxony at the Present Day, Vol. I*. London: W. H. Allen & Co., 1864.

McCrum, Robert, Robert MacNeil, and William Cran, *The Story of English*. London, 1992.

Meek, James. "Rise Up, Rebel, Revolt: How the English Language Betrays Class and Power," *The Guardian*, September 6, 2019.

Melinkoff, David. *The Language of the Law*. Wipf and Stock Publishers, 2004.

Miller, Eugene F. *Hayek's The Constitution of Liberty: An Account of Its Argument*. Institute of Economic Affairs. London: The Institute of Economic Affairs, 2010.

More, Thomas. *The Utopia of Sir Thomas More*, William Dallam Armes (ed.). New York: Macmillan, 1912.

Morely, John. *The Life of Richard Cobden*. Cambridge University Press, 2010.

Morier, Robert B. D. "The Agrarian Legislation of Prussia during the Present Century," *Systems of Land Tenure in Various Countries*. London: Cobden Club, 1870.

Morris, Marc. *Castle: A History of the Buildings that Shaped Medieval Britain*. London: Cornerstone, 2012.

———. *The Norman Conquest*. London: Hutchinson, 2012.

Morrison, Blake. "How the Other Half Lives," *Independent*, October 23, 2011.

Mount, Ferdinand. "Wedded to the Absolute," *London Review of Books*, September 26, 2019.

Napier, William. *History of General Sir Charles Napier's Administration of Scinde*. London: 1851.

Neeson, J. M. *Commoners: Common Right, Enclosure and Social Change in England, 1700–1820*. Cambridge University Press, 1996.

New World Encyclopedia, "Richard I of England."

Newbolt, Henry. *The Teaching of English in England*. London, 1921.

———. "Vitai Lampada," 1892.

North, Roger. *A Discourse on the Study of the Laws*. London: 1824.

Ogden, H. J. *The War Against the Dutch Republics in South Africa*. Taylor, Garnett, Evans & Co., 1901.

Olusoga, David. "Black and British: A Forgotten History," BBC, November 29, 2016.

———. "The History of British Slave Ownership Has Been Buried: Now Its Scale Can Be Revealed," *The Guardian*, July 11, 2015.

———. "The Windrush Story Was Not a Rosy One Even Before the Ship Arrived." *The Guardian*, April 22, 2018.

"On the Designs for the New Houses of Parliament," *Architectural Magazine, Vol. 3*, 1836.

Orange, William. "Declaration of the Prince of Orange," October 10, 1688.

Orwell, George. *The Road to Wigan Pier*. New York: Harcourt Brace, 1958.

Otis, James. "The Rights of the British Colonies Asserted and Proved." Boston: 1764.

Parker, George, Sarah Gordon, and Elizabeth Rigby. "Cameron Campaign Strategy Splits Opinion," *Financial Times*, April 23, 2015.

Pickard, Jim. "How Ukip Surge Came Despite Referendum Pledge and Immigration Fall," *Financial Times*, March 1, 2013.

Peat, Jack. "This Clement Attlee Quote on Referendums Is Going Viral," *The London Economic*, February 9, 2019.

Pepys, Samuel. *The Diary of Samuel Pepys: Selected Passages*, Richard Le Gallienne (ed.). Dover Publications, 2004.

Pope Pius V. "Regnans in Excelsis: Excommunicating Elizabeth I of England, 1570," Papal Encyclicals, 1570.

Powell, David. *British Politics, 1910–1935: The Crisis of the Party System*. London and New York: Routledge, 2004.

Powell, Enoch. "Rivers of Blood," speech to Parliament, 1968.

———. Speech to the Royal Society of St. George, April 23, 1961.

Powell, James. *The Triumph of Liberty*. New York: The Free Press, 2000.

Priestley, J. B. *The English*. Viking, 1973.

———. *English Journey*. London, 1935.

———, and Jacquetta Hawkes. *Journey Down a Rainbow*. New York: Heinemann-Cresset, 1955.

"Provisions of Oxford, The," UK Parliament, parliament.uk.

Puttenham, George. *The Art of English Poesy: A Critical Edition*, Frank Whigham and Wayne A. Rebhorn (eds.). Ithaca and London: Cornell University Press, 2007.

Ratcliffe, Susan. *Oxford Essential Quotations, 4th and 5th Editions*. Oxford University Press, 2016, 2017.

Reis, Sister Bernadette Mary. "St Thomas Becket, Sign of Contradiction," *Vatican News*, December 29, 2018.

Richards, Judith M. "The English Accession of James VI: 'National' Identity, Gender and the Personal Monarchy of England," *The English Historical Review* 117, no. 472, June 2002.

Riches, William Terence Martin. *The Civil Rights Movement: Struggle and Resistance*. New York: St. Martin's Press, 1997.

————. "White Slaves, Black Servants and the Question of Providence: Servitude and Slavery in Colonial Virginia 1609–1705," *Irish Journal of American Studies, Vol. 8*, 1999.

Robinson, Martin. "Maps Show How 'Youthquake' Would Have Won Election for Labour If 18 to 24-Year-Olds Had Been Only Voters—while Tories Would Have Been Even Bigger Winners If Over-65s Were the Only Ones to Go to the Polls," *Daily Mail*, December 31, 2019.

Rochford: Rediscovering a Lost Medieval English Family, 1066–1550, therochfords. wordpress.com.

Ross, Alan S. C. "Linguistic Class-Indicators in Present-Day English," *Neuphilologische Mitteilungen* 55, no. 1, 1954.

Rowse, A. L. *The Elizabethan Renaissance: The Cultural Achievement*. New York: Charles Scribner's Sons, 1972.

Ruddick, Andrea. *English Identity and Political Culture in the Fourteenth Century*. Cambridge, UK: Cambridge University Press, 2013.

Sabine, B. E. V., *A History of Income Tax*. Abingdon, 2006.

Salisbury, "Disintegration," *Lord Salisbury on Politics*, Paul Smith (ed.). Cambridge University Press, 2007.

Sampson, Anthony. *Anatomy of Britain*. London: Hodder & Stoughton, 1962.

Sandbrook, Dominic. *Seasons in the Sun: The Battle for Britain, 1974–1979*. Penguin UK, 2012.

Sayer, Derek. "A Notable Administration: English State Formation and the Rise of Capitalism," *American Journal of Sociology* 97, no. 5, 1992.

Scott, George Gilbert. "On the Present Position and Future Prospects of the Revival of Gothic Architecture," *Reports and Papers Read at the Meetings of the Architectural Societies, Vol. 4*. London: 1857.

Scruton, Roger. "How I Overcame My Class Stigma," *UnHerd*, March 28, 2019.

"Second Statute of Labourers, 1351," The National Archives.

Seeck, Otto (ed.), *Notitia Dignitatum: Accedunt Notitia Urbis Constantinopolitanae et Latercula Prouinciarum*. London: Forgotten Books, 2018.

Seton-Watson, R. W. *Disraeli, Gladstone, and the Eastern Question*. London and New York: Routledge, 2006.

Sex Pistols. "Anarchy in the UK," *Never Mind the Bollocks, Here's the Sex Pistols*, 1977.

Shah, Idries. *The Englishman's Handbook: or, How to Deal with Foreigners*. London, The Octagon, 2000.

Shaw-Taylor, Leigh. "Proletarianisation, Parliamentary Enclosure and the Household Economy of the Labouring Poor: 1750–1850," *The Journal of Economic History* 60, no. 2, 2000.

Short, Ian. "Patrons and Polyglots: French Literature in Twelfth Century England," *Anglo-Norman Studies, Vol. 14*, Marjorie Chibnall (ed.). Woodbridge, 1992.

Simms, Brendan. *Three Victories and a Defeat: The Rise and Fall of the First British Empire*. New York: Basic Books, 2008.

Snow, Dan. "Today in 1066 King Edward the Confessor Died Without an Heir. What Followed Makes *Game of Thrones* Look Like a Game of Musical Chairs," Twitter, @ thehistoryguy, January 5, 2021.

Somerset, Anne. *Elizabeth I*. London, Anchor: 2003.

Steerpike, "Fact Check: What Did Michael Gove Actually Say About 'Experts'?," *The Spectator*, September 2, 2021.

Stephens, Philip. "Brexit Has Read the Rites Over British Conservatism," *Financial Times*, September 5, 2019.

Stowe, John. "Historical Memoranda of John Stowe: On Cade's Rebellion (1450)." London: Camden Society, 1880.

Summerson, Henry, et al. (trans.), "The 1215 Magna Carta," The Magna Carta Project.

Tate Museum, "Art under Attack: Histories of British Iconoclasm; Religion: Reformation," tate.org.uk.

Tawney, Richard H. *The Agrarian Problem in the Sixteenth Century*. London, 1912.

———, and Eileen Power (eds.). "Acte Agaynst Pullyng Doun of Tounes," *Tudor Economic Documents, Vol. 1*. London: Longmans, Green and Co., 1924.

Taylor, John. "Taylor's Western Voyage to the Mount," *Works of John Taylor, The Water-Poet*, Charles Hindley (ed.). London: Reeves and Turner, 1872.

Thatcher, Margaret. "The Bruges Speech," College of Europe, September 20, 1988.

———. "The Choice Before Us," *Daily Telegraph*, June 4, 1975.

Thierry, Augustin. *History of the Conquest of England by the Normans*. London: Whittaker and Co., 1825.

Thrush, Dr. Andrew. "1614: The Beginning of the Crisis of Parliaments," *The History of Parliament*, May 7, 2014.

"Titulus Regius," The Richard III Society, richardiii.net.

de Tocqueville, Alexis. *Journeys to England and Ireland*, J. P. Mayer (ed.). New Haven, 1958.

Tombs, Richard. *The English and Their History*. New York: Vintage, 2016.

Trevelyan, G. M. *Illustrated History of England*. London: Longmans, Green and Co., 1956.

Tyndale, William. *The Obedience of a Christian Man*. London, 1582.

Vaughan, Robert. *The History of England Under the House of Stuart, Including the Commonwealth, Part 1*. London: Baldwin and Cradock, 1840.

Vinen, Richard. *National Service: A Generation in Uniform 1945–1963*. London: Penguin, 2014.

Vitalis, Ordericus. *The Ecclesiastical History of England and Normandy, vol. 1*, Thomas Forester (trans.). London: Henry G. Bohn, 1853.

Walker, Jonathan. "Boris Johnson Says It's His Government's Job to End the North-South Divide," *Chronicle Live*, October 2, 2019.

Walker, Julia M. *The Elizabeth Icon: 1603–2003*. Palgrave Macmillan, 2004.

Walpole, Horace. *The Letters of Horace Walpole, Vol. 3*, J. Wright (ed.). Philadelphia: 1842.

Watson, George. "Shakespeare and the Norman Conquest: English in the Elizabethan Theatre," *Virginia Quarterly Review*, Autumn 1990.

Watt, Nicholas and Patrick Wintour. "How Immigration Came to Haunt Labour: The Inside Story," *The Guardian*, March 24, 2015.

West, Ed. *My Kingdom for a Horse*. New York: Skyhorse, 2018.

Wheeldon, Tom. "Perfidious Albion: Napoléon and His British Nemesis," *France 24*, March 5, 2021.

Whelan, Charlie. "Labour's Great Divide," *The Guardian*, January 6, 1999.

Wickham, Chris. *The Inheritance of Rome: A History of Europe from 400 to 1000*. New York: Viking, 2009.

William of Malmesbury's Chronicle of the Kings of England, J. A. Giles (ed.). London, 1847.

Williams, Earnest Edwin. *Made in Germany*. London: William Heinemann, 1896.

Williamson, Peter, and Stephen Caunce. "History of the North South Divide," *UK North South Divide Conference Report*, Rustat Conference, November 26, 2015.

Winstanley, Gerrard. "A Declaration from the Poor Oppressed People of England," *Wistanley: "The Law of Freedom" and Other Writings*, Christopher Hill (ed.). London: Cambridge University Press, 2006.

———, and the Diggers. "The True Levellers Standard Advanced." London: Renascence Editions, 1649.

Woodruff, Philip. *The Men Who Ruled India: The Founders*. London: Jonathan Cape, 1953.

Wormald, Jenny. "The Creation of Britain: Multiple Kingdoms or Core and Colonies?," *Transactions of the Royal Historical Society, Vol. 2*. Cambridge University Press, 1992.

Wright, Robert. *The Life of Major-General James Wolfe*. London: Chapman and Hall, 1864.

Image Credits

Every effort has been made to trace and contact copyright holders. If an error or omission is brought to our notice, we will be pleased to correct it in future editions of this book. For further information, please contact the publisher.

p. 6 Coin of Carausius, late 3rd century. Private collection.

p. 24 Coin of King Athelstan, 9th century. Private collection.

p. 35 Detail from Scene 57 of the Bayeux Tapestry. 2011 Creative Commons, identified as own work by user Myrabella.

p. 44 The Sinking of the White Ship. c.1321; British Library, Cotton Claudius D. ii, fol. 45v; G70017-90.

p. 49 Henry II and Queen Eleanor. From a miniature of Philip Augustus sending an envoy, and the envoy being received by the King and Queen. in Les Grands Chroniques de France, 1332–1350; British Library Royal F 43v.

p. 54 Henry II with Thomas à Beckett. From Liber Legum Antiquorum Regum, British Library Cotton MS Claudius D. II, f.73.

p. 57 Clash of Cavalry at the Battle of Bouvines. Detail from Les Grands Chroniques de France, Royal G VI f 343 v.

p. 62 Chronica Roffense; drawing in lower margin: the Battle of Evesham and death of Simon de Montfort, August 4, 1265; British Library G70106-93; Cotton Nero D. II, f 177.

p. 67 Le danse macabre: from the Nuremberg Chronicle, 1493. Creative Commons. In the library of the Catholic seminary of Strasbourg. Identified as own work by photographer/uploader Claude Truong-Ngoc, 2013.

p. 68 Fan-vaulting at Gloucester Cathedral, 1351. Creative Commons. Identified as own work by photographer/uploader Zhurakovskyi, 2016.

p. 73 Richard II's 1395 portrait. At Westminster Abbey. London

p. 74 Coronation of Henry IV. From Harleian MS No.4679; from Charles Knight, Old England. A Pictorial Museum, 1845. Reproduced by kind permission of fromoldbooks.org.

p. 76 Bradmore's sketch of his surgical instrument. Bradmore's "Philomena," Middle English translation of the original Latin, within British Library MS Harleian 1736 (ff. 6-184v).

p. 78 Battle of Agincourt, from Chroniques d'Enguerrand de Monstrelet (early 15th century), BNF, département des Manuscrits, manuscrit Français 2680, folio 208.

p. 83 Towton skull. Reproduced by permission of Bradford University's Biological Anthropology Research Centre.

p. 86 Left: Tudor image of Richard III; 1520, Royal Collection, Windsor Castle, royalcollection. org.uk/collection/403436/richard-iii-1452-85. Right: Laurence Olivier in the title role of the 1956 film production of William Shakespeare's "Richard III." Contributor: Granger Historical

Picture Archive / Alamy Stock Photo.

p. 90 Tombs of Henry VII and Elizabeth of York; Westminster Abbey. Author's photograph.

p. 92 The Henri Grace a Dieu (1514) Creative Commons: reproduced in The Anthony Roll of Henry VIII's Navy: Pepys Library 2991; British Library Additional MS 22047 with Related Documents ISBN 0-7546-0094-7, p. 40. Own scan uploaded by user: Gerry Bye

p. 93 Enclosure of a Village—diagram from paper, "Enclosure Acts: Great Britain," Professor Robert Sirabian, University of Wisconsin.

p. 103 Holbein's Portrait of Thomas Cromwell; The Frick Collection. 1915.1.76.

p. 105 "Old Coppernose," debased shilling. From the Andrew Wayne Collection. Ex Spink Numismatic Circular vol. CXII/2 (April 2004), no. HS1626; K.A. Jacob Collection. Classical Numismatic Group cngcoins.com.

p. 110 Coronation of Queen Elizabeth I. National Portrait Gallery NPG 5175: npg.org.uk/collections/search/portrait/mw02070/Queen-Elizabeth-I.

p. 117 page from The great frost: cold doings in London, except it be at the lotterie. Printed at London: For Henry Gosson, 1608. Attributed to Thomas Dekker (approx. 1572–1632). STC 11403, Houghton Library, Harvard University, released to Creative Commons.

p. 124 Matthew Hopkins. Frontispiece to a tract entitled The Discovery of Witches, 1647, britishmuseum.org/collection/object/P_1868-0808-3233© The Trustees of the British Museum, released to Creative Commons.

p. 126 The Execution of Charles I, 1649. National Portrait Gallery. NPG D1306: Contemporary German print of the execution of Charles I outside the Banqueting House. Based on the earliest European depiction of the execution.

p. 134 The Prince of Orange, Welcome to London: to the tune of The Two English Travellers. Ballad dating to 1688. Bodleian Library, Wood E 25, f. 118

p. 140 The Pump Room at Bath. Author's photograph.

p. 148 The East Offering Her Riches to Brittania, Roma Spiridone, 1778, for the Revenue Committee Room in East India House, London. Uploaded to Flickr/Commons by British Library; BL I 0SM F425.

p. 149 Bricked-up windows, Bath. Attributed to Flickr photographer Jo Folkes on amusingplanet.com.

p. 157 "Slave Emancipation or John Bull Gulled Out Of Twenty Millions." Bodleian, John Johnson Coll of Political & Satirical Prints, Series: Political Drama No. 10. Shelfmark: Political Cartoons 4 (8).

p. 158 Left: The Capitol, Washington, D.C. John Plumbe's daguerreotype 1846, Creative Commons: US Lib Congress Prints & Photos Division, digital ID: cph.3c102103. Right: Buckingham Palace, London. Author's photograph.

p. 159 Palace of Westminster. Author's photograph. Below left: Trinity College, Toronto. 1881, engraving, pub. J.M. Dent & Sons. Below right. Christ Church, Simla, India. Creative Commons, own work Arne Hueckelheim, 2010.

p. 164 Left: Eton Chapel. Creative Commons, own work, jonrobb 2011 Right: Lancing Chapel. Creative Commons, own work, Bellminsterboy 2015.

p. 165 1st edition of Lawn Tennis by Walter Wingfield 1874; reprinted in Gillmeister: Kulturgeschichte des Tennis. Wilhelm Fink Verlag, München 1990.

p. 169 Palmerston Folly. Author's photograph.

p. 170 The Anglo-American Telegraph Company. Reproduced by kind permission of Bill Burns.

p. 170 1871 Pamphlet edition of Sir George Chesney's The Battle of Dorking, pub. Wm. Blackwood & Sons, 1871.

p. 172 Letter to Queen Victoria. Source: National Records Office. Quoted in Englanders and Huns: The Culture Clash Which Led To The First World War. James Hawes. Simon & Schuster 2014.

p. 176 England First XV 1871. Posted by Creative Commons by Clifton Rugby Football Club.

p. 178 Sir Nicolas Roderick O'Conor. Photographer, unknown, St. Petersburg 1895–1898.

p. 178 "The Alien Pauper Question." Illustration from Fun magazine, London, mid 1880s.

p. 181 Left: Made in Germany, by E. E. Williams; William Heinemann 1896. Center: War of the Worlds, by H.G. Wells; William Heinemann 1898. Right: Dracula, by Bram Stoker, Archibald Constable & Company, 1897.

p. 184 Aquascutum advertisement. From the German magazine Simplicissimus, Issue No. 52; 23 March 1914. Published by the Klassik Stiftung Weimar, the Duchess Anna Amalia Library in conjunction with the German Literature Archive Marbach, as well as the Institute for German and General Literary Studies and the teaching and research area of German-Jewish literary history, both at the Rheinisch-Westfälische Technische Hochschule Aachen.

p. 184 Spiel und Sport, early 20th century, published by J. Bloch, Berlin. Author's scan from Berliner Staatsbibliothek.

p. 185 "John Bull at the Start of the 20th Century." German satirical cartoon, Der wahre Jakob magazine, issue no. 353, January 30, 1900. Courtesy of Digitised Literature collection, University of Heidelberg.

p. 186 British Pluck—Boer War–era tobacco tin.

p. 187 The Invasion of 1910. Times advertisement, March 9, 1909, for the forthcoming serialization in The Daily Mail.

p. 188 Under Which Flag?/The Great Naval Eclipse—Liberal and Conservative election posters, 1910. Author's collection.

p. 198 Radio Times, May 7, 1937. Image reproduced by kind permission of the BBC Genome.

p. 202 Left: The Hoover Building, Perivale, London, designed by Wallis, Gilbert and Partners, opened May 1933. Creative Commons: own work, Ethan Doyle White, 2018 Right: Unilever House, Blackfriars, London, designed by James Lomax Simpson, John James Burnet, Thomas S. Tait, opened 1933. Creative Commons: own work, Arild Vagen, 2014

p. 207 "Peace For Our Time." Daily Express, October 1, 1938.

p. 209 Squadron Leader D. Finlay, C.O. of No. 41 Squadron RAF, standing with four of his pilots in front of a Supermarine Spitfire, Mk II, at Hornchurch, Essex, December 1940. Photograph by Daventry B J (Mr), Royal Air Force official photographer: media.iwm.org.uk/ iwm/mediaLib//52/media-52967/large.jpg. Photograph CH 1871 from the collections of the Imperial War Museums.

p. 210 A British officer armed with a revolver leading his men forward with fixed bayonets, El Alamein, 1942. National Army Museum collection.nam.ac.uk/detail.php?acc=2005-05-25-6,

p. 213 British airborne troops moving through a shell-damaged house in Oosterbeek near Arnhem during Operation "Market Garden," September 23, 1944. Photograph by Smith, D.M. (Sgt.), Army Film and Photographic Unit. Photograph BU1121, Imperial War Museum: media. iwm.org.uk/ciim.

p. 217 West Indian immigrants arrive at Tilbury on the Empire Windrush. June 22, 1948. © PA Images/Alamy.

p. 218 Top left: The first prototype de Havilland DH106 Comet at Hatfield, October 4, 1947. Photo ATP. 18376C from the collections of the Imperial War Museums. Top right: Peter Whitehead crosses the line to win the 24 Hrs Le Mans race in 1951, in a Jaguar C-type. Image © and reproduced by kind permission of Jaguar Daimler Heritage Trust Archive, at the British Motor Museum. Bottom left: New Rover gas turbine car surrounded by admirers at Silverstone © Trinity Mirror/Mirrorpix/Alamy. Bottom right: The Fairey Delta. Image reproduced by permission of Aviation Ancestry aviationancestry.co.uk.

p. 221 Top left: "Building the Welsh Autobahn." The Sphere, November 7, 1953. Top right: "The Dam Busters Are Back." Flight magazine, August 15, 1958. Image reproduced by kind permission of Aviation Ancestry. Bottom: Royal Navy passing-out parade, 1953. Author's photograph.

p. 223 James Ogston, in the aftermath of H-bomb testing during Operation Grapple. Photograph reproduced by kind permission of Callum Smith.

p. 224 Left: Garendon Hall, 1964. Photograph by Syd Hall, Loughborough Monitor. May 13, 1964. Right: The College Boys—unidentified newspaper cutting from June 1964; reproduced with kind permission of Jane Sellek, Eton College archivist etoncollegecollections.wordpress. com/2018/08/16/eton-had-talent.

p. 225 Left: The Beatles meet Harold Wilson at the Dorchester Hotel, March 19, 1964. ©

Keystone Press/Alamy. Right: Prime Minister Sir Alec Douglas Home at his mansion in Coldstream, Berwickshire, with his favorite Labrador gun dog, October 25, 1963. © Trinity Mirror/ Mirrorpix/Alamy.

p. 226 Left: Time magazine cover, April 15, 1966, Geoffrey Dickinson. ©Time USA, LLC . Right: England fans at the World Cup final, July 30, 1966. © PA/Alamy.

p. 228 Powell For PM. Graffiti. Evening Standard May 1, 1968. © Hulton Archive/Getty Images.

p. 229 Left: Varoomshka trailer ad, illustrator John Kent, Guardian, February 12, 1972. Right: Battle Picture Weekly cover, September 6, 1975. Image reproduced by permission of Rebellion/ treasuryofbritishcomics.com.

p. 231 Margaret Thatcher at a rally in Parliament Square, March 9, 1975. ©Harry Prosser. Mirrorpix.

p. 232 The Sex Pistols perform in Paradiso, Amsterdam, January 6, 1977. Released to Creative Commons by Anefo Nationaal Archief; photo by Koen Suyk.

p. 233 Youths clash with Police in Brixton, July 1981 ©David Hoffmann Photo Library.

p. 234 Left: Harpers & Queen Official Sloane Ranger Handbook, by Peter York. Ebury Publishing, 1982. Right: TV Times magazine cover from October 1981 for ATV region depicting Anthony Andrews as Sebastian Flyte in Granada Television's adaptation of Brideshead Revisited, by Evelyn Waugh.

p. 235 Arthur Scargill with miners at Barnsley, September 15, 1984. ©PA/Alamy.

p. 236 Harry Enfield's "Loadsamoney," April 25, 1988. ©Mirrorpix/Alamy.

p. 238 The Battle of Trafalgar Square/Poll Tax Riots, March 31, 1990. ©David Hoffmann Photo Library.

p. 239 Neil Kinnock at the Labour rally in Sheffield, April 2, 1992. ©Mirrorpix/Alamy.

p. 240 Left: Blur vs. Oasis, New Musical Express (NME) cover, December 9, 1995. Right: Northern Lights, by Philip Pullman. First edition cover, design by David Scutt and Philip Pullman. July 9 1995 © Scholastic UK.

p. 245 Left: New and Lingwood shop-front, Windsor. Author's photograph. Right: Ollivanders Wand Shop (of the Harry Potter film and book series), Universal Studios, Florida. Author's photograph.

p. 250 Private Eye cover, December 22, 2005.

p. 252 Tweet by Emily Thornberry, Labour MP for Islington South and Finsbury, November 20, 2014.

p. 253 2012 Olympics Opening Ceremony images, July 23, 2012. © Shimelle Laine.

p. 255 Right: Detail from Scene 57 of the Bayeux Tapestry. 2011 Creative Commons, identified as own work by user Myrabella.

p. 258 2015 Election poster by the Conservative Party, Loughborough, April 9, 2015. Photograph by Mark Severn. © Alamy/Daily Mail headline, April 21, 2015.

p. 260 The NHS/Brexit bus. © Christopher Furlong / Getty Images.

Index

Cabot, John, 89
Cade, Jack, 79–80
Cade's Rebellion, 79–80
Caelin (King of West Saxons), 14
Callaghan, James, 243
Cambridge University, 88, 97–98, 257
Cameron, David, 252, 257, 259
Cannadine, David, 238
Carausius, Marcus Aurelius, 6, 6
Catherine of Aragon, 89–90, 92, 97, 99, 100, 104
Catherine of Valois, 79
Catholic Church. *See also individual names of Holy Roman Emperors; individual names of popes*: appeal of laws against (1829), 157; Battle of Hastings and, 39, 99; Benedictines, 24–25; Charles II and, 130–31; Dissolution of the Monasteries, 101–2; Elizabeth I and, 111; England's introduction to, 14–18, 25–26; James II and, 132; Mary I and, 104, 107–8
Caxton, William, 82, 85, 88
Cazalet, Victor (Colonel), 211
Celts, 8, 11, *13*, 13–14, 16
Chamberlain, Neville, 207, 208
Charlemagne, 17, 21
Charles I (King), 61, 118–24, *119*, 126, *126*, 135
Charles II (King), 128–32
Charles V (Holy Roman Emperor), 92, 96, *96*, 97, 107
Chartism, 158, 163
China, 168–69
Churchill, Winston, 58, 128, 189–92, *190*, 207–10, 212, 214, 219, 243, 262, 264
Church of England, 54, *54*, 113, 121, 123, 161, *161*, 164, 175, 246, *247*. *See also individual names of archbishops of Canterbury*
Citizenship Act (1948), 216
Civil War, 118–27, *122*, *124*
Clare, John, 141
Claudius (Roman emperor), 3
Clinton, Bill, 245
Cnut (Danish King), 27–30, *29*, 39, 45, 60
coal, 146–48, *147*, 201–2, 204, 230, 235
Cobden, Richard, 165
Codex Amiatinus, 16
Coelfrid, 16
Cohen, Nick, 249
coins, 3, 6, 22, 24, *24*, 105
Coke, Edward, 116–17
Collins, Tim, 241
Commynes, Philippe de, 84
Conan Doyle, Arthur, 184
Congress of Berlin (1878), 171, *171*, 173
Constantin (King of Scotland), 24
constitution (1014–1016), *30*
Continental System, 155, *155*
Corn Laws, 156, 158
Covenant, 121, 123
Cranmer, Thomas (Archbishop of Canterbury), 100, 103

Cromwell, Oliver, 102, 121–29, 208
Cromwell, Richard, 129
Cromwell, Thomas, 99, 102, 103, *103*, 114, 124

Daunton, Martin, 183
Decline and Fall of the Roman Empire (Gibbon), 139
Deeds of Hereward (c. 1125), 46
Defoe, Daniel, 138, *138*
Dekker, Thomas, 115
De Montfort, Simon, 60–62, *62*
Denmark, 20, 22–31, *23*, *29*, 33, 37
The Dialogue of the Exchequer (FitzNigel), 50–51
Diana (Princess of Wales), 244
Dickens, Charles, 168
Disraeli, Benjamin, 163, 167, 171–73
Domesday Book, 37, 38
Dorling, Danny, 206, 251
Douglas-Home, Alec, 225, *225*
Doyle, Conan, 184
Drake, Francis, 111
Dreadnought (battleship), 187–88
Dunstan (Archbishop), 25

Eadwig (King), 24
Edelstein, Michael, 179
Edgar (King), 24–25, 29
Edgerton, David, 217
Edmund Ironside (King), 28, 43, 45
Edward I (King), 61–65, *63*
Edward II (King), 65–66
Edward III (King), 66–67, 70, 80
Edward IV (King), 83–86, 87
Edward VI (King), 101, 104, 105–7
Edward VII (King), 186
Edward the Confessor (King), 30–32, 60, *73*
Edward the Elder (King of Anglo-Saxons), 23
Edward (son of King Edgar), 25
Edwin (Earl of Mercia), 34, 36
Eleanor of Aquitaine (Queen), 49, *49*
Elizabeth I (Queen), 104, 107–13, *110*, *112*, 115–16
Elizabeth II (Queen), 262
Elizabeth (Henry VII's wife), 87, *90*
Elliott, Larry, 247
Emma of Normandy, 26–28
Empire Windrush (passenger ship), 216, *217*
enclosure system, 92–94, *93*, 110, 117, *117*, 126–27, 140–42
Engels, Friedrich, 160, 162
England (overview): British Empire, 91–144 (*See also* England [1509–1763]); Industrial Revolution, 145–92 (*See also* Industrial Revolution [1763–1914]); Roman founding through Battle of Hastings, 1–40 (*See also* England [55 BCE–1087 CE]); shortest history, summarized, 265–66; of two tongues, 41–90 (*See also* England [1087–1509]; language); uniqueness of, 9–11, 53; World War I to present day, 193–265 (*See also* England [1914–present])

Gillingham, John, 84
Gladstone, W. E., 167, 170–76, 243, 258
Gloucester Cathedral, 68, *68*
Godwin (Earl of Wessex), 29–32
gold standard, 201
Good Friday Agreement (1998), 245
Goodwin, George, 83
Gorbachev, Mikhail, 237
Gospatric (Earl of Northumberland), 51–52
Gove, Michael, 260
Great Death (Black Death), *67*, 67–70
Great Depression, 202
Green, Caitlin, 37
Green, J. R., 28
Gregory (Pope), 14–15
Grey, Edward, 192
Groans of the Britons, 8
Gulf Wars (1991, 2003), 241, 250
Guthrum (Danish leader), 20

Habsburgs, 89, 92, 96, 98, 133, 142
Hague, William, 249
Haig, Douglas, 195
Hakluyt, Richard, 110
Hannan, Daniel, 255–56, *256*
Harald Hardrada, 34
Hardie, Keir, 186
Harold Godwinson (King), 29, 32, 34, 35, *35*,
    36, 255. *See also* Hastings, Battle of
Harold Harefoot, 30
Harris, Bernard, 162
Harrison, William, 106, 110
Harry Potter (Rowling), *245*, 245–46, *246*
Harthacnut, 30–31
Hastings, Battle of, 32–40, *33*, *35*, *38*, 42–46,
    44, 51, 99, 125, 255, 257
Hastings, Max, 212
Hawkes, Jacquetta, 223
Hawkins, Angus, 158
Hayek, Friedrich von, 237
Hayward, John, 113
Healey, Denis, 219
Heath, Edward, 229
Heimskringla (Norwegian saga), 28
Henri Grace à Dieu (ship), *92*
Henry I (King), 43–47
Henry II (King, Henry of Anjou), 46–55, *49*,
    50, *54*
Henry III (King), 60–62
Henry IV (German emperor), 33
Henry IV (King), *74*, 74–75
Henry V (King) (Prince Hal), 76–79
Henry VI (King), 79–80, 84
Henry VIII (King), 87–90, 92, *92*, 95–102,
    104–5, 109, 116
Henry Hotspur (Percy family), 76
Hereward the Wake, 46
Hill, Christopher, 103, 121
Hitchens, Peter, 211
Hitler, Adolf, 207, 209, 210
Holbein, Hans, 103, *103*
Holinshed, Raphael, 71
Holland, 111, 128, 130–35, 142

Holland, Tom, 23
Holt, James, 53, 57
Home Rule, 175–77, *188*, 189–92, *190*, *191*
Hopkins, Mathew, 124
Hume, David, 142
Hundred Years' War, 66–80
Hunt, Henry "Orator," 156
Hurd, Douglas, 241, 264
Hyndman, H. J., 174

India, *159*, 160, 216–17
Industrial Revolution (1763–1914), 145–92;
    American Revolution and, 149–50, *150*;
    British racial superpower image, *185*, 185–
    87, *187*; Chartism, 158, 163; Disraeli and,
    163, 167, 171–73; *Dreadnought* (battleship),
    187–88; economies of Southeast *vs.* Outer
    Britain during, *180*, 180–81; as effect of
    modernization/empire building, 146–49,
    147, *148*; Empire growth and image,
    158–61, *159*, *160*; England's competition
    with other countries, 169–72, *169–72*,
    179–80, *181*, 187–88; Gladstone and, 167,
    170–76; Home Rule and, 175–77, *188*,
    189–92, *190*, *191*; *The Invasion of 1910* (Le
    Queux), 187, *187*; Manchesterism and, *161*,
    161–64; middle class elite, *164*, 164–69, *167*,
    168, 175, 182–85, *184*; Napoleon and Army
    recruitment, 154–57, *155*; nationalism in
    late 19th century, 174–79, *176*, *178*; natural
    resources of North, 146, 150–52, *151*; paper
    money and, 152–53; People's Budget (1909),
    188, *188*; Second Industrial Revolution, 180,
    180; slavery and, 147, *147*, 157, *157*; United
    Kingdom inception, 153–54, *154*, 262;
    urban population growth, *151*, 152, *180*;
    Victoria and, *159*, 171–73, 181, 186; World
    War I and, 173, *173*, 176, 192
Ine (King of Wessex), 14
Internet, inception of, 240
The Invasion of 1910 (Le Queux), 187, *187*
Ireland. *See also* Northern Ireland:
    assimilation of (1541), 101; Civil War
    and, 119, 123; conquered by Henry II,
    55; Cromwell's religious slaughter of, 127;
    Empire *vs.* English nationalism, 177–79;
    French invasion plans, 152; Home Rule,
    175–77, *188*, 189–92, *190*, *191*; Restoration
    and, 129–30; "Scots" and, 6; UK assumption
    of, 160; United Kingdom name/construct,
    153–54, *154*, 262; voting patterns
    (1885–1929), 174; War of Independence
    (1919–1921), 197; World War I, 195
Isabella (Queen), 66
Israel, Jonathan, 134
Italy, 210–11

James I (King) , 115–18, 136
James II (King), 131–33
James Francis Edward Stuart, 133–35
James of St. George, 62–63
Jane Grey (Nine Day Queen), 107, *108*
Japan, 210, 213

North, Roger, 130
Northern Ireland, 206, 227, 231, 235, 245
Northern Rebellion, 109
North-South divide, overview, 17–22, *18*. *See also* Ireland; Scotland; Wales
Northumberland, 17, 23, 24, 37–38, 40, 76–77, *77*, 87
Notitia Dignitatum, 7

Oasis, 240, *240*
O'Conor, Nicolas Roderick, *178*
Odo (Bishop), 42
Offa (King of Mercia), 17
Olaf Guthfrithsson (Viking warlord), 24
Olaf (King of Norway), 28
Olivier, Laurence, as Richard III, *86*
Olusoga, David, 147, 155, 216
Ompteda (Count), 166
Ordericus Vitalis, 34, 39, 42
Orwell, George, 205
Otis, James, 149, 150
Otto IV (Holy Roman Emperor), 57
Owain Glyndwr of Wales, 76, *77*
Owain (King of Strathclyde), 24
Oxford University, 88, 257

paganism, 11, 14–16, 19, 22
Paine, Tom, 142
Palmerston's Follies, *169*
Paris, Matthew, 59
Parliament: architecture of, 158–59, *159*; Chartism, 158, 163; Civil War and, 118–27, *122*, *124*; as co-ruler with sovereign (1567), 108–9; EEC referendum and, *230*, 230–31; Henry IV and, 77; Henry VIII and, 99–100; inception of, 64–65; Magna Carta, 58–59; populism and, 227–29
Peasants' Revolt (14th century), 70–74
Pembroke (Earl), 55
Penda (King of Mercia), 16
People's Budget (1909), 188, *188*
Pepys, Samuel, 129
Percys of Northumberland, 76, *77*, 81
Perkins, John "Jack Punch," 143
Peter (Saint), 16
Philip (King of France), 56–57
Philip of Spain (Philip II), 107–8
Picts, 6–9, 17
Piers Plowman (Langland), 70
Poland, immigration from, 251–52, *253*
Popish Plot, 131
Portugal, Napoleon's invasion, 155
Powell, Enoch, 85, 228, *228*, 230
Prayer Book Rebellion, 106
Price, Richard, 142
Pride and Prejudice (Austen), 153
Pride's Purge, 126
Priestley, J. B., 142, 203–4, 223
Protestant Reformation, 97–106, *103*, 110, 115, 125
Provisions of Oxford (1258), 60–62, *62*
Pullman, Philip, 240, *240*
Putney Debates, 125

Puttenham, George, 109

Readwald of East Anglia (King), 15
"Recessional" (Kipling), 182
The Recuyell of the Historyes of Troye (Caxton), 85
Reform Act (1832), 157
religion. *See* Catholic Church; Church of England; Protestant Reformation
Restoration, 129
Richard I (King), 55–57, 62
Richard II (King), 70–75, *73*, 76
Richard III (King), 85–86, *86*, 87
Richard (Duke of Normandy), 26, 28
Richard (Duke of York), 80, 81
Richard Neville (Warwick the Kingmaker), 81, 84
Riches, William Terence Martin, 118
Robert Bruce, 65
Robert of Gloucester, 64
Roberts (Lord), 187
Robert (son of William the Conqueror), 42–44
Robin Hood legend, 56, 70
Romano-Britons, 2–14, *3–13*
Roosevelt, Franklin D., 207, 212
Ross, Alan, 222
Rowling, J. K., 245–46, *246*
Rowse, A. L., 114
royal assizes, 53–55, *54*
Ruddick, Andrea, 18
Rufus (King), 42–43, 47
The Ruin of Britain (Gildas), 8
"Rule, Britannia" (anthem), 142
Rule of the Major-Generals, 128–29
Russia, 156, 171, *171*, 173, 209–10, 237
Rye House Plot, 131

Saddam Hussein, 241
Salisbury (Lord), 115, 177
Sampson, Anthony, 222
Sandbrook, Dominic, 230
Savile, Jimmy, 229
Saxons, 6, 6–9, *7*, *9*
Saxon Shore, 7
Sayer, Derek, 52
Scargill, Arthur, 235, 239
Schröder, Gerhard, 245
Scotland: assimilation of (1542), 101; Battle of Culloden, 143; Battle of the Standard, 47–48, *48*; Civil War and, 119–20; Constantin (king), 24; Cromwell and, 127–28; Empire *vs.* English nationalism, 177–79; Great Britain inception, 137–39; Home Rule, 175–77, *188*, 189–92, *190*, *191*; James VI of, 115; Midlothian Campaign, 172; modern-day nationalism of, 257–58; Picts and, 6; Restoration and, 129–30
Scott, Gilbert, 159
Seasons in the Sun (Sandbrook), 230
Second Opium War, 168–69
Sermon of the Wolf (Wulfstan), 27
Seven Years' War, 143–44
Sex Pistols, *232*

About the Author

JAMES HAWES studied at University of Oxford and University College London, then held lectureships at the universities of Maynooth, Sheffield, and Swansea. He has published six novels with Jonathan Cape, and is also the author of *The Shortest History of Germany*. He leads the MA in creative writing at Oxford Brookes University. He is Series Story Consultant, on-screen contributor, and writer of the associated book for the major eight-episode BBC TV history of British creativity, *These Brilliant Isles: Art That Made Us*, to be screened in spring 2022.

jameshawes.org.uk | 🐦 jameshawes2

Also available in the Shortest History series

Trade Paperback Original | 256 pages
$15.95 US | $21.00 CAN
978-1-61519-569-5

Trade Paperback Original | 288 pages
$15.95 US | $21.00 CAN
978-1-61519-820-7